# The Blender Way to Better Cooking

# The Blender Way to Better Cooking

FOR EVERY DAY...EVERY MEAL...EVERYBODY

Edited by Betty Sullivan

*Illustrated by Eric Mulvaney* *Photographs by Foster Ensminger*

Golden Press • New York

All recipes have been tested in the Hamilton Beach kitchens at Racine, Wisconsin.

 PRINTED IN THE U. S. A. BY WESTERN PUBLISHING COMPANY, INC. PUBLISHED BY GOLDEN PRESS, NEW YORK, N.Y.

LIBRARY OF CONGRESS CATALOG CARD NUMBER: 65-25358
EIGHTH PRINTING, 1969

# Contents

# An Introduction

For years I have had a blender. I used it seldom, and then only to make fruit drinks, frozen daiquiris or a party sauce.

I was a little afraid of the blender, and preferred the old slow way to what was for me a quick trick with who-knew-what result. I didn't know just what a blender would do, and never felt that I could control it.

As a matter of fact, when I saw the recipes that were to make up this book, I couldn't believe they would work. But they did! After a few basic tests, I decided that the blender should be at work all day, every day—from breakfast to dinner.

I should confess that much of my enthusiasm was awakened by the new multi-speed blender that came to me with the recipes. You can now get more power in a blender than ever before, so that mixtures that once required many stops and starts blend smoothly and steadily. I am enthusiastic about the cutting element that separates from the container. In the past, I have wasted much precious time trying to rescue mixtures from between attached blades, and often have had to wash away precious food.

My new blender has a slide speed control, making possible a steady and gradual increase in speed, or an instantaneous halt in the blending process. When chopping fruits or nuts in a mixture, or vegetables in water for a relish, the instant response of the slide control bar gives absolute control of the texture. It isn't necessary to get hold of a tiny knob or switch. A sweep of the hand, and the motor stops.

Use it to make breakfast, whether you prefer it in liquid form as a breakfast-in-a-glass or in the shape of pancakes, scrambled eggs, muffins or waffles. Use it to prepare lunch box sandwich fillings and salads. Use it to chop the onion and parsley for meat loaf, as well as to make the bread or cracker crumbs. Use it to prepare the flavoring vegetables for a stew. Adding nuts to a cake? Blender combine fat, sugar, eggs and milk; add the *whole* nut meats and run blender just seconds to incorporate chopped nuts in the mixture. Dates may be chopped this way, too, and raisins, apricots or prunes. My new multi-speed blender is really seven appliances in one.

*Time Saving Is Incredible*

I found that tasks which ordinarily would require 15 minutes to a half hour were completed in seconds—that I could grind a pound of liver to a butter-smooth purée in two minutes. Think what the blender could do for a woman who prepares three family meals a day, plus snacks and perhaps even foods for a baby or an invalid!

*With a Blender You'll Acquire New Skills*

Without a moment's practice, you can make chef's specialties like Hollandaise sauce and fresh mayonnaise. There is no risk of the separating that has haunted chefs and homemakers alike in the past. Minutes after you assemble ingredients the sauce can be on the table.

From each of these two basic sauces, one hot and one cold, a dozen other gourmet sauces can be blender-prepared almost instantaneously.

*Meals Can Be More Nutritious*

The foods necessary for good nutrition can be offered in a variety of interesting forms when the blender works for you. Vitamin-rich perfection salad and raw vegetable slaws can be made in minutes, with only a knife, a rubber spatula and the blender container to rinse. You will be encouraged to make them more often, once you have tried the blender way. Your own nut butters will improve lunches and snacks. Cheesecake, delicious but so time-consuming that you rarely bother with it, practically makes itself in the blender.

*Blender Shortcuts Save Time and Trouble*

Make potato pancakes without a grater, chocolate treats without melting chocolate, freshly ground coffee without a coffee grinder, puréed fruits and vegetables without sieving.

*A Busy Blender Can Save Money for You*

Odd bits of food that are now left to spoil will find their way into soups, sauces, dips, sandwich spreads, beverages. Baby foods prepared from foods provided for the rest of the family cost about half what you pay for commercially prepared baby foods, and they are fresh instead of canned. More variety is possible, since you can make your own combinations.

*Special Diets Can Be More Attractive*

When a member of the family goes on a soft or low-calorie diet, blender preparation can create more interesting combinations, more attractive dishes. A creamed soup, vegetable and egg may be presented as a soufflé, as an omelet with sauce, as sliced hard-cooked egg in vegetable sauce on toast. Boring cooked fruit may be used in a whip with custard sauce, or as a purée to sauce ice cream or custard. Raw or cooked vegetables, cheese or fish may be combined in a molded salad.

*Speaking Personally—I Love My Blender*

Suddenly my diet is better, my menus more varied, and the routine business of getting meals to the table has become as much fun as a new game. I use it every day and for every meal—you will, too. Browse through the book and mark for trial the recipes that seem especially intriguing. Check the introductory paragraphs to each chapter; you will find useful hints for saving work or preventing disappointment. After you have tried a few of the recipes in the book, you will see ways of adapting the procedures to your own favorites. Happy Blending!

Eleanor Crook

# What to Look For in a Blender

**TWO-PIECE COVER**

*Make sure cover fits container tightly.*

*Removable center allows for easy addition of ingredients while blender is in operation.*

**CONTAINER**

*Clear, so you can watch blender action.*

*Open at both ends: spout end for "easy-pouring" mixtures; use spatula to push non-pouring mixtures out bottom—with no waste.*

**GASKET**

*No-leakage insurance.*

**CUTTING ASSEMBLY**

*Good blades. Removable assembly for easy and thorough cleaning. Greater versatility, too, since you can fit it on a Mason or canning jar for jobs such as puréeing baby foods, grinding coffee.*

**MULTI-SPEED SLIDE CONTROL BAR**

*Allows for easy selection of correct speed plus better control of blender operation. Easy on-off action.*

# Now That You Have a Blender...

Keep your blender handy, right on the countertop. No matter how often you cook—no matter how many you cook for—you'll want to use it every single day. Use it whenever you have something to whip, grate, chop, purée, mix or blend. Pulverize sugar for beverages. Grind coffee for the freshest brew you've ever tasted. You can liquefy fruits and vegetables with the blender, too. Forget you ever used graters or sieves; a kitchenful of bowls, spoons and clutter will be a thing of the past. What you used to think of as chores are now adventures—and easy, speedy adventures, at that!

## Blender Shortcuts and Speed-ups

As you experiment with your blender and the recipes in this book, you will discover lots of easy shortcuts and speed-ups for everyday cooking tasks. You will probably notice, too, that there is sometimes a difference in the order of adding ingredients in *these* recipes and the ones you now follow. There is a reason for this. For example, in blender cooking, liquids usually go into the container before solids; they help feed the solids into the blades and prevent "traffic jams." Solids which are to be *blended smooth* may be added piece by piece while the motor runs. Solids which are to be *chopped* are added after the base is smoothly blended.

The blender is incredibly fast, so be conservative about timing. Many jobs are done in 1, 2 or 3 seconds; *slow* operations generally require only 30-60 seconds. Remember, you can't unchop or unblend, so don't run the blender too long.

## To Control Texture

The fineness or coarseness of ingredients in a finished mixture depends largely on the length of time the blender is run. If you want a creamy, smooth base (i.e., sharp cheese blended with cream cheese) with chopped pieces of another ingredient (such as olive, nut or radish), combine the smooth mixture first, then add the other ingredient and run blender only until chopped to the coarseness desired.

For a coarse chop, turn blender to speed 2 or 3 (or low) for just a few seconds. Or turn to speed 3 or 4 (or low) and turn off at once; repeat until texture is right.

## One Utensil: A Spatula

A rubber spatula is the best kind to use. (You probably have one; if not, they are easily available in novelty and hardware stores.) When you work with thick mixtures, you may find that the food clings to the sides of the container, leaving the blades uncovered and thus causing the motor to race. If this happens, stop the blender and use the spatula to push the ingredients back toward the blades. The spatula also helps you remove the blended mixture from the container into a serving dish or cooking vessel. You will find the spatula especially useful if the cutting blades of your blender are not detachable.

## How Much Goes into the Blender?

The blender should not be more than half full of a thick mixture like a sandwich spread. For thinner mixtures, the container may be filled right up to the useable capacity of your particular blender.

Be sure to follow the manufacturer's instructions regarding the capacity of your blender. Such care will help you avoid overflows. And never start the motor until the cover is tightly fitted.

## Beating Egg Whites? Mashing Potatoes?

There are two jobs the blender can't do. It can't beat egg whites stiff—the blender's great speed breaks down the tender foam as fast as it builds up. (Whole eggs, however, may be beaten with other ingredients.)

Freshly boiled potatoes also respond better to slower beating and should not be blender-mashed. On the other hand, fresh cooked potatoes may be puréed for a blender soup, raw potatoes grated for potato pancakes; packaged instant mashed potatoes are improved by blender preparation (see page 127).

## Always Start with a Covered Container

Even small quantities of ingredients, wet or dry, may be thrown by the sudden impact of the blades. Put the cover on and press firmly into place before turning on power.

## If Your Blender Has a One-Piece Cover

When a recipe calls for adding ingredients through the center opening of the cover, tear a square of heavy duty aluminum foil, or doubled ordinary foil, large enough to cover the top and come well down over the sides of container. Cut a small hole in center, if adding liquids, and pour liquids through funnel fitted into hole. For adding solids, such as ice cubes, make the opening in the foil just large enough to admit the pieces. Some manufacturers recommend lifting a corner of the lid; with certain ingredients this is satisfactory. However, you may get some spattering.

## Care of the Container

Carefully read the booklet the manufacturer has supplied for your blender. Follow it carefully for instructions. If your blender has a plastic container, chances are you can pour boiling liquids into it. However, most plastic containers should never be immersed in boiling water or subjected to the high temperatures of an electric dishwasher.

# Blender Basics

Blender cooking is truly the new-fashioned way to make delicious meals for your family and friends. Practically any dish you now prepare the old-fashioned no-blender way can be blender-improved—made in a fraction of the time and with much less fuss and muss. And what could be better for the fast-moving pace set by modern homemakers?

If you cannot locate a specific recipe on the following pages, find one that would call for similar methods. For example, if a mushroom omelet is one of your favorites, turn to the Omelet with Spanish Sauce; the method will be similar. Simply use common sense and substitute ingredients.

If the blender is always handy, even the newest blender-cook will turn to it daily for blending beverages, scrambling eggs, puréeing cooked fruits and vegetables for the baby, for making salad dressings and sauces. But the blender can do much more for you. Master the following basics, adapt them to your needs—and, perhaps, to different ingredients—and you will be on your way to happier, faster and more modern cooking.

---

## CHOPPING VEGETABLES

Ingredients chopped just as you want them—fine or coarse—are an everyday necessity. Here's how to chop carrots, peppers, onions (even apples) and any other *solid* ingredient you may need for a salad, soup or relish—and no nicked fingers!

**"Dry" Method**

- Cut the ingredients to be chopped into 1" pieces (approximately). Pieces that are too large may prevent all the material from going through the blades.
- Process only small amounts at one time—about ½ cup, or enough to cover the blades.

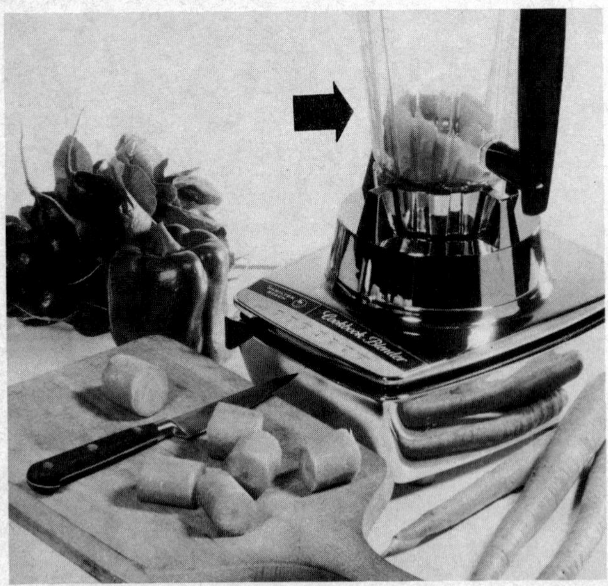

- Cover container and run on speed 4 (or low) then turn off quickly. Repeat several times. (This on-off action will help you control the texture of the chopped vegetables.)

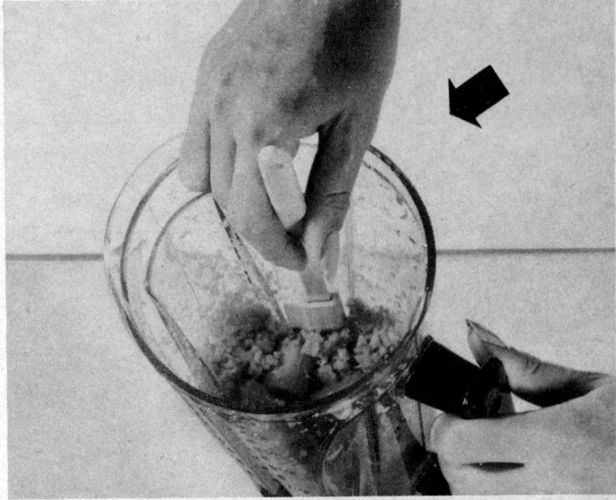

- If necessary, when blender is stopped, push ingredients toward blades with a rubber spatula.
- Empty into a measuring cup or mixing bowl. Repeat entire procedure, chopping only small amounts each time, until desired quantity is obtained.

### Water Method

A real time-saver. Perfect for cabbage slaws, for chopping several ingredients at one time, or large amounts of a vegetable.

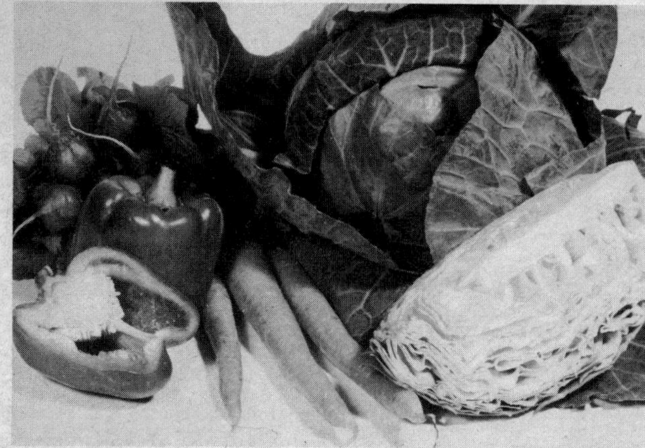

- Fill blender container to top cup marking with cut-up ingredients.
- Add just enough cool water to cover.

- Cover container and run on speed 7 (or high) about 5 seconds. Repeat, if necessary, until all ingredients are chopped. (Do not run too long or vegetables may be liquefied.)
- Drain in a colander or sieve. Repeat entire process, if necessary, until desired amount is obtained.

## CRUMBING

*Fresh* bread crumbs can make a great difference in your cooking—they have that "something special" that packaged crumbs seem to lack. Since you'll probably need them for so many of your favorite dishes, why not crumb a large quantity of bread and store it in your freezer in a tightly covered container. The crumbs will stay fresh and be ready to use to top your favorite casserole, to bread tasty chops and to coat chicken or croquettes before frying. Use leftover dry bread and crusts for dry crumbs—easy, and thrifty, too. Cooky and cracker crumbs make wonderful pie crusts and toppings for your favorite desserts—and they're indispensable for cheesecake.

### Bread

- Crumb only 1 slice of bread, fresh or dry, at a time. Tear the slice into 5 or 6 pieces and drop them into the blender container.
- Cover container and run on speed 4 (or low) until crumbed to the consistency desired.

***For buttered bread crumbs,*** simply spread soft butter on the bread before tearing it into pieces.

***For cheese crumbs,*** drop a few cubes of hard cheese into the blender container and process them with the bread.

**1 slice bread = about ½ cup crumbs**

### Cookies

● You can crumb about 5 wafer-type cookies at one time. Break them into the blender container.

● Cover container and run on speed 4 (or low) until crumbed to the texture desired.

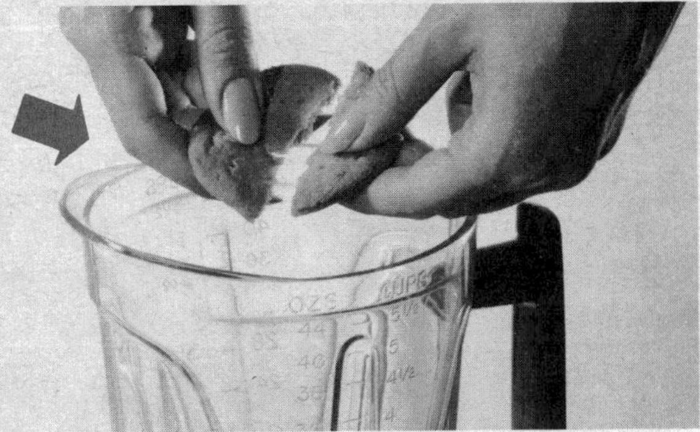

8 wafer-type cookies = about 1 cup crumbs

### Crackers

● You can crumb about 6 soda crackers or graham crackers at one time. Break them into the blender container.

● Cover container and run on speed 4 (or low) until crumbed as desired.

NOTE: *Remember, the longer you run the blender, the finer the crumbs will be.*

18 crackers = about 1 cup crumbs

## GRATING CHEESE

Freshly grated cheese can add much to any dish you prepare—as a golden garnish or as an integral part of the recipe.

● Cut hard cheese into 1″ cubes (approximately) and drop a few into blender container.

● Cover container and run on speed 4 (or low) until cheese is grated as desired.

3 ounces cheese = about 1 cup grated cheese

## CHOPPING NUTS

Chopped nuts are necessary for many of your favorite cookies, cakes and other desserts.

● Process about 1 cup shelled nuts at a time. Cover container and run on speed 4 (or low) until chopped as desired.

● Remember, the longer you run the blender the finer the grind.

NOTE: *In a blender you can chop nuts at the same time you mix batter for cake or breads.*

## USE OF ICE

### Ice Cubes

- Never try to chop or crush ice cubes in your blender. (If your blender has an ice crusher attachment, you can, of course, use it for this purpose.)
- You can, however, liquefy the cubes—if you add them, one at a time, to at least 2 cups liquid in the container. Add while the blender is running on speed 7 (or high). Always wait until each cube is liquefied before adding another.

### Crushed Ice

- When preparing a recipe that calls for crushed ice, add it last, and run blender until mixture is blended to a smooth texture.
- You can also use crushed ice with gelatin to speed jelling time (see recipe for Fruit Chiffon, page 143).

## USE OF GELATIN

For light and delicious chiffon puddings and pies and handsome molded salads—blender-dissolve your gelatin! When possible, follow specific recipe instructions. But here are some general rules:

### Flavored Gelatins

- Add the required amount of liquid to gelatin in blender container. Follow package directions for the amount of liquid.
- Cover and run on speed 1 (or low) until dissolved.

### Unflavored Gelatins

No need to dissolve unflavored gelatin over heat if you heat a portion (at least 3 tablespoons) of the required liquid.

- First put cold liquid in blender container (about ¼ cup). Add gelatin (Important: add the gelatin to the cold liquid; never add cold liquid to gelatin).
- Let stand for a few minutes to soften. Add remaining liquid—it must be *hot*.
- Cover container and run on speed 1 (or low) until gelatin is dissolved.

## ONE-STEP MIXING AND GRATING

You can assemble the ingredients for a batter (or gelatin) and the ingredients to be chopped and process them in one easy step. See Perfection Salad (page 76), Potato Pancakes (page 111) and Raisin Bars (page 175).

## LIQUEFYING

- To liquefy fruits and vegetables, follow the "Water Method" for chopping vegetables (page 11)—but run the blender until ingredients are liquefied. You need not fill the container to capacity, but be sure ingredients are covered by water.
- If drinking consistency is not obtained, simply add more liquid or ice while blender is running on speed 7 (or high).

## GRINDING COFFEE

The best tasting coffee is freshly ground coffee. For this reason, grind only as much as you will use at one time.

- You can process about 1 cup of coffee beans at a time. Cover container and run on speed 3 (or low) until ground to texture desired.
- If your blender has a detachable cutting unit, this is the perfect opportunity to do your grinding in a small Mason jar. No container to wash and any coffee that is left over can stay right in the jar to be ground with your next batch of coffee beans.

# Beverages Galore

*The creation of an almost limitless number of beverage combinations is possible when you use a blender. In addition to the ever-present milk shakes and daiquiris, you will find about 100 beverage recipes on the following pages: recipes for hot drinks—made with milk, chocolate, coffee and the classic heart-warming alcoholic liquors; recipes for cold drinks—made with the same ingredient bases, plus fruit; and, of course, recipes for beverages that rely on ice creams and sherbets. Another section is comprised of interesting combinations of vegetable drinks. (The blender can even liquefy carrots, if given a compatible liquid to start the process.) What a painless way to consume part of your daily quota of vitamins and minerals!*

Hints for Making Beverages

• *Blending on highest speed makes the smoothest beverage.*

• *Chocolate need not be melted when used to make any drink that includes hot milk or hot water.*

• *As long as you use twice as much liquid as solids, any preferred combination of ingredients may be used in a beverage. To some drinks, you may have to add an ice cube or two to achieve drinking consistency (see below).*

• *Add carbonated beverages just before pouring drinks from blender container. Or add to other ingredients in glass.*

• *Fruits may be used in sections or slices. Remove seeds, thick or coarse rinds, and bitter white fiber from surface of citrus fruits.*

• *In most instances when ice is used in drink preparation, it should be crushed. Ice cubes, however, can be added one at a time (to two cups or more liquid) while blender is running, to cool or thin the beverage.*

## Specially for Summer

### COFFEE COOLER

1 cup milk
2 cups cold water
4 teaspoons vanilla
1 cup nonfat dry milk solids
1 tablespoon instant cocoa
2 teaspoons instant coffee
1 teaspoon cinnamon
¼ teaspoon nutmeg
1 banana, peeled and cut into 1-inch pieces

Put all ingredients in blender container in order listed; cover and run on speed 7 (or high) until smooth. To serve, pour over ice cubes in tall glasses. *Makes 1 quart.*

### SPICED ICED COFFEE

1 cup cold water
1 6-ounce bottle cola
¼ cup light cream
1 cup crushed ice
2 tablespoons sugar
1 tablespoon instant coffee
⅛ teaspoon cinnamon

Put all ingredients in blender container; cover and run on speed 5 (or high) until smooth. *Makes about 3 servings.*

### FROSTY MINTED CHOCOLATE

¼ cup semisweet chocolate pieces
½ cup sugar
½ cup boiling water
¼ teaspoon salt
¼ teaspoon vanilla
1 13-ounce can evaporated milk
5–6 fresh mint sprigs OR ¼ teaspoon peppermint extract
1 cup crushed ice

Put chocolate, sugar and boiling water in blender container; cover and run on speed 1 (or low) for 30 seconds. Add remaining ingredients except crushed ice; cover and run on speed 1 (or low) for 1 minute. Add crushed ice and run on speed 7 (or high) until smooth. Serve in tall glasses. If desired, whipped cream (page 139) or a small spoonful of ice cream and a mint sprig may be used as a garnish. *Makes 3½ cups.*

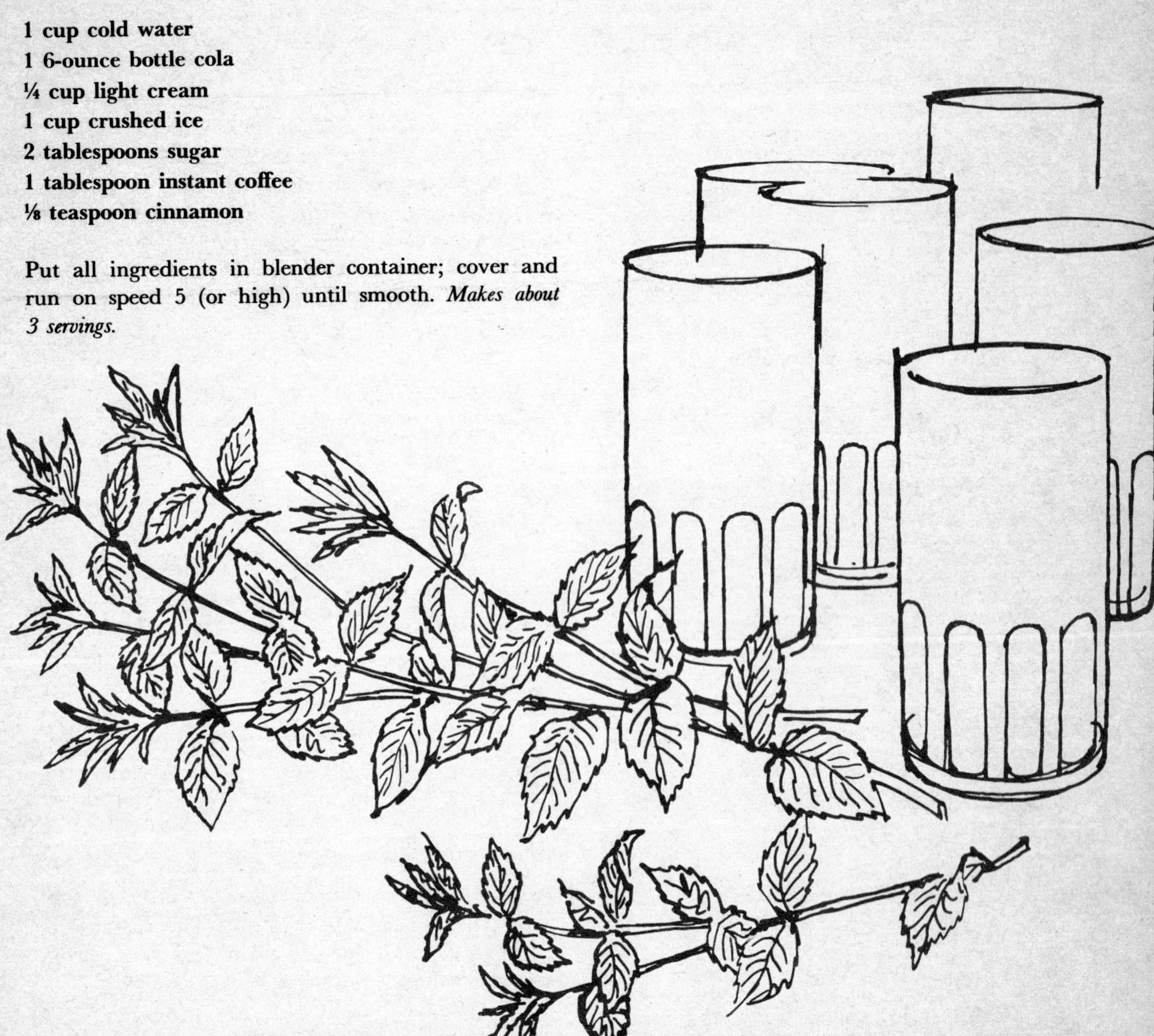

## Smooth Refreshers

### FRESH APPLE COOLER

½ cup water
1 tablespoon lemon juice
1 teaspoon sugar
1 apple, pared, cored and cut into 1-inch cubes
½ cup crushed ice

Put all ingredients except ice in blender container; cover and run on speed 7 (or high) until apple is liquefied. Add crushed ice; cover and run on speed 7 (or high) until ice is liquefied. Taste and add 1–2 additional teaspoons sugar, if necessary. *Makes 1½ cups; about 2 servings.*

### APPLE LIMEADE

½ cup sugar
12 mint leaves
½ cup lime juice
¼ teaspoon salt
2 large eating apples, pared, cored and cut up
½ cup boiling water
1 12-ounce bottle sparkling water, chilled

Put sugar, mint, lime juice, salt, apples and boiling water in blender container; cover and run on speed 5 (or high) until smooth. Cool and chill. At serving time, fill each of 3 tall glasses half full of apple mixture. Add sparkling water to fill each glass. *Makes 3 servings.*

### CHERRY TEA

1 cup water
½ cup sugar
1 cup double-strength tea, cooled
1 cup canned pitted sour cherries
¾ cup cherry juice
¼ cup lemon juice
2 tablespoons pineapple juice
1 quart cold water

Put 1 cup water and sugar in a small saucepan; bring to a boil, stirring to dissolve sugar. Boil 5 minutes. Set aside to cool. Put tea, cherry juice, cherries, lemon juice and pineapple juice in blender container; cover and run on speed 7 (or high) until cherries are liquefied. Pour into a pitcher; stir in syrup and 1 quart cold water. Chill. To serve, stir and pour over ice cubes in tall glasses. *Makes 8 servings.*

### CRANBERRY PUNCH

2¼ cups cold water
½ cup lemon juice
2 7-ounce cans jellied cranberry sauce
1 teaspoon almond extract
1 cup orange juice
1 6-ounce bottle ginger ale

Put cold water, lemon juice, cranberry sauce and almond extract in blender container; cover and run on speed 7 (or high) until smooth. Pour into a pitcher or small punch bowl; stir in orange juice and ginger ale. To serve, pour over ice cubes in tall glasses. *Makes 6 large servings.*

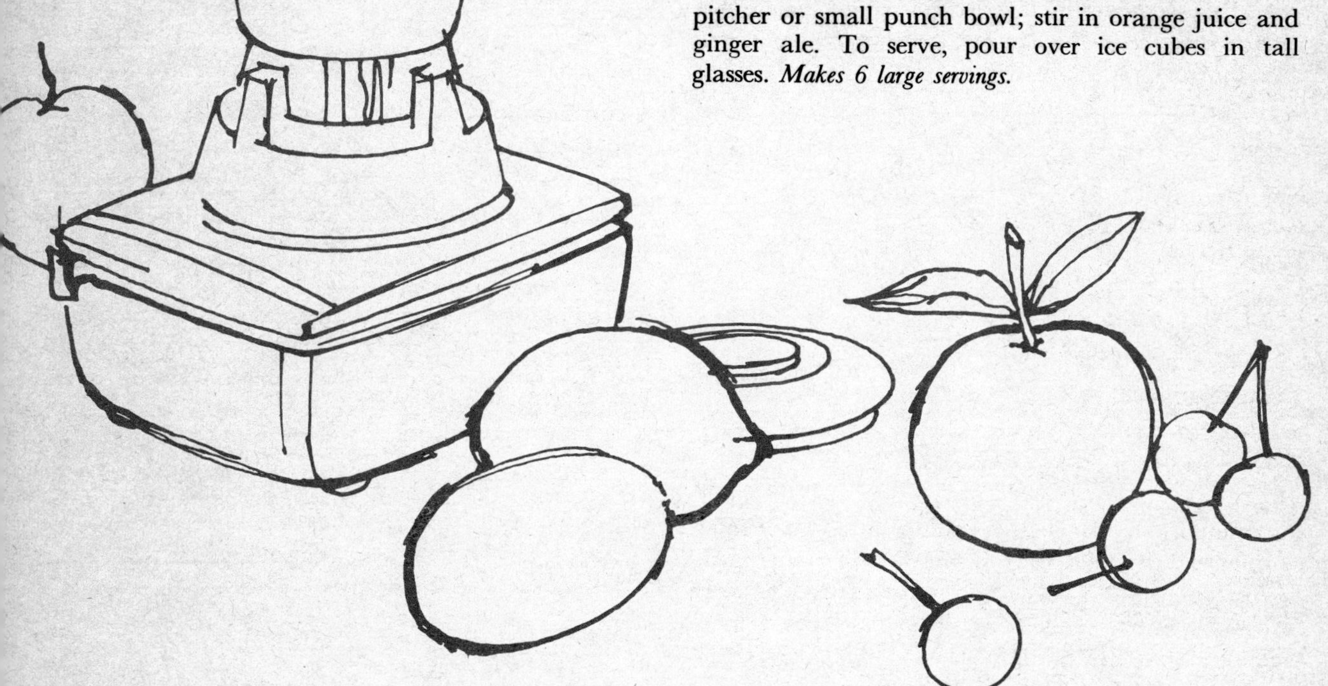

## LEMONADE

**½ cup lemon juice, fresh, frozen or canned**
**½ cup sugar**
**2 cups crushed ice**

Put all ingredients in blender container; cover and run on speed 7 (or high) about 10 seconds. Pour into 4 tall glasses and fill with water. *Makes 4 servings.*

### PINK LEMONADE

Add ¾ cup sweet cherry juice or ¾ cup frozen strawberries to ingredients before blending; blend until smooth.

## NUTRITIOUS LEMONADE

**1 egg**
**¼ cup sugar**
**¼ cup lemon juice**
**¼ cup water**
**1 cup crushed ice**

Put all ingredients in blender container; cover and run on speed 7 (or high) until ice is very fine. *Makes 2 servings.*

## LIME MINTADE

**1 cup mint leaves**
**1 cup sugar**
**1 cup boiling water**
**1 quart cold water**
**1¼ cups crushed ice**
**1 cup lime juice**
**¼ cup lemon juice**
**Few drops green food coloring**

Put mint leaves, sugar and boiling water in blender container; cover and run on speed 5 (or high) until mint is chopped. Cool; strain into a large pitcher. Add cold water, crushed ice, fruit juices and food coloring; mix well. Pour into ice cube-filled glasses and garnish with fresh mint. *Makes 8 servings.*

## ORANGE-APRICOT NECTAR

**3 cups orange juice**
**¾ cup cooked apricots, pitted**
**1½ cups crushed ice**

Put all ingredients in blender container; cover and run on speed 7 (or high) until smooth and frothy. *Makes 6 servings.*

## PINEAPPLE-APRICOT NECTAR

**6–7 canned apricot halves**
**2½ cups pineapple juice, chilled**
**1 cup crushed ice**

Put apricots in blender container; cover and run on speed 3 (or low) to make ¾ cup purée. Add remaining ingredients; cover and run on speed 7 (or high) for 1 minute or until smooth and frosty. *Makes 2–3 servings.*

## STRAWBERRY EGG SHAKE

**½ cup frozen strawberries, thawed**
**1 egg**
**1 tablespoon lemon juice**
**1 tablespoon sugar**
**½ cup crushed ice**

Put all ingredients in blender container; cover and run on speed 6 (or high) until smooth. Serve immediately. *Makes 1 serving.*

## STRAWBERRY LIMEADE

**½ cup lime juice**
**2 cups cold water**
**¼ cup sugar**
**1 10-ounce package frozen strawberries, thawed**
**5 ice cubes**

Put all ingredients except ice cubes in blender container; cover and run on speed 7 (or high) until smooth. While blender is running, add ice cubes, one at a time. *Makes 6 servings.*

*From left to right: Apple Limeade (p. 17), Cranberry Punch (p. 17), Orange-Apricot Nectar (p. 18), Strawberry Egg Shake (p. 18)*

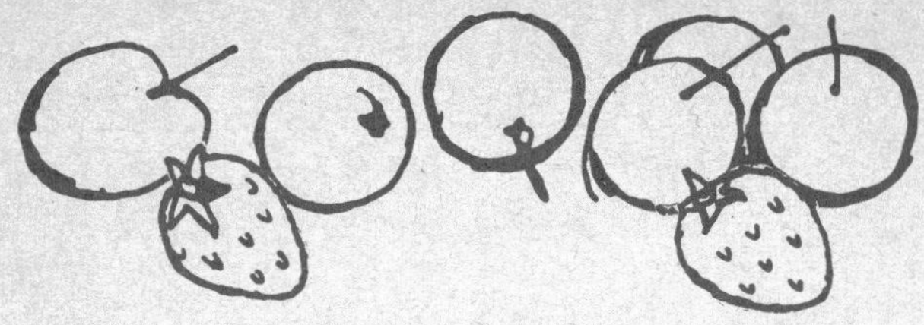

## SUMMER DREAM

**¼ cup heavy cream**
**1 10-ounce package frozen strawberries, partially thawed**
**1 9-ounce can crushed pineapple**
**Ginger ale, chilled**

Put all ingredients except ginger ale in blender container; cover and run on speed 7 (or high) until mixture is smooth. Divide among 6 glasses; fill with ginger ale and stir. *Makes 6 servings.*

## TROPICAL BLEND

**2 cups tropical-flavored fruit punch, chilled**
**2 small bananas, peeled and quartered**

Put fruit punch and bananas in blender container; cover and run on speed 2 (or low) until smooth. *Makes 2 servings.*

## SILVER FIZZ

**1 egg white**
**2 tablespoons lemon juice**
**1 tablespoon sugar**
**½ cup crushed ice**
**Ginger ale, chilled**

Put all ingredients except ginger ale in blender container; cover and run on speed 6 (or high) until frothy. Pour into a glass; add ginger ale. Garnish with a maraschino cherry. *Makes 1 serving.*

## APRICADO COOLER

**2 tablespoons lemon juice**
**1 12-ounce can apricot nectar**
**⅓ cup instant dry milk solids**
**½ medium avocado, peeled, seeded and cubed**
**1 cup crushed ice**

Put all ingredients in blender container; cover and run on speed 7 (or high) until very smooth. Pour over ice cubes to serve. *Makes 4 servings.*

### RECONSTITUTE DRY MILK SOLIDS

Measure desired amount of water into blender container; add dry milk solids. Cover and run on speed 3 (or low) and then run on speed 5 (or high) until completely blended.

## APRICOT-CRANBERRY CHILLER

**2 cups cranberry juice**
**1 cup canned apricot halves, drained**
**½ cup instant dry milk solids**
**½ teaspoon cinnamon**
**½ cup crushed ice**

Put all ingredients in blender container; cover and run on speed 7 (or high) until smooth. Serve immediately. *Makes 3 servings.*

## BUTTERMILK SHAKE

**½ cup chilled pineapple juice**
**⅛-inch thick slice lemon, with rind**
**1 tablespoon sugar**
**1 cup buttermilk**

Put all ingredients in blender container; cover and run on speed 7 (or high) until lemon is liquefied. *Makes 2 servings.*

## CREAMY FRUIT PUNCH

**3 cups cold milk**
**1 teaspoon rum flavoring**
**1 10-ounce package frozen strawberries, thawed**
**1 cup canned peach slices, drained**

Put 2 cups milk and remaining ingredients in blender container; cover and run on speed 7 (or high) until smooth. Pour into a punch bowl; add remaining 1 cup milk and stir well. *Makes 6 cups.*

### RECONSTITUTE FROZEN FRUIT JUICES

Put one 6-ounce can of frozen fruit juice concentrate in blender container; add required amount of cold water. Cover and run on speed 3 (or low) until completely blended.

## BASIC EGGNOG

**2 cups cold milk**
**2 eggs**
**4 teaspoons sugar**
**1 teaspoon vanilla**
**Nutmeg**

Put all ingredients except nutmeg in blender container; cover and run on speed 5 (or high). Pour into serving glasses; sprinkle with nutmeg, if desired. *Makes 3 cups.*

### FRUIT EGGNOG

Use Basic Eggnog recipe and add 2–3 tablespoons frozen fruit juice concentrate, such as pineapple or orange, or ½–¾ cup bottled fruit juice, such as grape, pineapple, cranberry or orange.

### EXTRA-RICH EGGNOG

Use Basic Eggnog recipe and add 2 scoops of any flavor ice cream.

### CARAMEL EGGNOG

Substitute 2 tablespoons maple syrup for sugar in Basic Eggnog recipe.

### PEACH EGGNOG

Use Basic Eggnog recipe, omitting sugar and vanilla. Add ½ cup frozen peaches, ½ teaspoon lemon juice and ⅛ teaspoon almond extract before blending.

## LEMONADE PUNCH

**1 lemon, quartered and seeded**
**2 tablespoons lemon juice**
**1 cup sugar**
**2 cups milk**
**1 tablespoon lemon extract**
**Lemon-lime carbonated beverage, chilled**

Put lemon, lemon juice, sugar, milk and lemon extract in blender container; cover and run on speed 5 (or high) until lemon rind is finely grated. Chill. At serving time, put 2 tablespoons of lemon mixture in each glass and fill with lemon-lime beverage. Store in covered jar. *Makes 1½ cups lemon base (enough for 12 servings).*

## LIME FREEZE

**1 egg**
**2 tablespoons lime juice**
**¼ cup sugar**
**1 cup cold milk**
**3 ice cubes**

Put all ingredients except ice cubes in blender container; cover and run on speed 6 (or high) until frothy. While blender is running, add ice cubes, one at a time. *Makes 3 servings.*

## HONEY BANANA SHAKE

**1 cup cold milk**
**2 tablespoons orange juice**
**2 tablespoons honey**
**1 ripe banana, peeled and quartered**

Put all ingredients in blender container; cover and run on speed 7 (or high) until smooth. *Makes 2 servings.*

## BANANA MILK SHAKE

**1 banana, peeled and cut into 1-inch pieces**
**1½ cups instant dry milk (approximately)**
**2 tablespoons sugar**
**1 teaspoon vanilla**
**½ cup cold water**
**Crushed ice**

Put banana and dry milk (to the 2-cup marking) in blender container. Add sugar, vanilla, water and enough crushed ice to fill container. Cover and run on speed 7 (or high) until smooth. *Makes 6 servings.*

***BREAKFAST IN A HURRY***

*Banana Milk Shake*
*over crisp cereal with berries*
*or sliced fresh nectarines or peaches*

## MILK 'N' FRUIT SMOOTHEES

**General Method:** To prepare Milk Smoothees, put all ingredients in blender container; cover and run on speed 7 (or high) until smooth and ice is completely liquefied, about 30 seconds.

### APRICOT SMOOTHEE

**1 cup milk**
**1 cup canned apricot halves OR ½ cup soaked dried apricots**
**⅛ teaspoon almond extract**
**Sugar to taste**
**1 cup crushed ice**

Prepare according to general method. *Makes 2 cups.*

### BANANA SMOOTHEE

**2 cups cold milk**
**2 ripe bananas, peeled and quartered**
**¼ teaspoon vanilla**
**1 tablespoon sugar**
**1 cup crushed ice**

Prepare according to general method. *Makes 4 cups.*

### BERRY SMOOTHEE

**2 cups cold milk**
**1 cup any fresh or frozen berries**
**1 tablespoon lemon juice**
**1-3 tablespoons sugar**
**Ice cubes**

Prepare according to general method. To cool, add 1 ice cube at a time while blender is running on speed 7 (or high). *Makes 2½ cups.*

## CARNIVAL MILK SHAKE

**1 cup fruit cocktail, drained**
**½ pint vanilla ice cream, cut into chunks**
**½ cup milk**
**Nutmeg OR 3 dashes aromatic bitters**

Reserve about ¼ cup fruit cocktail; put remainder in blender container; cover and run on speed 2 (or low) about 30 seconds or until smooth. Add ice cream and milk; cover and run on speed 3 (or low) until ice cream is soft. Pour into glasses. Add reserved fruit cocktail. Sprinkle with nutmeg. *Makes 3 servings.*

## PINEAPPLE-LEMON SHAKE

**1 cup cold milk**
**1 9-ounce can crushed pineapple**
**2 teaspoons lemon juice**
**1 pint vanilla ice cream, cut into chunks**

Put all ingredients in blender container in order listed; cover and run on speed 6 (or high) until smooth and frothy. Pour into tall glasses. *Makes 4 servings.*

## PEACH MILK SHAKE

**2 cups milk**
**½ cup light cream**
**1 1-pound can sliced peaches, drained**
**¼ cup sugar**
**Dash salt**
**Nutmeg**

Pour milk and cream into refrigerator tray; freeze until edges are icy. Put drained peaches in blender container; cover and run on speed 4 (or high) until puréed. Add frozen milk and cream, sugar and salt; cover and run on speed 3 (or low) until smooth. Sprinkle with nutmeg. *Makes 4 servings.*

## ORANGE-STRAWBERRY BREAKFAST IN A GLASS

**1 cup orange juice**
**1 cup frozen strawberries**
**1 egg**
**2 tablespoons nonfat dry milk solids**
**2 tablespoons sugar**

Put all ingredients in blender container; cover and start on speed 1 (or low) then run on speed 7 (or high) until smooth. *Makes 2 servings.*

## APPLE LIME FROST

**1 cup apple juice, chilled**
**1 pint lime sherbet, cut into chunks**
**2 drops peppermint extract**

Put all ingredients in blender container in order listed; cover and run on speed 5 (or high) until smooth. *Makes 4 servings.*

## BANANA-ORANGE SHAKE

**2 cups orange juice**
**2 bananas, peeled and cut into 1-inch pieces**
**½ pint vanilla ice cream, cut into chunks**

Put all ingredients in blender container in order listed; cover and run on speed 7 (or high) until smooth. Pour into tall glasses. *Makes 4 servings.*

## BLUEBERRY FLIP

**1½ cups whipping cream**
**1 egg**
**¾ cup canned or cooked fresh blueberries (with syrup)**
**2 tablespoons sugar**
**2 cups milk**
**½ pint vanilla ice cream**

In a chilled bowl whip cream with electric mixer until it will hold soft peaks; set aside. Put egg, blueberries, sugar and milk in blender container; cover and run on speed 7 (or high) until very smooth. Pour carefully over whipped cream and gently fold together. Pour into 6 glasses; top each with a scoop of ice cream. *Makes 6 servings.*

*Banana-Orange Shake, Blueberry Flip*

## CRANBERRY FREEZE

**2 cups cranberry juice**
**3 tablespoons frozen orange juice concentrate**
**1 pint vanilla ice cream, cut into chunks**

Put all ingredients in blender container in order listed; cover and run on speed 6 (or high) until smooth and frothy. *Makes 6 servings.*

## COCONUT PINEAPPLE FLOAT

**2 cups cold milk**
**¼ cup moist shredded coconut**
**1 tablespoon sugar**
**½ teaspoon vanilla**
**¼ teaspoon nutmeg**
**¼ cup crushed pineapple**
**Vanilla ice cream**

Put all ingredients except ice cream in blender container; cover and run on speed 7 (or high) until coconut is very fine. Pour into 3 tall glasses; top each with a scoop of ice cream. *Makes 3 servings.*

## CHOCOLATE-CHERRY SODA

**½ cup instant chocolate-flavored drink mix**
**2 cups milk**
**¼ cup light cream**
**1 teaspoon almond extract**
**1 pint cherry vanilla ice cream**
**2 7-ounce bottles cherry soda, chilled**

Put chocolate drink mix, milk, cream and almond extract in blender container; cover and run on speed 5 (or high) for 1 minute or until well mixed. Pour into 4 tall glasses. Add a scoop of ice cream to each. Pour cherry soda into the glasses. Top each soda with whipped cream (page 139 ) and toasted almonds, if desired. *Makes 4 servings.*

## MOCHA PUNCH

**1 cup cold water**
**1 cup crushed ice**
**1 tablespoon instant coffee**
**¼ teaspoon almond extract**
**Dash salt**
**1 pint chocolate ice cream, cut into chunks**
**½ cup whipping cream, whipped**
**¼ teaspoon nutmeg**

Put water, ice, instant coffee, extract and salt in blender container; cover and run on speed 6 (or high) until smooth. Add half the ice cream; cover and run on speed 6 (or high) until smooth. Fold in whipped cream and remaining ice cream. Top with nutmeg. *Makes 8 servings.*

## ORANGE CREAM FREEZE

**2 cups orange juice**
**1 pint vanilla ice cream, cut into chunks**

Put ingredients in blender container; cover and run on speed 6 (or high) until smooth and frothy. *Makes 4 servings.*

## ORANGE-PINEAPPLE CREAM

**1¾ cups pineapple juice, chilled**
**¼ pint orange sherbet**
**½ pint vanilla ice cream, cut into chunks**
**1 6-ounce bottle ginger ale, chilled**

Put first 3 ingredients in blender container in order listed; cover and run on speed 6 (or high) until smooth. Pour into a small punch bowl; stir in ginger ale. Serve immediately. *Makes 6 small servings.*

## PEACHY SHAKE

**1 10-ounce package frozen sliced peaches, thawed**
**¼ cup lemon juice**
**2 tablespoons honey**
**1 pint vanilla ice cream, cut into chunks**

Put all ingredients in blender container; cover and run on speed 7 (or high) until smooth and thick. If necessary, stop blender during processing and push ingredients toward blades with rubber spatula. Pour into tall glasses. *Makes 4 servings.*

## BANANA GINGER FIZZ

**1½ cups milk**
**3 ripe medium bananas, peeled and cut up**
**Lime sherbet**
**Ginger ale, chilled**

Put milk, bananas and 3 scoops sherbet in blender container; cover and run on speed 2 (or low) until smooth. Divide among 4 tall glasses and add ginger ale to fill. *Makes 4 servings.*

## PINEAPPLE PUFF

**1 egg**
**¼ cup crushed canned pineapple (with syrup)**
**1 scoop vanilla ice cream**
**½ cup ginger ale, chilled**

Put all ingredients except ginger ale in blender container; cover and run on speed 6 (or high) until smooth. Add ginger ale; cover and run on speed 1 (or low) for 5 seconds. Serve immediately. *Makes 1 serving.*

## PRUNE FROST

**⅓ cup orange juice, chilled**
**½ cup cooked pitted prunes**
**1 cup cold milk**
**1 teaspoon lemon juice**
**1 tablespoon sugar**
**1 large scoop vanilla ice cream**

Put all ingredients except ice cream in blender container; cover and run on speed 7 (or high) until perfectly smooth. Add ice cream; cover and run on speed 5 (or high) just until smooth. *Makes 2 large servings.*

## RASPBERRY REFRESHER

**1 cup pineapple juice, chilled**
**½ cup frozen raspberries, thawed**
**1 pint lemon sherbet, cut into chunks**

Put pineapple juice and raspberries in blender container; cover and run on speed 7 (or high) until raspberries are liquefied. Strain to remove seeds. Return mixture to blender container; add sherbet; cover and run on speed 5 (or high) until smooth. *Makes 4 servings.*

## STRAWBERRY-PINEAPPLE SHAKE

**1 cup milk**
**1 9-ounce can crushed pineapple**
**1 pint strawberry ice cream**

Put milk and pineapple in blender container; cover and run on speed 7 (or high) until smooth. Spoon in ice cream; cover and run on speed 4 (or low) until smooth. Garnish with fresh mint leaves. *Makes 4 servings.*

## STRAWBERRY MINT FLOAT

**2 cups milk**
**1 pint vanilla ice cream, cut into chunks**
**1 10-ounce package frozen strawberries, thawed**
**1 pint peppermint ice cream**

Put all ingredients except peppermint ice cream in blender container; cover and run on speed 7 (or high) until smooth. Pour into 6 glasses; float a heaping spoonful of peppermint ice cream in each glass. *Makes 6 servings.*

## TUTTI-FRUTTI FLOAT

**3 cups orange juice**
**1 cup canned fruit cocktail, drained**
**1 pint vanilla ice cream**

Put orange juice and fruit cocktail in blender container; cover and run on speed 4 (or low) until fruit is finely chopped. Pour into 4 tall glasses; top each with a scoop of ice cream. *Makes 4 servings.*

## Soda Fountain Specials

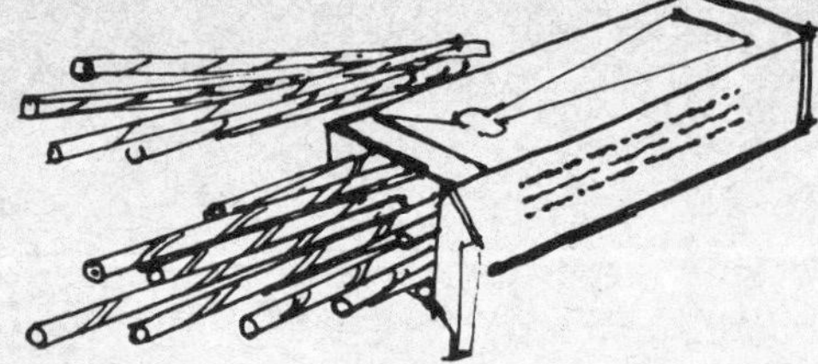

## VANILLA MILK SHAKE

**1 cup cold milk**
**½ pint vanilla ice cream**

Put ingredients in blender container; cover and run on speed 5 (or high) about 30 seconds or until smooth and fluffy. *Makes 2 cups.*

#### CHOCOLATE MILK SHAKE

Add ¼ cup chocolate syrup to Vanilla Milk Shake before blending; or substitute chocolate ice cream for vanilla ice cream.

#### STRAWBERRY MILK SHAKE

Add ½ cup sweetened fresh or frozen strawberries to Vanilla Milk Shake before blending.

#### BANANA MILK SHAKE

Add 1 ripe banana, peeled and quartered, to Vanilla Milk Shake before blending.

#### MOCHA MILK SHAKE

Add 2 teaspoons instant coffee to Vanilla Milk Shake and substitute chocolate ice cream for vanilla ice cream.

#### MALTED MILK SHAKE

Add 1 tablespoon malted milk powder to any of the above Milk Shakes before blending.

## QUICK SHAKE

**1 13-ounce can evaporated milk, chilled**
**½ cup instant cocoa**
**1 pint vanilla ice cream, cut into chunks**

Put all ingredients in blender container; cover and run on speed 5 (or high) until thick and smooth. Serve immediately, or pour into a chilled vacuum bottle for later use. Shake before serving. *Makes 4–5 servings.*

## ICE CREAM SODAS

**General Method:** To prepare the following ice cream sodas, put the milk, fruit or flavoring and ice cream in blender container; cover and run on speed 2 (or low) about 30 seconds or until smooth. Pour into a tall glass and fill with chilled ginger ale or carbonated soda.

#### CHOCOLATE ICE CREAM SODA

**2 tablespoons milk**
**2 tablespoons chocolate syrup**
**2 scoops chocolate or vanilla ice cream**
**Ginger ale or carbonated soda, chilled**

Prepare according to general method. *Makes 1 serving.*

#### FRESH STRAWBERRY SODA

**3 tablespoons milk**
**⅓ cup frozen or crushed sweetened fresh strawberries**
**2 scoops vanilla or strawberry ice cream**
**Ginger ale or carbonated soda, chilled**

Prepare according to general method. *Makes 1 serving.*

*Fresh Strawberry Soda, Mocha Milk Shake*

*Hot Cocoa*

## Chocolate Favorites

### HOT COCOA

**1 cup hot water**
**4 tablespoons cocoa**
**4 tablespoons sugar**
**¼ teaspoon salt**
**½ teaspoon vanilla**
**3 cups scalded milk**

Put all ingredients except milk in blender container; cover and run on speed 2 (or low). While blender is running, slowly add hot milk. Serve immediately or keep hot in top of double boiler. *Makes 5 servings.*

### HOT MINTED CHOCOLATE

**2½ cups hot milk**
**½ cup light cream**
**15 chocolate mint wafers**

Put all ingredients in blender container; cover and start blender on speed 1 (or low), then run on speed 7 (or high) until chocolate is liquefied. Serve immediately. *Makes 4 servings.*

### QUICK HOT CHOCOLATE

**¾ cup hot water**
**3 tablespoons sugar**
**Dash salt**
**1 teaspoon vanilla**
**2 squares (2 ounces) unsweetened chocolate, cut up**
**2¾ cups scalded milk**

Put water, sugar, salt, vanilla and chocolate in blender container; cover and run on speed 7 (or high) until chocolate is liquefied, about 1 minute. Run on speed 2 (or low) and, while running, slowly add hot milk. Serve immediately or keep hot in top of double boiler. *Makes 6 servings.*

### HOT CHOCO-MINT FLUFF

**8 round peppermint hard candies**
**½ cup whipping cream, whipped**
**¼ cup chocolate syrup**
**3 cups hot milk**

Put candy in blender container; cover and run on speed 3 (or low) until finely crushed. Fold into whipped cream. Put chocolate syrup, milk and half the whipped cream in blender container; cover and run on speed 2 (or low) until smooth. Fill cups with chocolate mixture and top with remaining peppermint whipped cream. *Makes 5–6 servings.*

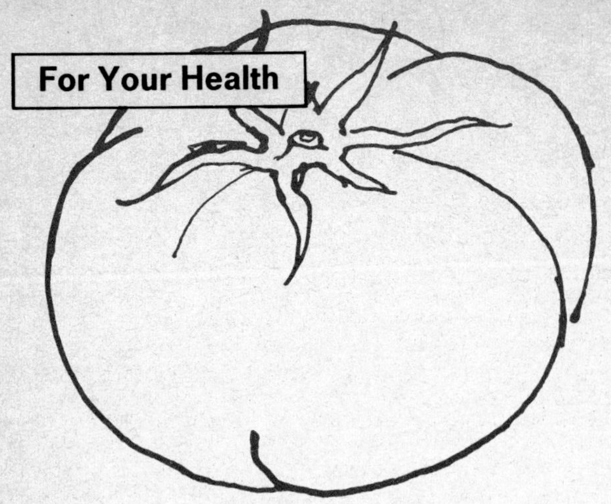


## PINEAPPLE-CARROT COCKTAIL

**2 cups pineapple juice**
**3 medium carrots, cut into 2-inch pieces**
**1 small banana, peeled and cut up**
**4–6 ice cubes**

Put all ingredients except ice cubes in blender container; cover and run on speed 7 (or high) until carrots are completely liquefied. While blender is running, add ice cubes, one at a time. Drink should be chilled and thinned to drinking consistency. *Makes about 4–6 servings.*

## TOMATO JUICE COCKTAIL

**1½ cups tomato juice**
**½ cup evaporated milk**
**¼ teaspoon celery salt**
**¼ teaspoon salt**
**Dash black pepper**
**½ cup crushed ice**

Put all ingredients in blender container; cover and run on speed 6 (or high) until smooth and frothy. *Makes about 4 servings.*

## CARROT MILK

*An excellent drink for children.*

**2 cups milk**
**3 medium carrots, cut into 1-inch pieces**

Put ingredients in blender container; cover and run on speed 7 (or high) until carrots are liquefied. *Makes 4 servings.*

## TOMATO VEGETABLE COCKTAIL

**2 cups tomato juice**
**½ teaspoon salt**
**2 tablespoons lemon juice**
**1 teaspoon Worcestershire**
**3 sprigs parsley**
**1 small stalk celery, cut into 2-inch pieces**
**1 small raw carrot, cut into 2-inch pieces**
**1 slice onion**
**4 ice cubes**

Put all ingredients except ice cubes in blender container; cover and run on speed 7 (or high) until vegetables are liquefied. While blender is running, add ice cubes, one at a time. *Makes 3 servings.*

## TOMATO JUICE CUCUMBER COCKTAIL

**½ small cucumber, pared**
**2½ cups tomato juice**
**1 teaspoon prepared horseradish**
**2 tablespoons lemon juice**
**1 small green onion with top, cut into 1-inch pieces**
**½ teaspoon salt**
**⅛ teaspoon pepper**
**1 cup crushed ice**

Cut 4 thin slices from cucumber and set aside. Dice remaining cucumber, removing seeds, and put in blender container with remaining ingredients. Cover container and run on speed 7 (or high) until all ingredients are liquefied. Garnish with cucumber slices. *Makes 4 servings.*

***LITTLE MEAL***

*Tomato Juice Cocktail*
*Surprise Deviled Eggs (p. 43)*

***LITTLE MEAL***

*Carrot Milk*
*Crackers and Peanut Butter (p. 54)*

***LITTLE MEAL***

*Pineapple Carrot Cocktail*
*Ham Salad Spread (p. 50)*
*on shredded wheat wafers*

## Punches for Parties

### ORANGE EGGNOG

6 eggs
¼ cup sugar
¼ teaspoon cinnamon
¼ teaspoon ginger
¼ teaspoon cloves
½ cup lemon juice
2 quarts orange juice, chilled
1 quart vanilla ice cream, cut into chunks
1 quart ginger ale, chilled
Nutmeg

Put eggs, sugar, cinnamon, ginger, cloves, lemon juice and 3 cups orange juice in blender container; cover and run on speed 7 (or high) for 1 minute. Pour into a punch bowl. Stir in remaining orange juice, ice cream and ginger ale. Sprinkle with nutmeg. *Makes 20 servings.*

### FRUITED TEA PUNCH

2 cups pineapple juice
1 10-ounce package frozen strawberries, thawed
1 6-ounce can frozen lemonade concentrate, thawed
5 tablespoons instant tea
1½ quarts water

Put all ingredients except water in blender container; cover and run on speed 7 (or high) until strawberries are liquefied. Pour into a punch bowl; add water and stir. Add ice cubes to chill. *Makes 20 small servings.*

### LEMON-STRAWBERRY PUNCH

1½ cups fresh strawberries, hulled
3 6-ounce cans frozen lemonade concentrate, partially thawed
½ cup sugar
2 quarts ice water
1 quart ginger ale, chilled

Put strawberries in blender container; cover and run on speed 3 (or low) a few seconds or until fruit is puréed. Add lemonade concentrate and sugar; cover and run on speed 3 (or low) to mix. Let stand 30 minutes. At serving time, add water and ginger ale. Pour over a block of ice in punch bowl. *Makes 32 servings.*

### GOLDEN MINT RECEPTION PUNCH

30–35 sprigs mint
2 cups sugar
2 quarts boiling water
2 quarts orange juice, chilled
1 1-pound 4-ounce can (2⅓ cups) pineapple juice, chilled
2⅓ cups lemon juice, chilled
1 quart ginger ale, chilled
1 quart sparkling water, chilled

Put half the mint sprigs, 1 cup sugar and 1 quart boiling water in blender container; cover and run on speed 5 (or high) until mint is chopped. Pour into a large pitcher. Repeat with remaining mint, sugar and boiling water. Cool and pour through a very fine strainer. At serving time, pour mint syrup and remaining ingredients into punch bowl; stir to mix. If desired, float mint sprigs and lemon slices on punch. *Makes 50 servings.*

### THREE-FRUIT PUNCH

1 6-ounce can frozen lemonade concentrate
1 8-ounce can crushed pineapple
1 10-ounce package frozen strawberries, thawed
3 quarts ginger ale, chilled
Crushed ice

Put lemonade concentrate, pineapple and strawberries in blender container; cover and run on speed 7 (or high) until completely smooth. Combine with ginger ale and pour over crushed ice in a punch bowl. *Makes 1 gallon (32 servings).*

**Note:** Fruit mixture can be made in advance and stored in a covered jar in refrigerator. Combine with ginger ale just before serving.

## Blender Bartending

*For alcoholic drinks you will find most of the standard formulas are included in this section. But there are some new tricks, too. You will discover after-dinner drinks as smooth as velvet that are best made with the blender. And there is an array of impressive liqueur frappés, which might act as low-calorie but high-glamor substitutes for dessert — and they can be made only with the blender.*

## Standard Cocktails

### DAIQUIRIS

Most people like them of a slushy consistency, but others prefer them like sherbet. Serve in champagne glasses with short straws. If you don't want your daiquiri frozen, run blender only a few seconds.

#### FROZEN DAIQUIRIS

**1½ ounces light rum or Bacardi rum**
**¾ tablespoon lime juice**
**1 teaspoon sugar**
**3 ounces ice for slushy consistency OR**
**10 ounces ice for frozen consistency**

Put all ingredients in blender container. Cover and run on speed 6 (or high) until desired consistency is obtained. For sherbet consistency, it may be necessary to stop the blender during processing and push frozen mixture toward blades with rubber spatula. *Makes 2 servings.*

#### FRUIT DAIQUIRI

Bananas, peaches, strawberries, apricots, pineapple or cherries all may be added individually to make delicious daiquiris that could be used as a dessert. All should be added before the ice.

**Use ½ banana per daiquiri**
**Use about 2 ounces (4 tablespoons) fruit or berries (fresh or frozen)***

*If fruit is sweetened, omit sugar in recipe.

**Note:** Top a frozen daiquiri in a champagne glass with a dash of grenadine and a red or green cherry. Serve slushy daiquiri with a slender pineapple stick.

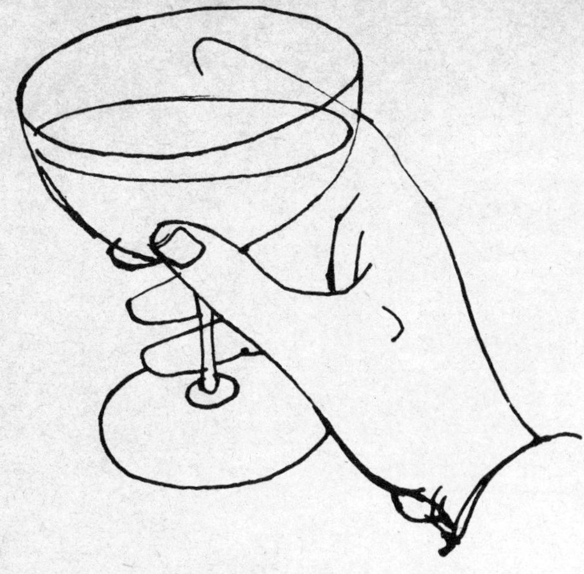

## EGGNOG

**1½ ounces rum, brandy, whiskey, sherry or Cognac***
**1 teaspoon sugar**
**1 egg**
**5 ounces milk**
**2 ice cubes, crushed**

Put all ingredients in blender container. Cover and run on speed 1 (or low) for 5 seconds. Strain into glasses and top each with dash of nutmeg. *Makes 2 servings.*

* Half rum and half brandy is another popular combination for eggnogs.

### HOT EGGNOG

Use above ingredients except heat milk, sugar and liquor. Do not boil. Put eggs in blender container; cover and run on speed 1 (or low). While blender is running, gradually add hot ingredients. Serve in warm mugs topped with dash of nutmeg.

**Note:** Recipes may be doubled or quadrupled.

## NEW YEAR'S MORNING MILK PUNCH

**1 cup milk**
**2 ounces light rum**
**1 teaspoon sugar**
**2 drops almond extract**
**Dash aromatic bitters**
**Dash nutmeg**
**1 cup crushed ice**

Put all ingredients in blender container; cover and run on speed 6 (or high) for 3 seconds. Strain into highball glasses. *Makes 2 servings.*

## BACARDI COCKTAIL

**3 ounces Bacardi rum**
**Juice of 2 limes**
**2 dashes grenadine**
**1 teaspoon sugar**
**1 cup crushed ice**

Put all ingredients in blender container; cover and run on speed 3 (or low) for 30 seconds or until of drinking consistency. (Double ice if a frappé is desired.) Serve with straws. *Makes 2 servings.*

## JAMAICA SWIZZLE

**1½ ounces Jamaica rum**
**6 dashes aromatic bitters**
**1½ tablespoons lime juice**
**1 teaspoon sugar**
**½ cup crushed ice**

Put all ingredients in blender container; cover and run on speed 6 (or high) for 15 seconds. Serve in cocktail glass. *Makes 1 serving.*

## PINEAPPLE PASSION

**1 13½-ounce can pineapple tidbits**
**½ cup light rum**
**¼ cup lime juice**
**1 tablespoon sugar**
**1 teaspoon grenadine**
**6 ice cubes**

Put all ingredients except ice cubes in blender container; cover and run on speed 5 (or high) until pineapple is finely crushed. While blender is running, add ice cubes, one at a time. *Makes 3–4 servings.*

## RUM FLIP

**1 teaspoon sugar**
**1½ ounces light rum**
**1 egg**
**½ cup crushed ice**

Put all ingredients in blender container; cover and run on speed 6 (or high) for 15 seconds. Serve in cocktail glass and sprinkle with nutmeg. *Makes 1 serving.*

## PINK LADY

3 ounces dry gin
1 egg white
1–2 teaspoons grenadine
½ cup crushed ice

Put all ingredients in blender container. Cover and run on speed 3 (or low) for 10–20 seconds or until contents are blended. Serve in cocktail glasses. *Makes 2 servings.*

## WHITE LADY

8 ounces gin
2 ounces lemon juice
1 ounce Cointreau
2 egg whites
2 cups crushed ice

Put all ingredients in blender container; cover and run on speed 6 (or high) for 15 seconds. Serve in cocktail glasses. *Makes 4 servings.*

## SHAMROCK FROST

3 ounces gin
3 tablespoons lime juice
1 ounce green crème de menthe
1 egg white
1½–2 cups crushed ice

Put all ingredients in blender container. Cover and run on speed 7 (or high) until of sherbet consistency. Serve in champagne glasses with short straws. *Makes 2 servings.*

## BACARDI GIN COCKTAIL

Juice of 2 limes
2 teaspoons grenadine
1½ ounces gin
3 ounces Bacardi rum
1 cup crushed ice

Put all ingredients in blender container; cover and run on speed 3 (or low) for 30 seconds or until of drinking consistency. (Double ice if a frappé is desired.) Serve with straws. *Makes 2 servings.*

## GRAPE-VODKA FROTH

3 ounces vodka
8 ounces grape juice
1½ tablespoons fresh lemon juice
1 egg white
1 cup crushed ice

Put all ingredients in blender container. Cover and run on speed 3 (or low) for 15 seconds or until frothy and smooth. Pour into chilled cocktail glasses. *Makes 4 servings.*

## BLOODY MARY

8 ounces tomato juice
3 ounces vodka
6 tablespoons lemon juice
1 egg white
½ teaspoon salt
Dash freshly ground pepper
2 fresh celery leaves
4 dashes Worcestershire
1 cup crushed ice

Put all ingredients in blender container; cover and run on speed 6 (or high) until ice is completely liquefied. *Makes 4 servings.*

## GREEN COOLER

1 6-ounce can frozen limeade concentrate
1 can vodka
5 cans crushed ice

Put all ingredients in blender container; cover and run on speed 6 (or high) for 15 seconds. Serve in highball glasses with straws. *Makes 4 servings.*

## BRANDY FLIP

**1¼ ounces brandy**
**1 egg**
**½ teaspoon sugar**
**⅓ cup crushed ice**

Put all ingredients in blender container. Cover and run on speed 1 (or low) until smooth. Pour into champagne glasses. Sprinkle with nutmeg. *Makes 2 servings.*

## EARLY BIRD COCKTAIL

**1½ ounces frozen grapefruit juice concentrate, thawed**
**1½ ounces gin**
**¼ cup crushed ice**

Put all ingredients in blender container; cover and run on speed 6 (or high) for 15 seconds. Serve in old fashioned glass. *Makes 1 serving.*

## TOMATO JUICE MIST

**½ medium green pepper, seeded and cut up**
**½ cup dry vermouth**
**2 tablespoons lemon juice**
**1 teaspoon Worcestershire**
**Dash Tabasco**
**¾ teaspoon celery salt**
**¼ teaspoon onion powder**
**¼ teaspoon garlic salt**
**2 13½-ounce cans tomato juice, chilled**
**4–6 thin lemon slices**

Put all ingredients except tomato juice and lemon slices in blender container; cover and run on speed 5 (or high) until smooth. Pour through a strainer into a pitcher; stir in tomato juice. Chill. Pour over ice cubes in tall glasses and garnish with lemon slices. Serve with straws. *Makes 4–6 servings.*

## SHERRY SHAKE

**1½ cups orange juice**
**½ cup lemon juice**
**1 cup dry sherry**
**½ cup sugar**
**1 egg**
**6 ice cubes**

Put all ingredients except ice cubes in blender container; cover and run on speed 5 (or high) until foamy and well mixed. While blender is running, add ice cubes, one at a time. Serve immediately. *Makes 8 servings.*

## TOM AND JERRY

**2 eggs**
**2 tablespoons sugar**
**2 ounces rye whiskey or brandy**
**2 ounces Jamaica rum**
**1½ cups hot milk**

Put eggs, sugar and liquor in blender container; cover and run on speed 1 (or low). While blender is running, gradually add hot milk. Serve in warm mugs and sprinkle with nutmeg. *Makes 4 servings.*

## RUM RUNNER

*A perfect cocktail for the ladies.*

**1½ ounces white rum**
**1½ ounces orange juice**
**Dash grenadine**
**½ cup crushed ice**
**½ slice orange**

Put all ingredients except orange slice in blender container; cover and run on speed 6 (or high) for 10 seconds. Strain into a champagne glass and garnish with orange slice. *Makes 1 serving.*

## SCOTCH FROST

1½ ounces Scotch whiskey
¾ ounce lemon juice
1 teaspoon sugar
1 cup crushed ice

Put all ingredients in blender container; cover and run on speed 6 (or high) for 8 seconds. Serve with straw in old fashioned glass. *Makes 1 serving.*

## WHISKEY SOUR

2 tablespoons lemon juice
1 teaspoon sugar
4 ounces whiskey
1 cup crushed ice

Put all ingredients in blender container. Cover and run on speed 3 (or low) for 10–20 seconds. Serve in whiskey sour glasses. *Makes 2 servings.*

*Whiskey Sour (p. 34)*

*Bloody Mary (p. 32)*

*Shamrock Frost (p. 32)*

*From left to right: Chocolate Mocha Dream (p. 36), Orange Blossom (p. 35), Lovely (p. 36)*

## Cordial Desserts

### ALEXANDER

**4 ounces gin**
**4 ounces whipping cream**
**4 ounces crème de cacao**
**1 cup crushed ice (approximately)**

Put all ingredients in blender container; cover and run on speed 3 (or low) for 5–10 seconds or until blended. Strain into cocktail glasses; serve immediately. *Makes 4 servings.*

**Variations:** For a Southern Alexander substitute 4 ounces Southern Comfort for the gin. For a Brandy Alexander, substitute 4 ounces brandy for the gin.

### GOLDEN GLOW

**3 ounces gin, light rum or Southern Comfort**
**½ pint orange ice or sherbet, cut into chunks**

Put ingredients in blender container. Cover and run on speed 1 (or low) until smooth. Serve in champagne glasses. *Makes 2 servings.*

### GRASSHOPPER

**4 ounces green crème de menthe**
**4 ounces white crème de cacao**
**4 ounces light cream**
**1 cup crushed ice**

Put all ingredients in blender container; cover and run on speed 3 (or low) for 5–10 seconds or until blended. Strain into cocktail glasses. *Makes 4 servings.*

### ORANGE BLOSSOM

**1 scoop vanilla ice cream**
**½ scoop orange sherbet**
**1½ ounces gin**
**½ slice orange**

Put ice cream, sherbet and gin in blender container; cover and run on speed 5 (or high) for 15 seconds. Serve in champagne glass; garnish with orange slice. *Makes 1 serving.*

## LAMPLIGHTER

*A nice after-dinner drink.*

**1 ounce bourbon**
**1 tablespoon orange curacao**
**1 ounce light cream**
**½ teaspoon green crème de menthe**
**½ cup crushed ice**

Put all ingredients in blender container; cover and run on speed 6 (or high) for 15 seconds. Serve in a champagne glass. *Makes 1 serving.*

## LOVELY

*A delightful after-dinner drink.*

**1 ounce bourbon**
**1 tablespoon cherry liqueur**
**1 ounce light cream**
**½ cup crushed ice**

Put all ingredients in blender container; cover and run on speed 6 (or high) for 15 seconds. Serve in a cocktail glass. *Makes 1 serving.*

## CRÈME DE CAFÉ

**1 ounce bourbon**
**1 ounce triple-strength cold coffee**
**¼ cup vanilla ice cream**

Put all ingredients in blender container; cover and run on speed 6 (or high) for 8 seconds. Serve in place of dessert. *Makes 1 serving.*

## COFFEE COCKTAIL

**1 tablespoon coffee liqueur**
**1 ounce port**
**1 ounce brandy**
**½ teaspoon sugar**
**½ cup crushed ice**

Put all ingredients in blender container; cover and run on speed 6 (or high) for 15 seconds. *Makes 1 serving.*

## CHOCOLATE MOCHA DREAM

**1 cup strong warm coffee**
**1 ⅞-ounce almond chocolate bar**
**1 cup bourbon**
**1 pint vanilla ice cream, cut into chunks**

Put coffee and chocolate bar in blender container; cover and run on speed 7 (or high) until chocolate is liquefied. Add bourbon and ice cream; cover and run on speed 5 (or high) until smooth. Attractive when served in wine glasses. *Makes 8 servings.*

## JAMAICA SPICE

*(After-dinner drink)*

**1 ounce dark rum**
**1 ounce brandy**
**1 ounce coffee**
**1 ounce honey**
**½ cup crushed ice**

Put all ingredients in blender container; cover and run on speed 6 (or high) for 15 seconds. Serve in cocktail glass. *Makes 1 serving.*

## PINK SQUIRREL

*(After-dinner drink)*

**¼ cup vanilla ice cream**
**1 ounce crème De Noyaux**
**1 ounce white crème de cacao**

Put all ingredients in blender container; cover and run on speed 5 (or high) for 10 seconds. Serve in place of dessert. *Makes 1 serving.*

# Starters and Spreads

*The custom of blending mayonnaise, sour cream, cheeses, fish and meat into savory mixtures to spread on or dip with crackers, chips and vegetables is not more than a generation old. It grew out of the recognized need to provide food to accompany the beverages served before dinner or during cocktail parties.*

*In this chapter you will find such gourmet specialties as Baked Liver Pâté for the first course at a meal. You will find showpieces for the cocktail party in Filled Edam Cheese and Appetizer Cheesecake. There are dips, which can be turned into spreads by reducing liquids and seasonings, and spreads, which can become dips if made more liquid and more spicy. Also included are tidbits and nibbles, both hot and cold.*

*To go with these tasty snacks, try one of the blender beverages or soups, especially before dinner. It's a good way to raise spirits and heighten appetites while dinner cooks.*

Use Up Bits and Pieces

*The bowl of ham bits or the piece of dried cheese can find glamorous transformation in a dip or spread. The recipes collected here were designed, in large part, to make the most of what you have. Devise your own combinations if you don't find one that is exactly suitable.*

Dippers Galore

*When planning for dips, keep in mind potato chips, corn chips, a variety of small crackers and pretzels. Always have at least one vegetable dipper, such as thin slices of carrot or cucumber, celery, green pepper sticks, cauliflower flowerets or raw mushrooms in slices.*

*Mid-morning, mid-afternoon, pre-lunch, pre-dinner or late at night—whenever you have a taste for "something special," turn to the pages ahead.*

*From left to right: Snowball Pâté (p. 39), Appetizer Cheesecake (p. 39)*

## SNOWBALL PÂTÉ

**2 tablespoons mayonnaise**
**2 tablespoons lemon juice**
**½ pound liver sausage, cut up**
**2 green onions, cut up**
**4 ounces cream cheese, cubed**
**2 tablespoons milk or cream**

Put first 4 ingredients in blender container; cover and run on speed 4 (or high) until smooth. If necessary, stop blender during processing and push ingredients toward blades with rubber spatula. Pack in a small bowl and cover; chill for at least 2 hours or overnight.

Unmold on serving plate. Put cream cheese and milk in blender container; cover and run on speed 4 (or high) until smooth. Spread over mold and chill until serving time. *Makes a mold about 3 inches in diameter.*

## BAKED LIVER PÂTÉ

**½ pound beef liver, cut into 2-inch cubes**
**2 pieces zwieback**
**1 egg**
**1 tablespoon cornstarch**
**¾ teaspoon salt**
**¼ teaspoon pepper**
**1¼ cups hot milk**
**½ medium onion, cut up**
**¼ pound ground lean pork**
**Bay leaves**

Preheat oven to 325°. Cook liver in boiling salted water for 6–8 minutes; drain and cool. Meanwhile, break zwieback into blender container; cover and run on speed 3 (or low) until crumbed. If necessary, stop and start blender to toss pieces toward blades. Set aside.

Put egg, cornstarch, salt and pepper in blender container; cover and run on speed 3 (or low) a few seconds. Add a small amount of hot milk; cover and run on speed 3 (or low) a few seconds. Add remaining milk, onion and pork; cover and run on speed 2 (or low) until onion is chopped. Remove cover and slowly add liver while blender is running on speed 6 (or high). When all liver is chopped, add zwieback crumbs; cover and run on speed 5 (or high) until smooth. Pour into a 1-quart casserole or 9x5x3-inch loaf pan. Arrange bay leaves on top in a petal design. Set in a shallow pan and add hot water to ½-inch depth. Bake for 1½ hours or until a knife inserted in center comes out clean. Cool. Cover and refrigerate until ready to serve. *Makes about 3 cups.*

## SARDINE PÂTÉ

**2 tablespoons lemon juice**
**1 thin slice onion**
**4 sprigs parsley**
**1 8-ounce package cream cheese, cubed**
**2 4-ounce cans sardines in oil, drained**

Put all ingredients in blender container in order listed; cover and run on speed 6 (or high) until smooth. If necessary, stop blender during processing and push ingredients toward blades with rubber spatula. Chill. Form into a ball. Serve with parsley and radish garnish, if desired. *Makes about 1 cup.*

## APPETIZER CHEESECAKE

**Melted butter or margarine**
**1 6-ounce box cheese crackers**
**2 cups dairy sour cream**
**½ cup green salad olives OR 10–12 large stuffed green olives**
**1 medium green pepper, seeded and cut up**
**1 small onion, cut into quarters**
**2 tablespoons lemon juice**
**1 teaspoon salt**
**1 teaspoon Worcestershire**
**¼ teaspoon paprika**
**Dash Tabasco**
**1 large stalk celery, cut into 1-inch pieces**
**2–3 pitted ripe olives, cut into rings**
**7–8 pimiento strips**
**Chicory or parsley**

Brush bottom and sides of 9-inch spring form pan (or pan with removable bottom) with melted butter. Put ⅓ of the crackers in blender container; cover and run on speed 4 (or low) until crumbed. Pour crumbs into bowl and repeat with remaining crackers until all have been crumbed. Cover bottom of prepared pan with half the cracker crumbs. Reserve the remaining crumbs for top.

Put sour cream, green olives, green pepper, onion, lemon juice, salt, Worcestershire, paprika, Tabasco and celery in blender container. Cover and run on speed 2 (or low), until vegetables are finely chopped. If necessary, stop blender and push ingredients toward blades with rubber spatula. Spread this mixture over cracker crumb base. Scatter remaining cracker crumbs evenly over the top. Cover with waxed paper and refrigerate for at least 24 hours. Remove sides of pan; place cake (still on pan bottom) on serving dish. Garnish with ripe olive rings and pimiento strips. Border dish with chicory. Serve with thin pumpernickel or crisp rye crackers. *Makes 12 servings.*

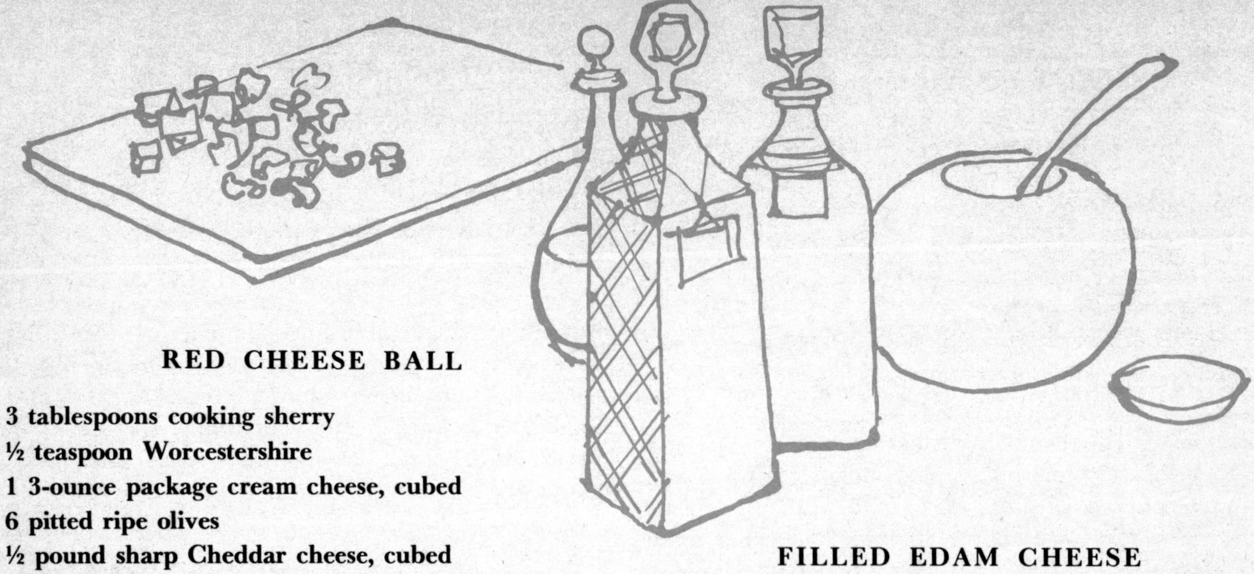

## RED CHEESE BALL

**3 tablespoons cooking sherry**
**½ teaspoon Worcestershire**
**1 3-ounce package cream cheese, cubed**
**6 pitted ripe olives**
**½ pound sharp Cheddar cheese, cubed**
**Dash each onion salt, garlic salt and celery salt**
**½ cup dried beef, coarsely snipped**

Put sherry, Worcestershire, cream cheese and olives in blender container; cover and run on speed 4 (or high) until smooth. Add Cheddar cheese and salts and run on speed 4 (or high) until smooth. If necessary, stop blender during processing and push ingredients toward blades with rubber spatula. Turn mixture out onto foil or waxed paper and use hands to round it into a ball. Wrap in the foil or waxed paper and refrigerate (for several days if possible, so the flavors will blend).

About 30 minutes before serving, unwrap and reshape ball, if necessary. Then roll in dried beef until completely coated. Serve with crackers or small rye bread slices. *Makes a ball about 3 inches in diameter.*

## CHILI AND CURRY CHEESE SLICES

**2 tablespoons milk**
**4 ounces cream cheese, cubed**
**4 ounces Cheddar cheese, cubed**
**½ clove garlic**
**½ cup walnuts**
**2 teaspoons curry powder**
**2 teaspoons chili powder**

Put milk, cheeses and garlic in blender container; cover and run on speed 6 (or high) until smooth. If necessary, stop blender during processing and push ingredients toward blades with rubber spatula. Add walnuts; cover container and run on speed 4 (or low) until walnuts are chopped. Chill mixture 2 hours; shape into 2 rolls, each 1½ inches in diameter. Sprinkle curry powder and chili powder on separate sheets of waxed paper; roll one cheese roll in each spice. Wrap and chill. Slice into ⅛-inch-thick rounds and serve on round crackers. *Makes about 75 slices.*

## FILLED EDAM CHEESE

**1 ½-pound Edam cheese**
**2 or more tablespoons beer**
**½ teaspoon prepared mustard**
**Few grains cayenne**
**1 tablespoon chopped chives**
**1 tablespoon canned pimiento strips**

Let cheese soften for several hours at room temperature. Cut a 3-inch round from top of cheese. Lift off this "lid" and scoop out center, leaving a ¼-inch wall. Put scooped out cheese with beer, mustard and cayenne in blender container; cover and run on speed 2 (or low) until smooth, adding beer as necessary to make of spreading consistency. If necessary, stop blender during processing and push ingredients toward blades with rubber spatula. Add chives and pimiento; run on speed 1 (or low) just to mix. Return seasoned cheese to shell and refrigerate. Remove from refrigerator 1 hour before serving. Serve with crackers.

## SNAPPY CHEESE BALL

**½ cup walnuts**
**3 tablespoons brandy or gin**
**½ cup very soft butter or margarine**
**½ cup crumbled blue cheese**
**½ cup cubed brick cheese**

Put walnuts in blender container; cover and run on speed 4 (or high) until finely chopped. Spread nuts evenly on a 12x12-inch piece of waxed paper. Put brandy, butter and blue cheese in blender container; cover and run on speed 6 (or high) until smooth. Add brick cheese and continue to run on speed 6 (or high) until smooth. Scrape cheese mixture from container onto chopped nuts. Put hands under waxed paper and shape cheese into a ball. Wrap in foil and chill until firm. *Makes a ball about 3 inches in diameter.*

**Tasty Tidbits**

## LAYERED HAM CUBES

**2 tablespoons mayonnaise**
**2 tablespoons prepared horseradish**
**1 teaspoon Worcestershire**
**½ teaspoon seasoned salt**
**1 8-ounce package cream cheese, cubed**
**6 thin slices boiled ham**

Put all ingredients except ham in blender container; cover and run on speed 6 (or high) until smooth. If necessary, stop blender during processing and push ingredients toward blades with rubber spatula. Place one slice ham on waxed paper; spread with 1/5 of cheese mixture. Put another slice ham on top of cheese mixture and spread with more cheese. Repeat process, ending with a ham slice. Wrap firmly in aluminum foil or waxed paper and place in freezer for 2 hours or more. About an hour before serving, remove from freezer and cut into ½-inch cubes. Pierce each cube with a toothpick to serve. *Makes about 54 cubes.*

## OLIVE FILLED CHEESE BALLS

**½ pound softened sharp Cheddar cheese, cubed**
**2 tablespoons soft butter**
**½ cup flour**
**Dash cayenne**
**25 large pitted ripe or stuffed green olives, well drained**

Preheat oven to 400°. Put cheese and butter in blender container; cover and run on speed 4 (or high) until smooth. Add flour and cayenne; cover and run on speed 2 (or low) until blended. If necessary, stop blender during processing and push ingredients toward blades with rubber spatula. Push the cheese mixture out of container onto a sheet of waxed paper. Wrap about 1 tablespoon of the mixture around each olive, completely covering it. Bake for 15 minutes. Serve hot. *Makes 25 balls.*

## CHEESE-BACON BROIL

**1 slice bacon**
**1 egg**
**¼ cup very soft butter or margarine**
**1 3-ounce package pimiento cream cheese, cubed**
**¼ green pepper, seeded**
**½ clove garlic**
**8 thin slices bread, with crusts removed**

Dice bacon and fry until crisp; cool slightly in drippings. Put bacon, drippings and remaining ingredients except bread in blender container; cover and run on speed 4 (or low) until green pepper is finely chopped. Toast one side of bread under broiler; cut each slice into quarters. Spread cheese mixture on untoasted side. Return to broiler and broil until cheese bubbles and browns slightly. Serve hot. *Makes 32 hors d'oeuvres.*

**Note:** Cheese mixture will be thin when spread on bread and will thicken as it broils.

## CHEESE AND HAM APPETIZERS

**1 3-ounce package cream cheese, cubed**
**5–6 large stuffed green olives**
**2 tablespoons mayonnaise**
**½ teaspoon prepared mustard**
**4 thin slices cold boiled ham**

Put first 4 ingredients in blender container; cover and run on speed 5 (or start on low, then move to high) until smooth. If necessary, stop blender during processing and push ingredients toward blades with rubber spatula. Spread mixture ⅛ inch thick on ham slices; roll each slice as for jelly roll. Wrap in waxed paper or aluminum foil. Chill an hour or two. Slice in ¼-inch slices. Place slices on small crackers to serve. *Makes 15–20 appetizers.*

*Filled Edam Cheese (p. 40)*

*Cheese and Ham Appetizers (p. 41)*

*Olive Filled Cheese Balls (p. 41)*

## HOT LOBSTER CANAPÉS

**1 teaspoon soft butter**
**1 slice dry bread**
**2 tablespoons cooking sherry**
**½ cup canned condensed cream of mushroom soup, undiluted**
**¼ canned pimiento**
**¼ teaspoon salt**
**3 drops Tabasco**
**1 5-ounce can (1 cup) lobster meat, drained (bony tissue removed)**
**30 melba toast rounds**

Spread butter on bread; break into 6 pieces and drop into blender container; cover and run on speed 4 (or low) until finely crumbed; empty into a small bowl and set aside. Put remaining ingredients except melba toast in blender container; cover and run on speed 4 (or low) until lobster is chopped. Spread mixture on melba toast rounds and sprinkle buttered crumbs over top. Broil 2–3 minutes or until crumbs are browned. *Makes 30 canapés.*

## CRAB MEAT AND WATER CHESTNUT NIBBLES

**2 tablespoons soy sauce**
**½ cup Blender Mayonnaise (page 79)**
**2 small green onions, cut up**
**½ cup water chestnuts**
**1 pound (2 cups) cooked crab meat (fresh, frozen or canned)**

Put all ingredients except crab meat in blender container; cover and run on speed 3 (or low) until water chestnuts are finely minced. Add half the crab meat; cover container and run on speed 4 (or high) until crab meat is chopped. Add remaining crab meat; cover container and run on speed 4 (or high) just until crab meat is coarsely chopped. If necessary, stop blender during processing and push ingredients toward blades with rubber spatula. Spread on crisp crackers. *Makes about 36 nibbles.*

## SURPRISE DEVILED EGGS

**6 hard-cooked eggs, shelled and cut in half lengthwise**
**2 tablespoons mayonnaise**
**1 teaspoon vinegar**
**½ teaspoon salt**
**½ teaspoon dry mustard OR 1 teaspoon prepared mustard**
**Filling such as caviar, anchovy, stuffed olive, deviled ham, blue cheese, fish or meat paste**
**Paprika**

Remove yolks from eggs; put in blender container with the next 4 ingredients; cover and run on speed 2 (or low) until smooth. If necessary, stop blender during processing and push ingredients toward blades with rubber spatula. Put a small amount of one of the savory fillings (caviar, anchovy, etc.) in each egg-white half; top with egg yolk filling and sprinkle with paprika. *Makes 12.*

## ARTICHOKE APPETIZERS

**1 large artichoke**
**1 teaspoon salad oil**
**1 bay leaf, crushed**
**½ teaspoon salt**
**1 3-ounce package cream cheese, cubed**
**2–3 drops Tabasco**
**½ teaspoon garlic salt**
**1 tablespoon light cream**
**18–20 (about ¼ pound) small shrimp, cleaned**
**Paprika**

Cook artichoke in enough water to cover in tightly covered container; add oil, bay leaf and salt to the cooking water. Simmer 30 minutes or until tender. Drain; cool and remove leaves. (Use leaves that are firm and have a good edible portion on ends.)

Put cream cheese, Tabasco, garlic salt and cream in blender container; cover and run on speed 4 (or high) until well blended. If necessary, stop blender during processing and push ingredients toward blades with rubber spatula. Spread some of the cream cheese mixture on each artichoke leaf; top with a small shrimp and sprinkle with paprika. Arrange on plate in the shape of a sunflower so each leaf is easy to pick up. *Makes about 18.*

## Dips and Dunks

### COTTAGE CHEESE DIP

**2 tablespoons milk**
**½ teaspoon Worcestershire**
**1 12-ounce carton creamed cottage cheese**
**Dash salt**

Put ingredients in blender container in order listed. Cover container; start on speed 1 (or low), then run on speed 6 (or high) until smooth. If necessary, stop blender and push ingredients toward blades with rubber spatula. Refrigerate. *Makes 1 cup.*

#### CHEDDAR DIP

**1 cup cubed sharp Cheddar cheese**
**Small piece onion (optional)**

Prepare as for Cottage Cheese Dip, adding cheese a few cubes at a time. *Makes 2 cups.*

#### LIVER SAUSAGE DIP

**¼ pound smoked liver sausage, cut up**
**2 sweet pickles, cut up**
**Small piece onion**
**¼ teaspoon monosodium glutamate**

Prepare as for Cottage Cheese Dip. *Makes 2 cups.*

#### ONION DIP

**1 small onion, cut up**
**1 beef bouillon cube**

Add bouillon cube to milk in container before adding other ingredients. Then prepare as for Cottage Cheese Dip. *Makes 1 cup.*

#### BLUE CHEESE DIP

**2 ounces blue cheese, crumbled (¼ cup)**
**Small piece onion (optional)**
**⅛ teaspoon monosodium glutamate**

Prepare as for Cottage Cheese Dip. *Makes 1¼ cups.*

#### CLAM DIP

**2 tablespoons clam liquid**
**1 teaspoon lemon juice**
**Dash Tabasco**
**1 7-ounce can minced clams**
**½ clove garlic**

Drain clams, reserving liquid. Use 2 tablespoons liquid in place of milk in Cottage Cheese Dip. Prepare as for Cottage Cheese Dip. *Makes 2 cups.*

#### ANCHOVY DIP

**¼ teaspoon prepared mustard**
**1 2-ounce can anchovy fillets**
**¼ cup stuffed green olives**

Prepare as for Cottage Cheese Dip. *Makes 1½ cups.*

#### TUNA DIP

**1 7-ounce can tuna, drained**
**1 tablespoon capers**
**1 teaspoon prepared horseradish**
**¼ teaspoon celery salt**
**2 teaspoons garlic salt**
**¼ teaspoon monosodium glutamate**

Prepare as for Cottage Cheese Dip. *Makes 2 cups.*

## SEAFOOD DIPPING SAUCE

½ cup catsup
1 small sweet pickle
1 teaspoon Worcestershire
½ cup chili sauce
1 teaspoon prepared horseradish
½ thin slice lemon with rind

Put all ingredients in blender container; cover and run on speed 4 (or low) until pickle and lemon are finely chopped. Serve with chilled shrimp, lobster meat or crab meat. *Makes 1 cup.*

## HOT BEAN DIP

2 tablespoons tomato juice
2 tablespoons vinegar
2 teaspoons Worcestershire
1 No. 2½ can (3½ cups) pork and beans in tomato sauce
½ cup cubed process American cheese
1 teaspoon garlic salt
1 teaspoon chili powder
½ teaspoon salt
Dash cayenne
4 slices bacon, fried crisp

Put all ingredients except bacon in blender container; cover and run on speed 7 (or high) until smooth. If necessary, stop blender during processing and push ingredients toward blades with rubber spatula. Pour into chafing dish or double boiler and serve hot. Crumble bacon over top. Serve with potato chips, crackers or corn chips. *Makes 3 cups.*

## CAMEMBERT DIP

2 tablespoons milk
1 12-ounce carton creamed cottage cheese
1 8-ounce package cream cheese, cubed
1 5½-ounce package Camembert cheese
⅓ cup grated Parmesan cheese
1 teaspoon seasoned salt

Put all ingredients in blender container in order listed; cover and run on speed 7 (or high) until smooth. If necessary, stop blender during processing and push ingredients toward blades with rubber spatula. Serve on crackers or melba toast rounds. *Makes about 3½ cups.*

## GARLIC-CHEESE DIP

⅓ cup dairy sour cream
2 tablespoons pineapple juice
5 drops Tabasco
1 sprig parsley
⅓ clove garlic
½ teaspoon Worcestershire
1 3-ounce package cream cheese, cubed
⅓ cup crumbled Roquefort or blue cheese

Put all ingredients except cheeses in blender container; cover and run on speed 4 (or high) until garlic is liquefied. Add cheeses; cover and run on speed 4 (or high) until smooth. If necessary, stop blender during processing and push ingredients toward blades with rubber spatula. Chill at least 2 hours to blend flavors. Serve with crisp crackers or potato chips. *Makes about 1 cup.*

## CHEESE 'N' BACON DIP

¼ cup milk
1 8-ounce package cream cheese, cubed
Small piece onion
3 ounces Camembert cheese, crumbled
1 tablespoon lemon juice
½ pound bacon, fried crisp and crumbled

Put all ingredients in blender container in order listed; cover and run on speed 6 (or high) until smooth. If necessary, stop blender during processing and push ingredients toward blades with rubber spatula. *Makes 2 cups.*

## BLUE CHEESE DIP FOR VEGETABLES

3 tablespoons dry vermouth
2 tablespoons sour cream
4 ounces blue cheese, crumbled (½ cup)
4 ounces cream cheese, cubed

Put all ingredients in blender container in order listed; cover and run on speed 6 (or high) until smooth. Use as a dip for fresh celery, carrots, green onions, sliced raw turnips, cauliflower, zucchini sticks, etc. *Makes about 1 cup.*

## DEVILED HAM DIP

½ cup Blender Mayonnaise (page 79)
1 8-ounce package cream cheese, cubed
1 4½-ounce can deviled ham
Small piece onion
¼ teaspoon garlic salt
¼ canned pimiento

Put all ingredients except pimiento in blender container; cover and run on speed 6 (or high) until smooth. Add pimiento; run on speed 4 (or low) just until chopped. Serve with potato chips or crackers. *Makes 2 cups.*

## CREAMY AVOCADO DIP

2 tablespoons milk
½ teaspoon Worcestershire
1 ripe avocado, pitted, peeled and quartered
1 12-ounce carton creamed cottage cheese
½ teaspoon salt
¼ teaspoon monosodium glutamate
¼ small onion

Put all ingredients in blender container; cover and run on speed 6 (or high) until smooth. If necessary, stop blender during processing and push ingredients toward blades with rubber spatula. Serve with assorted crackers, potato chips, etc. *Makes about 1½ cups.*

## HARLEQUIN DIP

2 tablespoons milk
1 12-ounce carton creamed cottage cheese
1 teaspoon lemon juice
½ teaspoon salt
1 teaspoon prepared horseradish
1 medium carrot, cut into 1-inch pieces
3 radishes, halved
3 sprigs parsley

Put milk, cottage cheese, lemon juice, salt and horseradish in blender container; cover and run on speed 6 (or high) until smooth. Add remaining ingredients; cover and run on speed 4 (or low) just until vegetables are chopped. *Makes 1½ cups.*

## GUACAMOLE

1 tablespoon lemon juice
½ cup Blender Mayonnaise (page 79)
Small piece onion
1 teaspoon salt
¼ teaspoon chili powder
2 ripe avocados, peeled, pitted and quartered

Put all ingredients in blender container in order listed; cover and run on speed 6 (or high) until smooth. Empty into small bowl. Press waxed paper or plastic wrap against surface; chill. Serve with crackers, potato chips or corn chips. (Guacamole will discolor if stored longer than 12 hours or if not protected against air.) *Makes 1½ cups.*

*Harlequin Dip (p. 46)*

*Guacamole (p. 46)*

*Deviled Crab Meat Dip (p. 47)*

## LOBSTER-CHEESE DIP

1 tablespoon lemon juice
1 tablespoon water
½ cup dairy sour cream
1 green onion with top, cut into 1-inch pieces
½ clove garlic
1 8-ounce package cream cheese, cubed
2 tablespoons crumbled blue cheese
1 6-ounce can lobster meat, drained (bony tissue removed)

Put all ingredients except lobster meat in blender container; cover and run on speed 6 (or high) until smooth. Add lobster meat; cover and run on speed 4 (or low) just until lobster is chopped. Pile into serving dish or lobster shell. *Makes about 2 cups.*

## AVOCADO SHRIMP DIP

2 ripe avocados, peeled, pitted and quartered
1 cup dairy sour cream
2 tablespoons chili sauce
½ teaspoon salt
1 4½-ounce can deveined shrimp, drained

Put first 4 ingredients in blender container; cover and run on speed 4 (or high) until smooth. Add shrimp; cover and run on speed 4 (or high) until shrimp is chopped. If necessary, stop blender during processing and push ingredients toward blades with rubber spatula. Pour into bowl and chill. Serve with potato chips, crackers and crisp vegetables. *Makes 2½ cups.*

## DEVILED CRAB MEAT DIP

⅔ cup (½ of a 10½-ounce can) condensed tomato soup, undiluted
½ cup Blender Mayonnaise (page 79)
1 3-ounce package cream cheese, cubed
½ clove garlic
⅛ teaspoon salt
6 drops Tabasco
Dash monosodium glutamate
1 7½-ounce can crab meat, drained (bony tissue removed)

Put all ingredients except crab meat in blender container in order listed; cover and run on speed 6 (or high) until smooth. Add crab meat and run on speed 4 (or low) just until crab meat is chopped. Serve as a dip for potato chips. *Makes about 2 cups.*

## CREAMY SHRIMP DIP

1 10¼-ounce can frozen cream of shrimp soup, thawed
2 3-ounce packages cream cheese, cubed
3 tablespoons chili sauce
⅛ teaspoon Tabasco

Put all ingredients in blender container; cover and run on speed 6 (or high) just until smooth. Chill. Serve with potato chips, crackers, raw vegetables or cooked shrimp. *Makes 1½ cups.*

*Hot Bean Dip (p. 45)*

*…e Cheese Dip (p. 45)*

## CHICKEN LIVER PÂTÉ WITH BACON

1 pound chicken livers
1 cup chicken broth (1 chicken bouillon cube dissolved in 1 cup hot water)
¼ medium onion, sliced
⅛ teaspoon rosemary
6 slices bacon, fried crisp and crumbled
½ cup very soft butter or margarine
½ teaspoon dry mustard
¼ teaspoon salt
⅛ teaspoon pepper

Simmer chicken livers in the chicken broth with onion and rosemary until livers are tender, about 15 minutes. Let cool in broth; drain and reserve broth. Put ¼ cup of the broth, the chicken livers, onion and all other ingredients in blender container; cover and run on speed 6 (or high) until smooth. Refrigerate in a covered container at least 24 hours to blend flavors. Serve on toast or crackers. *Makes about 2 cups.*

## NIPPY CLAM SPREAD

¼ cup dairy sour cream
1 green onion, cut up
1 ounce blue cheese, crumbled
Dash white pepper
1 7½-ounce can minced clams, drained

Put all ingredients in blender container; cover and run on speed 4 (or high) until thoroughly combined. Refrigerate 2 hours before serving to allow flavors to blend. *Makes 1 cup.*

## SALMON-RIPE OLIVE SPREAD

1 small carrot, cut into ¾-inch pieces
1 teaspoon lemon juice
¼ cup mayonnaise
½ cup canned salmon, drained, skin and bones removed
¼ cup pitted ripe olives
Pinch salt
⅛ teaspoon monosodium glutamate

Run blender on speed 4 (or high); drop carrot pieces into container while blender is running and cover quickly. Turn off blender as soon as carrot is coarsely chopped. Add remaining ingredients in order listed; cover container and run on speed 6 (or high) just until well mixed. *Makes 1 cup.*

## CRAB-AVOCADO SPREAD

1 tablespoon lemon juice
Dash Tabasco
3 tablespoons mayonnaise
1 ripe avocado, pitted, peeled and quartered
1 cup cooked crab meat

Put all ingredients except crab meat in blender container; cover and run on speed 3 (or low) until smooth. Add crab meat; cover and run on speed 4 (or high) until crab meat is chopped. *Makes about 1½ cups.*

## CHEDDAR SHRIMP SPREAD

1 tablespoon milk
½ cup Blender Mayonnaise (page 79)
2 drops Tabasco
¼ small onion
½ cup cooked cleaned shrimp, fresh or canned
¼ pound Cheddar cheese, cubed

Put all ingredients in blender container; cover and run on speed 6 (or high) until smooth, about 1½ minutes. If necessary, stop blender during processing and push ingredients toward blades with rubber spatula. *Makes 1½ cups.*

## CHABLIS-CHEESE SPREAD

**¼ cup Chablis**
**8 ounces Liederkranz cheese, cubed**
**¼ teaspoon celery salt**
**¼ teaspoon garlic salt**
**2 8-ounce packages cream cheese, cubed**

Put wine, Liederkranz cheese and seasonings in blender container; cover and run on speed 3 (or low) until smooth. If necessary, stop blender during processing and push ingredients toward blades with rubber spatula. Set aside half this mixture. Add a few pieces of cream cheese to the mixture remaining in blender container; cover and run on speed 3 (or low). Repeat until one 8-ounce package of cream cheese has been blended in. If necessary, stop blender during processing and push ingredients toward blades with rubber spatula. Empty into a bowl.

Return reserved Chablis-cheese mixture to blender container and process remaining cream cheese as directed above. Pack into 1 large dish or several small ones. Cover tightly and refrigerate at least a week so that flavors can blend. Serve with crackers. *Makes 3½ cups.*

## PORT WINE CHEESE SPREAD

**¼ cup port wine**
**3 ounces cream cheese, cubed**
**½ pound sharp Cheddar cheese, cubed**
**Dash onion salt**

Have all ingredients room temperature. Put all ingredients in blender container in order listed; cover and run on speed 4 (or high) until blended. Stop blender when necessary and push ingredients toward blades. *Makes about 1½ cups.*

## SMOKY CHEESE SPREAD

**¼ cup lemon juice**
**1 teaspoon Worcestershire**
**6 ounces cream cheese, cubed**
**1 6-ounce roll smoky cheese, cut into pieces**
**1 clove garlic**
**¼ cup stuffed green olives**

Put all ingredients except olives in blender container in order listed; cover and run on speed 6 (or high) until smooth. Stop blender when necessary and push ingredients toward blades with rubber spatula. Stop blender and add stuffed olives; cover and run on speed 6 (or high) just until olives are coarsely chopped. *Makes 1½ cups.*

## CHEDDAR RUM SPREAD

**2 tablespoons rum**
**⅛ teaspoon cayenne**
**½ pound sharp Cheddar cheese, cubed**
**¼ pound very soft butter or margarine**

Put all ingredients in blender container; cover and run on speed 6 (or high) until smooth. If necessary, stop blender during processing and push ingredients toward blades with rubber spatula. Spread on crackers or crisp toast. *Makes about 2 cups.*

## TRI-CHEESE SPREAD

**½ cup dairy sour cream**
**1½ teaspoons Worcestershire**
**¼ teaspoon garlic salt**
**1 teaspoon paprika**
**½ cup crumbled blue cheese**
**½ cup cubed Swiss cheese**
**¼ cup cubed sharp Cheddar cheese**

Have cheeses room temperature. Put all ingredients in blender container in order listed; cover and run on speed 6 (or high) until smooth. *Makes 1½ cups.*

## Hearty Spreads

*Almost any spread can make a perfect party canapé when atop a thin, crisp wafer or cracker. More important, however, delicious spreads can make every sandwich lunch an adventure. There is no need for monotony, even in a lunchbox. Tuna, egg salad, salami, sliced processed cheese, cold meat or peanut butter may be combined in minutes with flavor builders found in almost every kitchen, producing an endless variety of appetite-teasing sandwiches. Twenty spreads are offered here as a foundation on which you can build countless combinations. Use your favorite main dishes and salads as further inspiration. Any combination that tastes good to you offers a possible pattern. Try adding a little mint sauce to the chopped roast lamb, or catsup to replace part of the mayonnaise in egg salad. Chop a bit of cucumber into tuna salad.*

Turn Leftovers into Treats

*One hamburger patty, some shreds of pot roast or ham, a couple of olives—these are not very inspiring and are often left in the refrigerator until they spoil. They can be used to add flavor, substance and nutrition to sandwich mixtures.*

Vary the Bread

*In addition to the ever-present white, whole wheat and rye breads, consider using soft rolls, hard rolls hollowed to contain the filling; experiment with Boston brown bread, orange bread, date nut bread; try oatmeal bread, pumpernickel bread. Banana bread, nut bread and cinnamon loaf are also suitable for cream or cottage cheese mixtures. (See recipes for Blender Breads on pages 132 and 136.)*

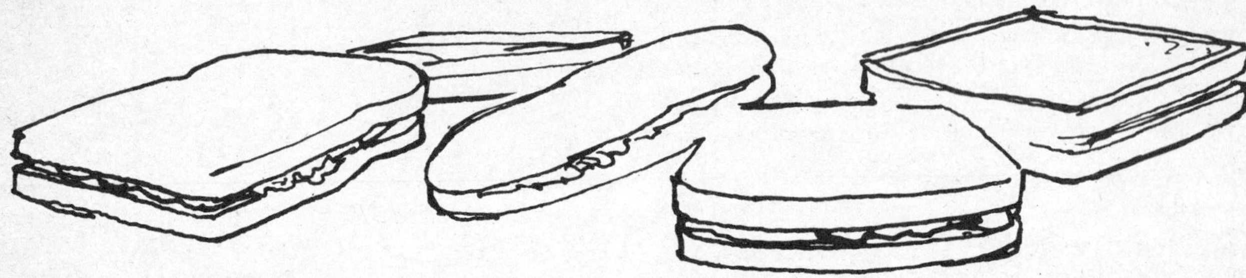

### MEAT SPREAD

**¼ cup mayonnaise**
**1 teaspoon prepared horseradish**
**½ teaspoon salt**
**½ stalk celery, cut into 1-inch pieces**
**1 cup cubed cooked meat (beef, veal, pork or lamb)**
**1 slice onion**

Put all ingredients in blender container; cover and run on speed 4 (or high) until meat and celery are chopped. Stop blender when necessary and push ingredients toward blades with rubber spatula. *Makes about 1 cup.*

**Note:** 4–5 stuffed olives or half a large dill pickle may be substituted for the horseradish and celery; with the olives, add salt to taste.

### HAM HORSERADISH SPREAD

**⅓ cup dairy sour cream**
**5 sprigs parsley**
**1 tablespoon prepared horseradish**
**1 cup cubed cooked ham**

Put all ingredients in blender container in order listed; cover and run on speed 4 (or high) until ham is finely chopped. Serve on crackers or thin slices of rye bread. Chill. *Makes 1 cup.*

### HAM AND CHEESE SPREAD

**2 tablespoons milk**
**1 3-ounce package cream cheese, cubed**
**½ teaspoon dry mustard**
**1 cup cubed cooked ham**

Put all ingredients in blender container; cover and run on speed 5 (or high) until ham is chopped. If necessary, stop blender during processing and push ingredients toward blades with rubber spatula. *Makes about 1¼ cups.*

### HAM SALAD SPREAD

**3 tablespoons mayonnaise**
**1 teaspoon Worcestershire**
**1 small sweet pickle**
**1 cup cubed cooked ham**

Put all ingredients except ham in blender container; cover and run on speed 2 (or low) until smooth. Add ham; cover and run on speed 4 (or high) until ham is chopped. If necessary, stop blender during processing and push ingredients toward blades with rubber spatula. *Makes 1 cup.*

*Ham Salad Spread (p. 50)*

## TROPICAL CHICKEN SANDWICH SPREAD

**½ cup Blender Mayonnaise (page 79)**
**1 8¾-ounce can crushed pineapple, drained**
**¼ cup blanched almonds**
**1 stalk celery, cut into 1-inch pieces**
**1 thin slice onion**
**1 cup cubed cooked chicken**

Put all ingredients in blender container; cover and run on speed 4 (or high) until ingredients are chopped and thoroughly mixed. If necessary, stop blender during processing and push ingredients toward blades with rubber spatula. Chill. *Makes about 2 cups.*

## CHICKEN SALAD SPREAD

**3 tablespoons mayonnaise**
**1 medium stalk celery, cut up**
**1 teaspoon Worcestershire**
**¼ teaspoon salt**
**1 cup cubed cooked chicken**

Put all ingredients except chicken in blender container; cover and run on speed 2 (or low) until smooth. Add chicken; cover container and run on speed 4 (or high) until chicken is chopped. Stop blender during processing and push ingredients toward blades with rubber spatula. *Makes 1 cup.*

## RAISIN-CARROT SPREAD

**3 tablespoons mayonnaise**
**½ cup creamed cottage cheese**
**Dash Tabasco**
**Dash salt**
**½ cup raisins**
**1 small carrot, cut into 1-inch pieces**

Put first 4 ingredients in blender container; cover and run on speed 5 (or high) until smooth. Add raisins and carrot; cover and run on speed 4 (or high) just until raisins and carrot are chopped. If necessary, stop blender during processing and push ingredients toward blades with rubber spatula. *Makes about 1½ cups.*

## BACON 'N EGG SPREAD

**3 hard-cooked egg yolks**
**3 slices bacon, fried crisp and crumbled**
**2 tablespoons mayonnaise**
**2 ounces cream cheese, cubed**

Put all ingredients in blender container; cover and run on speed 4 (or high) until smooth. Stop blender when necessary and push ingredients toward blades with rubber spatula. *Makes ¾ cup.*

## DEVILED EGG SPREAD

**1 tablespoon mayonnaise**
**1 tablespoon chili sauce**
**1 2¼-ounce can deviled ham**
**4 large ripe olives, pitted**
**2 hard-cooked eggs, shelled and quartered**

Put mayonnaise, chili sauce and deviled ham in blender container; cover and run on speed 3 (or low) until thoroughly mixed. Add olives and eggs; cover and run on speed 4 (or high) until eggs and olives are chopped. *Makes about 1 cup.*

## EGG SALAD SPREAD

**¼ cup mayonnaise**
**¼ teaspoon salt**
**¼ teaspoon onion salt**
**⅛ teaspoon pepper**
**⅛ teaspoon paprika**
**½ stalk celery, cut into 2-inch pieces**
**4 hard-cooked eggs, shelled**

Put all ingredients except eggs in blender container in order listed. Quarter eggs and separate the yolks from the whites. Add yolks to ingredients in container; cover and run on speed 3 (or low) until celery is chopped. Stop blender during processing and push mixture toward blades with rubber spatula. Add egg whites; cover and run on speed 4 (or low) just until egg whites are coarsely chopped. Chill. *Makes 1½ cups.*

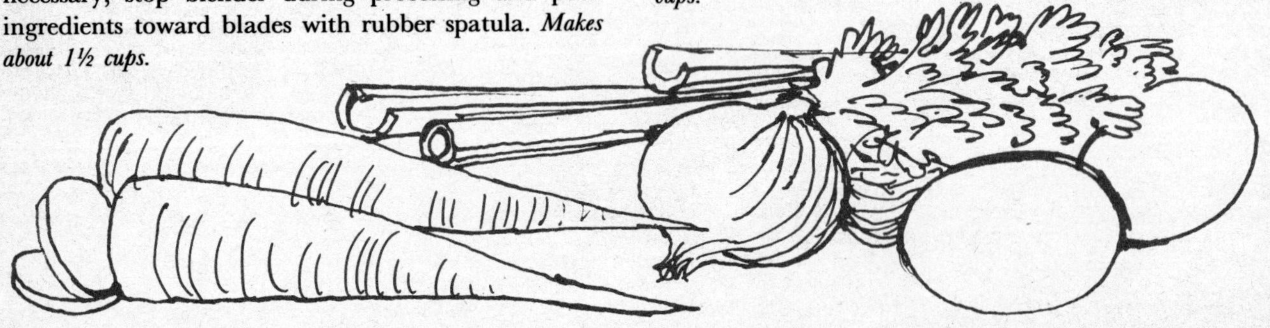

## LOBSTER SPREAD

**2 tablespoons milk**
**¼ cup mayonnaise**
**3 drops Tabasco**
**½ teaspoon onion salt**
**1 teaspoon capers**
**1 6-ounce can lobster meat, bony portion removed**

Put all ingredients in blender container in order listed; cover and run on speed 4 (or low) until lobster is finely chopped. If necessary, stop blender during processing and push ingredients toward blades with rubber spatula. Chill. *Makes ¾ cup.*

## SARDINE SPREAD

**1 3¾-ounce can sardines, drained**
**2 tablespoons mayonnaise**
**1 teaspoon Worcestershire**
**1 teaspoon lemon juice**
**3–5 drops Tabasco**
**1 hard-cooked egg, shelled and sliced**

Put all ingredients in blender container in order listed; cover and run on speed 4 (or high) until blended. If necessary, stop blender during processing and push ingredients toward blades with rubber spatula. Chill. *Makes ⅔ cup.*

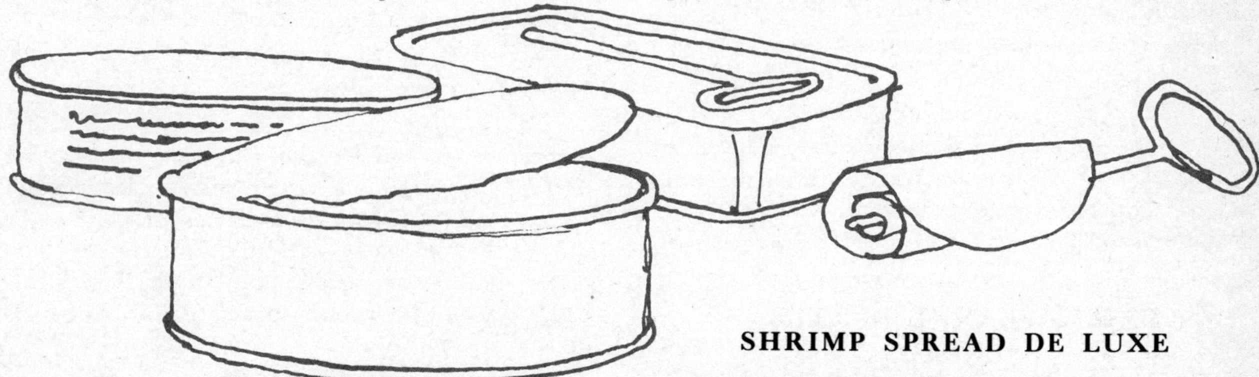

## SALMON-EGG SPREAD

**2 tablespoons mayonnaise**
**1 teaspoon prepared horseradish**
**¼ teaspoon celery salt**
**⅛ teaspoon pepper**
**1 7-ounce can red salmon, drained, skin and bones removed**
**2 hard-cooked eggs, shelled and quartered**

Put all ingredients except eggs in blender container in order listed; cover and run on speed 4 (or high) until smooth. Add eggs; run on speed 4 (or low) until eggs are chopped. *Makes about 1 cup.*

## SALMON PÂTÉ

**1½ tablespoons tarragon vinegar**
**1 teaspoon caper liquid**
**1 tablespoon cut chives**
**3 tablespoons mayonnaise**
**1 1-pound can red salmon, drained, skin and bones removed**

Put all ingredients in blender container; cover and run on speed 6 (or high) until smooth. If necessary, stop blender during processing and push ingredients toward blades with rubber spatula. Use as spread on crackers or bread. Chill. *Makes 1½ cups.*

## SHRIMP SPREAD DE LUXE

**2 tablespoons mayonnaise**
**1 tablespoon catsup**
**1 teaspoon prepared mustard**
**Dash garlic salt**
**1 3-ounce package cream cheese, cubed**
**1 5-ounce can shrimp, drained and rinsed**
**1 stalk celery, cut into 1-inch pieces**

Put first 5 ingredients in blender container; cover and run on speed 3 (or low) until smooth. Add shrimp and celery; cover and run on speed 4 (or high) until celery is chopped. If necessary, stop blender during processing and push ingredients toward blades with rubber spatula. *Makes about 1½ cups.*

## SPICY TUNA SPREAD

**1 tablespoon chili sauce**
**1 teaspoon Worcestershire**
**5 drops Tabasco**
**1 3-ounce package cream cheese, cubed**
**Small piece onion**
**1 7-ounce can tuna, drained**

Put all ingredients in blender container in order listed; cover and run on speed 6 (or high) until smooth. If necessary, stop blender during processing and push ingredients toward blades with rubber spatula. Chill thoroughly before serving. *Makes about 1¼ cups.*

## PEANUT AND OTHER NUT BUTTERS

Put 2 cups shelled, salted peanuts in blender container; cover and run on speed 4 (or low) until finely chopped, then move to speed 7 (or high) until smooth. Stop blender when necessary and push peanuts from sides of container toward blades. (Cashews and peanuts require no additional oil, but add 1 tablespoon non-flavored salad oil for each cup of all other nuts.) *Makes about 1½ cups.*

## CASHEW BANANA SPREAD

**1 ripe banana, peeled and quartered**
**1 teaspoon orange juice concentrate or lemon juice**
**½ cup salted cashews**

Put banana and orange juice concentrate in blender container; cover and run on speed 4 (or high) until smooth. Stop blender and add nuts; cover and run on speed 7 (or high) until smooth. *Makes ⅔ cup.*

## BACON-PEANUT BUTTER SPREAD

**½ cup chili sauce**
**8 slices bacon, fried crisp and crumbled**
**½ cup peanut butter***

Put all ingredients in blender container; cover and run on speed 6 (or high) until bacon is finely chopped. *Makes about 1 cup.*

*You can make your own peanut butter, you know—see the recipe above.

### CHURN BUTTER FROM CREAM

Put two cups heavy cream in blender container; cover and run on speed 5 (or high) until butter forms. Drain butter and rinse with cold water.

## HONEY BUTTER

*Good on toast, pancakes and waffles.*

**½ cup soft butter or margarine**
**½ cup honey**

Put ingredients in blender container; cover and run on speed 4 (or high) until blended. Stop blender when necessary and push ingredients toward blades with rubber spatula. *Makes 1 cup.*

## STRAWBERRY BUTTER

*A perfect spread for toast, muffins and waffles.*

**1 10-ounce package frozen strawberries, thawed**
**½ pound soft sweet (unsalted) butter**
**1 cup confectioners' sugar**

*Important: Be sure thawed strawberries and sweet butter are room temperature.* Put all ingredients in blender container in order listed; cover and run on speed 6 (or high) until completely smooth. If necessary, stop blender during processing and push ingredients toward blades with rubber spatula. Chill. *Makes 2½ cups.*

# Soup, Soup, Beautiful Soup

*Let your blender make your soups. In seconds it can produce perfectly blended cream soups. It can also take over the laborious task of chopping vegetables for a soup, and blender-chopped vegetables cook in a few minutes.*

*With the blender to speed up the preparation and modern ways to serve it, soup can provide one of the easiest and most nutritious answers to any meal. Serve it in mugs; carry it to the living room or porch and offer it with a tasty nibble (see pages 37-54) or with interesting crackers. Or serve soup at the table before a complementary main course.*

## Blender Soups Save Waste

*The recipes in this section will suggest ways of using some of the otherwise uninspiring remnants that accumulate in a family refrigerator. Usually discarded because they are coarse or torn, the vitamin-A-rich green outside leaves of lettuce and romaine may be washed, trimmed and coarsely shredded, then chopped or puréed into any soup except a sweet one. Heat or not, as you prefer.*

## Hints for Making Soup

- *For satin-smooth cream soups, blend liquids, vegetables and thickening ingredients on high speed until all solid particles disappear.*

- *For soups in which ingredients are to be merely chopped, put soup liquid into container, add solids and run on speed 3 or 4 (or low) for a few seconds.*

- *When making large quantities of soup, divide liquid and solids into several portions and empty each containerful into cooking vessel after chopping or blending is completed.*

- *When combining hot and cold ingredients, put cold ingredients into blender container first.*

## Hot—With Meat and Without

### DUTCH CARROT SOUP

**4 medium carrots, cut up**
**½ medium onion, quartered**
**2 stalks celery, cut up**
**¼ cup butter or margarine**
**2 cans condensed consommé**
**2 cans water**
**3 tablespoons farina**
**⅛ teaspoon pepper**
**⅛ teaspoon mace**

Put a few pieces of carrot in blender container; cover and run on speed 4 (or high) until chopped. Empty into a frypan. Repeat process with remaining carrots. Repeat process with onion and celery. Sauté vegetables in butter until onion is lightly browned; add 1 can consommé and 1 can water and simmer until tender, about 8 minutes. Put mixture in blender container; cover and run on speed 2 (or low) until vegetables are puréed. Empty into a saucepan and add 1 can consommé, 1 can water, farina, pepper and mace. Simmer, stirring occasionally, for 20 minutes. *Makes 6 servings.*

### CAULIFLOWER CREAM SOUP

**1 10-ounce package frozen cauliflower, thawed**
**1 10½-ounce can chicken broth**
**1 cup light cream**
**1 teaspoon salt**
**⅛ teaspoon white pepper**
**1 egg yolk**
**1 10¼-ounce can frozen cream of potato soup**

Put cauliflower and chicken broth in a saucepan and bring to a boil; cover and cook over low heat for 8 minutes. Put remaining ingredients except cream of potato soup in blender container; add cooked cauliflower and broth. Cover and run on speed 7 (or high) until smooth. Pour into saucepan and add potato soup; cook over low heat until hot, being careful not to let the soup boil. *Makes 4-5 servings.*

***QUICK SUPPER***

*Hamburger Soup (p. 58)*
*Alsatian Pudding (p. 145)*

## CANADIAN CHEESE SOUP

**2 green onions with tops, cut up**
**2 small carrots, cut up**
**2 stalks celery, cut up**
**1 cup water**
**1 chicken bouillon cube**
**¼ cup butter or margarine**
**8 ounces American cheese, cubed (1½ cups)**
**¼ cup flour**
**⅛ teaspoon pepper**
**3 cups milk**

Put onions, carrots, celery and water in blender container; cover and run on speed 4 (or high) until vegetables are finely chopped. Empty into a saucepan; add bouillon cube and butter. Simmer for 10 minutes.

Meanwhile, put ⅓ of cheese in clean, dry blender container; cover and run on speed 3 (or low) until grated. Empty into a bowl and repeat process until all cheese is grated. Put 1 cup milk, flour and pepper in blender container; cover and run on speed 5 (or high) a few seconds. Add with remaining milk to vegetables and cook, stirring constantly, until mixture thickens. Lower heat and add cheese. Stir until cheese is melted. *Makes 6–8 servings.*

## BLUE CHEESE-ONION SOUP

**2–3 large onions, cut up**
**⅓ cup butter or margarine**
**¼ teaspoon pepper**
**2 10½-ounce cans condensed beef bouillon**
**2 cans water**
**6 ounces blue cheese, crumbled (¾ cup)**
**Toasted French bread**

Put 2 onions in blender container and add water to cover; cover and run on speed 4 (or high) until chopped. Drain well in a colander or sieve; measure. If necessary, repeat process with additional onion until you have 4 cups. Sauté onion in butter until golden brown. Add pepper, beef bouillon and water; simmer, covered, for 30 minutes. Top each serving with blue cheese and serve with toasted French bread. *Makes 8 servings.*

## QUICKY CHEESE SOUP

**3 cups hot milk**
**1 beef bouillon cube**
**8 ounces American cheese, cubed (1½ cups)**
**1 10¼-ounce can frozen cream of potato soup**

Put milk, bouillon cube and cheese in blender container; cover and run on speed 6 (or high) until smooth. Pour into saucepan; add frozen soup. Cook over low heat, stirring frequently, until hot. Serve immediately. *Makes 4 servings.*

## COMPANY CHICKEN SOUP

**½ cup blanched almonds**
**1 cup chicken broth**
**1 10½-ounce can condensed cream of chicken soup, undiluted**
**6 stalks chives**
**3 sprigs parsley**
**½ teaspoon tarragon**
**½ cup whipping cream**

Put almonds and chicken broth in a saucepan and simmer 3-4 minutes. Put in blender container; cover and run on speed 2 (or low) until nuts are finely chopped. Add soup, chives, parsley and tarragon; cover and run on speed 3 (or low) a few seconds. While blender is running, slowly add whipping cream. Return to saucepan and heat to serving temperature. *Makes 4 servings.*

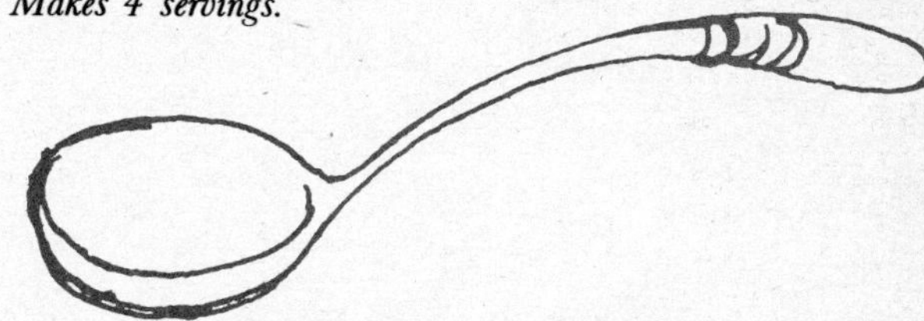

## SHERRY CONSOMMÉ

**¾ cup cut-up cooked chicken**
**1 13¾-ounce can chicken broth**
**1 12½-ounce can madrilene**
**¼ cup sherry**
**½ cup whipping cream, whipped**
**Chopped chives**
**Paprika**

Put chicken and broth in blender container; cover and run on speed 3 (or low) until chicken is finely chopped. Empty into a 1½-quart saucepan; add madrilene and heat to boiling. Remove from heat and add sherry. Ladle into soup cups; top with whipped cream and a sprinkling of chives and paprika. *Makes 6 servings.*

## CREAM CONSOMMÉ

**3 10½-ounce cans consommé**
**1 medium onion, quartered**
**1 unpeeled apple, cored and quartered**
**½ teaspoon salt**
**Dash paprika**
**Dash curry powder**
**1½ cups whipping cream**

Put 2 cans consommé, onion and apple in blender container; cover and run on speed 3 (or low) until apple and onion are finely grated. Pour into a saucepan; cook until onion and apple are tender, about 15 minutes. Return mixture to blender container; cover and run on speed 6 (or high) until very smooth. Return to saucepan; stir in remaining consommé, seasonings and whipping cream. Reheat slowly just until hot throughout. Serve in small cups. *Makes 10 servings.*

## CORN SOUP

**4 slices bacon**
**1 medium onion, cut up**
**1 stalk celery, cut up**
**1 bay leaf**
**4–5 sprigs parsley**
**1 1-pound can (2 cups) cream-style corn**
**1 tablespoon flour**
**1½ teaspoons salt**
**¼ teaspoon pepper**
**2 cups milk**

Cook bacon in a large frypan until crisp; remove bacon and reserve. Put a few pieces of onion and celery in blender container; cover and run on speed 4 (or high) until chopped. If necessary, stop blender during processing and push vegetables toward blades with rubber spatula. Empty into frypan with bacon fat and repeat until all vegetables are chopped. Add bay leaf and sauté vegetables until onion is tender; remove bay leaf. Put parsley, corn, flour, seasonings and milk in blender container; cover and run on speed 2 (or low) until mixed. Add to onion and celery. Cook, stirring constantly, until mixture boils and thickens. Top each serving with crumbled bacon. *Makes 6 servings.*

## CRAB MEAT-CORN CHOWDER

**1 1-pound can (2 cups) cream-style corn**
**2 cups milk**
**2 green onions with tops, cut up**
**1 chicken bouillon cube**
**2 tablespoons flour**
**2 tablespoons butter or margarine**
**1½ teaspoons salt**
**⅛ teaspoon pepper**
**Dash cayenne**
**1 7½-ounce can crab meat**
**Lemon wedges**

Put corn, milk, onions, bouillon cube and flour in blender container; cover and run on speed 6 (or high) for 3 minutes, until smooth. Empty into a saucepan and add butter and salt; cook, stirring constantly, until mixture thickens. Add pepper and cayenne. Flake crab meat, removing any bits of shell, and add to chowder; heat through. Serve with lemon wedges. *Makes 6 servings.*

## HAMBURGER SOUP

**1 1-pound 12-ounce can (3½ cups) tomatoes**
**2 cans condensed consommé**
**2 cups water**
**1 medium onion, quartered**
**4 carrots, cut up**
**4 celery tops**
**4 large sprigs parsley**
**10 peppercorns**
**1½ pounds ground beef**
**3 tablespoons salad oil**
**1 bay leaf**
**2 teaspoons salt**
**¼ teaspoon pepper**
**½ teaspoon sugar**
**⅛ teaspoon Tabasco**

Combine tomatoes, consommé, water, onion, carrots, celery tops, parsley and peppercorns in a large saucepan; simmer, covered, for 25 minutes. Put half of mixture in blender container; cover and run on speed 6 (or high) for 1 minute or until vegetables are puréed. Empty into large saucepan. Repeat process with remaining soup. Meanwhile, brown meat in oil, breaking it apart as it cooks. Add to soup with remaining seasonings; cover and simmer 20 minutes. *Makes 10–12 servings.*

Canadian Cheese Soup (p. 57)
Perfection Vegetable Soup (p. 62)
Corn Soup (p. 58)

## LEMON SOUP

**3 10½-ounce cans chicken broth**
**2 tablespoons uncooked rice**
**2 eggs**
**2 tablespoons lemon juice**

Cook broth and rice until rice is tender, about 20 minutes. Put eggs and lemon juice in blender container; cover and run on speed 6 (or high) for 1 minute. While blender is running, gradually pour in 2 cups of the hot broth; stir blended mixture into remainder of broth in saucepan. Do not heat further. Serve immediately. *Makes 4 servings.*

## MUSHROOM WINE SOUP

**2 quarts hot water**
**8 beef bouillon cubes**
**3 tablespoons cornstarch**
**1 pound fresh mushrooms, cleaned**
**1 medium onion, cubed**
**2 medium stalks celery, cut into 1-inch pieces**
**¼ cup butter or margarine**
**1 clove garlic, quartered**
**2 bay leaves**
**10 peppercorns**
**¾ teaspoon monosodium glutamate**
**¾ cup sauterne**

Put 1 quart hot water and 4 bouillon cubes in blender container; cover and run on speed 5 (or high) until bouillon cubes are dissolved. Pour into 4-quart saucepan. Repeat process with remaining water, bouillon cubes and cornstarch.

Put half the mushrooms and all the onion and celery in blender container; cover and run on speed 4 (or high) just until vegetables are chopped (do not over-blend or vegetables will be liquefied). Drain thoroughly in a colander or sieve. Repeat process with remaining mushrooms.

Melt butter in a frypan; add chopped vegetables, garlic, bay leaves, peppercorns and monosodium glutamate. Cook 10 minutes over moderate heat. Stir into bouillon; bring to a boil, stirring constantly, then reduce heat and simmer 50 minutes. Remove from heat and strain soup through a sieve; press lightly with back of a spoon to extract all liquid. Discard contents of sieve. Mix sauterne with strained soup. Serve immediately. *Makes 6–8 servings.*

## MUSHROOM SOUP SUPREME

**½ pound fresh mushrooms, sliced**
**¼ cup butter or margarine**
**2 cups chicken stock OR 2 chicken bouillon cubes dissolved in 2 cups hot water**
**3 egg yolks**
**1 cup light cream**
**¼ teaspoon salt**
**⅛ teaspoon pepper**
**2 tablespoons sherry**

Sauté mushrooms in butter for 5 minutes; set aside 6 slices for garnish. Put chicken stock and sautéed mushrooms in blender container; cover and run on speed 4 (or low) just until mushrooms are chopped, about 5 seconds. Add egg yolks; cover and run on speed 6 (or high) for 2 seconds. Pour into a saucepan. Add cream, salt and pepper and stir over low heat until hot and slightly thickened. Add sherry. Garnish each serving with a mushroom slice. *Makes 6 servings.*

## SPLIT GREEN PEA SOUP

**½ pound (1 cup) dried split green peas**
**3 quarts water**
**2 bay leaves**
**2 large potatoes, pared and diced**
**3 green onions, cut up**
**3 stalks celery, cut into 2-inch pieces**
**1 ham bone**
**2 teaspoons salt**
**¼ teaspoon pepper**

Soak peas overnight; drain. Add water and bay leaves; bring to a boil. Skim off foam. Add potatoes, onions, celery and ham bone; simmer 2 hours. Remove bay leaves and ham bone. Pour ¼ of the soup into blender container; cover and run on speed 6 (or high) until smooth. Repeat this process until all soup is blended smooth. Return soup to saucepan; add seasonings. Cook 15 minutes longer. *Makes 8 servings.*

## YELLOW SPLIT PEA SOUP

1 1-pound package quick-cooking dry yellow peas, rinsed
2 quarts boiling water
1 bay leaf
2 pounds pork shoulder or ham, cut up
1 medium onion, cut up
1 teaspoon marjoram
¼ teaspoon thyme
¼ teaspoon ginger
3 teaspoons salt
¼ teaspoon pepper

Combine peas with water and bay leaf; simmer, covered, for 1 hour, stirring occasionally. Add pork, onion, herbs and ginger; simmer, covered, for 1 hour and 15 minutes. Add salt and pepper. Remove bone, fat and bay leaf. Put 4 cups of mixture in blender container; cover and run on speed 5 (or high) for 3 minutes or until smooth. Empty into large saucepan and repeat with remaining soup. *Makes 10–12 servings.*

### BLENDER GRIND DRY PEAS OR BEANS

To cut cooking time or eliminate soaking overnight, blender grind dry peas or beans one cup at a time. Ground peas or beans will cook in approximately half the time.

If you prefer to rinse before using dried peas and beans, the following method will cut cooking time:

Put two parts water to one part dried peas or beans in blender container; cover and run on speed 6 (or high) until peas or beans are very fine. Repeat amount if necessary. Proceed as directed in recipe, adding any additional water called for. This method cuts cooking time approximately in half.

## PIMIENTO SOUP

1 canned pimiento
2 tablespoons butter or margarine
2 tablespoons flour
1¾ cups chicken broth
¼ teaspoon Tabasco
1 ounce Cheddar cheese, cubed (about ¼ cup)
Toast points

Put pimiento, butter, flour and ¾ cup broth in blender container; cover and run on speed 6 (or high) for 20 seconds. Empty into a saucepan; add remaining broth. Cook, stirring constantly, until thick. Add Tabasco. Put cheese in clean, dry blender container; cover and run on speed 3 (or low) until grated. Sprinkle cheese on toast points and broil until melted. Float 1 toast point in each bowl of soup and serve others alongside. *Makes 2–3 servings.*

## POTATO SOUP

3 cups milk
2 medium potatoes, pared and cubed
1 teaspoon salt
½-inch slice onion
2 tablespoons bacon fat
2 slices bacon, fried crisp
1 stalk celery, cut into 2-inch pieces

Put all ingredients in blender container in order listed; cover and run on speed 4 (or low) until vegetables and bacon are chopped. Pour into saucepan; simmer over low heat 30 minutes. *Makes 3–4 servings.*

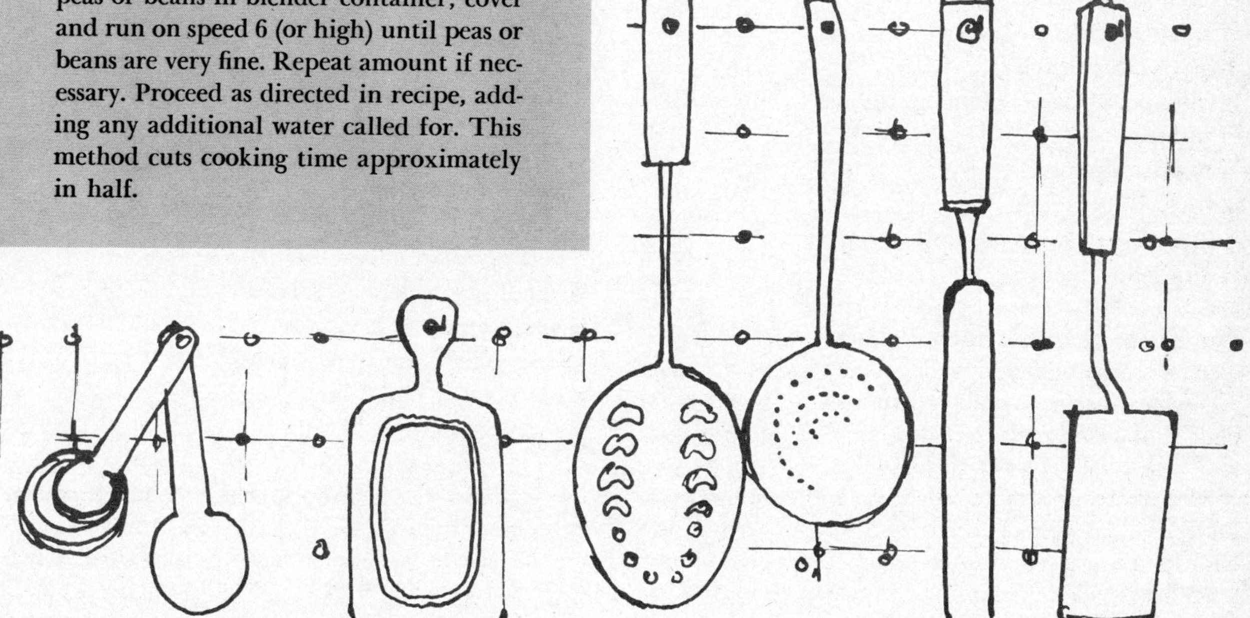

## PUMPKIN SOUP

2 cups chicken stock OR 2 chicken bouillon cubes dissolved in 2 cups hot water
½ green pepper, seeded and diced
1 large tomato, peeled and quartered
1 green onion
1 sprig parsley
¼ teaspoon thyme
1 1-pound can pumpkin OR 2 cups cubed cooked pumpkin
1 tablespoon flour
2 tablespoons butter
1 cup milk
½ teaspoon nutmeg
1 teaspoon sugar
½ teaspoon salt

Put 1 cup chicken stock, green pepper, tomato, onion, parsley and thyme in blender container; cover and run on speed 4 (or high) just until vegetables are coarsely chopped. Pour into a saucepan; simmer 5 minutes. Return mixture to blender container; add pumpkin and flour. Cover and run on speed 6 (or high) until mixture is very smooth. Pour into saucepan; stir in remaining 1 cup chicken stock and all remaining ingredients. Heat to a boil, stirring frequently; cook 3 minutes longer. Serve hot. *Makes 4–6 servings.*

## HERBED SPINACH SOUP

3 green onions with tops
3 sprigs parsley
2 tablespoons chives
¼ small head lettuce, sliced
1 cup fresh spinach
2 tablespoons butter or margarine
½ teaspoon salt
⅛ teaspoon pepper
½ teaspoon tarragon
4 10½-ounce cans consommé
½ cup light cream

Put onions, parsley, chives, lettuce and spinach in blender container; add enough cold water to cover vegetables. Cover container and run on speed 4 (or high) just until vegetables are finely chopped. Drain well in a colander or sieve.

Melt butter in a large saucepan; add chopped vegetables, salt, pepper and tarragon and cook over low heat for 15 minutes. Add consommé; cook 15 minutes longer. Just before serving, stir in cream and bring just to a boil. *Makes 8 servings.*

## CHEF'S PRIDE TOMATO SOUP

1 stalk celery, cut into 1-inch pieces
2 tablespoons butter or margarine
1 1-pound can (2 cups) tomatoes
1 10½-ounce can consommé
½ cup dry white wine
2 green onions
1 tablespoon lemon juice
1 tablespoon cornstarch
Cheese croutons

Sauté celery in butter until just tender. Put sautéed celery and remaining ingredients except croutons in blender container; cover and run on speed 4 (or low) just until onions and celery are chopped. Pour into a saucepan; simmer 15-20 minutes, stirring occasionally. Garnish with cheese croutons. *Makes 6 servings.*

## PERFECTION VEGETABLE SOUP

1 cup water
1½ cups tomato juice
½ teaspoon Worcestershire
2 beef bouillon cubes
¼ small green pepper, seeded
¼ small onion
1 stalk celery, cut into 2-inch pieces
2 carrots, cut into 2-inch pieces
1 sprig parsley

Put ingredients in blender container in order listed; cover and run on speed 4 (or low) until vegetables are chopped. If a smooth soup is desired, run on speed 7 (or high) until completely smooth. Pour into a saucepan and simmer 10 minutes. *Makes 3–4 servings.*

## LOBSTER BISQUE WITH LOBSTER BALLS

2 8-ounce packages lobster tails
½ teaspoon salt
2 cups boiling water
Lobster Balls (right)
½ cup flour
¼ cup salad oil
2⅓ cups water
¼ green pepper, seeded
½ small onion, diced
1 stalk celery, cut into 1-inch pieces
1 8-ounce can tomato sauce
1 tablespoon parsley
½ teaspoon pepper
1 teaspoon chili powder
¼ teaspoon thyme
⅛ teaspoon cayenne
1 teaspoon lemon juice

Put lobster tails and salt in boiling water; return water to boiling and cook 6-7 minutes or just until lobster tails turn red. Reserve lobster broth for later use. Rinse tails in cold water. Remove meat from shells; dice. Divide meat into 2 equal portions. Refrigerate one portion for use in bisque; make Lobster Balls with second portion.

Blend flour and oil in a 2-quart saucepan. Stir over low heat 15 minutes or until dark brown. Put ⅓ cup water, green pepper, onion and celery in blender container; cover and run on speed 4 (or high) just until vegetables are chopped. Add to mixture in saucepan; stir and cook 10 minutes. Gradually stir in 2 cups of the reserved lobster broth and 2 cups water; cook 20 minutes, stirring constantly, until thickened. Put remaining ingredients and lobster meat reserved for bisque in blender container; cover and run on speed 4 (or high) until lobster is chopped. Add to mixture in saucepan; bring to boiling. Add Lobster Balls and simmer 10 minutes. Serve immediately. *Makes 6 servings.*

### LOBSTER BALLS

2 slices dry white bread
¼ cup melted butter or margarine
¼ small onion, diced
2 eggs
½ teaspoon salt
¾ teaspoon chili powder
⅛ teaspoon thyme
⅛ teaspoon pepper
⅛ teaspoon cayenne
Lobster meat

Break 1 slice bread into 6 pieces and drop into blender container; cover and run on speed 4 (or low) until finely crumbed. Empty into a bowl. Repeat process with other slice bread.

Put butter and onion in blender container; cover and run on speed 4 (or low) until onion is chopped. Add to crumbs. Put eggs, seasonings and lobster meat reserved for balls in blender container; cover and run on speed 4 (or high) until lobster is chopped. Add to crumb mixture; mix well. Refrigerate at least one hour. Shape into 2-inch balls and add to bisque.

## HOT CREAM OF AVOCADO SOUP

**1 large ripe avocado, pitted, peeled and diced**
**2 14½-ounce cans evaporated milk**
**2 cups milk**
**½ teaspoon celery salt**
**½ teaspoon garlic salt**
**¼ teaspoon monosodium glutamate**
**¼ teaspoon salt**
**⅛ teaspoon pepper**

Put avocado and evaporated milk in blender container; cover and run on speed 7 (or high) until smooth. Pour into saucepan. Stir in milk and seasonings. Heat just until hot; do not boil. *Makes 6 servings.*

## CREAM OF CABBAGE SOUP

**½ medium head cabbage, cut up**
**2 stalks celery, cut up**
**1 small potato, pared and quartered**
**1 small onion, quartered**
**1½ cups water**
**4 sprigs parsley**
**1 cup light cream**
**1 teaspoon salt**
**¼ teaspoon black pepper**
**2 tablespoons butter or margarine**

Cook cabbage, celery, potato and onion in water until tender. Put in blender container; cover and run on speed 4 (or high) for 1½ minutes. Add remaining ingredients; cover and run on speed 2 (or low) for 15 seconds, until mixed. Reheat to serve. *Makes 4–5 servings.*

## GREEN PEA SOUP

**3 tablespoons soft butter or margarine**
**¼ cup flour**
**2 cups milk**
**1 10-ounce package frozen peas, thawed or broken apart**
**Small piece onion**
**2 teaspoons salt**
**2 cups water**

Put all ingredients except water in blender container; cover and run on speed 7 (or high) until smooth. Pour into saucepan, add water and cook over low heat, stirring frequently, about 20 minutes. *Makes 4–5 servings.*

## CARROT SOUP

**1¾ cups water**
**4 large carrots, cut into 1-inch pieces**
**½ teaspoon salt**
**1 14½-ounce can evaporated milk**
**¼ teaspoon pepper**
**¼ teaspoon nutmeg**

Put water, carrots and salt in saucepan; bring to a boil and cook about 20 minutes or until carrots are tender. Put carrots, cooking water and all other ingredients in blender container; cover and run on speed 6 (or high) until smooth. Return to saucepan and bring to a boil. Serve immediately. *Makes 6 servings.*

## CREAMY LIMA BEAN SOUP

**1 cup dry Lima beans, rinsed**
**6 cups water**
**½ small onion, cubed**
**1 carrot, cut into 1-inch pieces**
**3 sprigs parsley**
**¼ cup butter or margarine**
**1 teaspoon salt**
**½ teaspoon paprika**
**1 cup milk**

Put beans and 3 cups water in blender container; cover and run on speed 6 (or high) until beans are very fine. Pour into a large saucepan; simmer 20 minutes. Return to blender container; cover and run on speed 7 (or high) until smooth. Return to saucepan. Put remaining 3 cups water, onion, carrot and parsley in blender container; cover and run on speed 4 (or high) just until vegetables are chopped. Add vegetables and water to bean mixture; bring to boil, then cover and simmer 1 hour. Add remaining ingredients; heat through but do not boil. *Makes 6 servings.*

## FRENCH TOMATO SOUP

**2 medium tomatoes, cut up**
**2 medium carrots, cut up**
**2 small potatoes, pared and cut up**
**4 cups water**
**1 tablespoon butter or margarine**
**2 teaspoons salt**
**Dash tarragon**
**Dash marjoram**
**Dash cayenne**
**1 cup dairy sour cream**
**Croutons**

Put tomatoes, carrots and potatoes in blender container in order listed; cover and run on speed 4 (or high) until finely chopped. Empty into a large saucepan; add water, butter and salt; simmer for 30 minutes. Add seasonings and simmer 10 minutes longer. Put half of mixture in blender container; cover and run on speed 2 (or low) for 30 seconds. Add half of sour cream; cover and run on speed 2 (or low) a few seconds or until mixed. Pour into warmed soup tureen. Repeat process with remaining soup and sour cream. Serve with croutons. *Makes 6–8 servings.*

## CREAM OF TOMATO SOUP

**2 cups cold milk**
**2½ cups canned tomatoes**
**1 small onion**
**¾ teaspoon salt**
**⅛ teaspoon pepper**
**½ teaspoon celery salt**
**1 teaspoon sugar**
**3 tablespoons flour**
**2 tablespoons butter or margarine**

Pour milk into a 2-quart saucepan. Put remaining ingredients in blender container; cover and run on speed 7 (or high) until smooth. Slowly add tomato mixture to milk, stirring constantly. Place over low heat until hot. *Makes 6–8 servings.*

## CREAM OF VEGETABLE SOUP

**4 cups milk**
**2 tablespoons butter**
**1 tablespoon flour**
**½ teaspoon salt**
**¼ teaspoon pepper**
**1 cup cooked or canned vegetables**

Put all ingredients except 2 cups milk in blender container in order listed; cover and run on speed 6 (or high) until smooth. Pour into a saucepan and add remaining milk. Cook, stirring constantly, over low heat until hot. *Makes 4–5 servings.*

### CREAM OF CARROT SOUP

Use 1 cup cooked or canned diced carrots in Cream of Vegetable Soup. Substitute ½ cup carrot liquid for ½ cup milk. Add 2 sprigs parsley before blending.

### CREAM OF CELERY SOUP

Use 1 cup diced cooked celery and ½ teaspoon celery salt in Cream of Vegetable Soup.

### CREAM OF ASPARAGUS SOUP

Use 1 cup canned or cooked asparagus, drained, in Cream of Vegetable Soup.

### CREAM OF ONION SOUP

Substitute 1 cup beef stock for 1 cup milk in Cream of Vegetable Soup. Sauté 1 cup chopped onion in ¼ cup butter or margarine until transparent (omit 2 tablespoons butter in basic recipe); add to other ingredients and run on speed 4 (or low) until onions are finely chopped.

## Cold—With Meat and Without

### BLENDER BORSCHT

**3 cups dairy sour cream**
**1 thin slice lemon, peeled and seeded**
**½ teaspoon salt**
**½ small onion**
**1½ cups cooked diced beets**

Put 2½ cups sour cream and remaining ingredients in blender container; cover and run on speed 7 (or high) until perfectly smooth. Chill. Serve cold; garnish with remaining ½ cup sour cream and sprigs of parsley. *Makes 3–4 servings.*

### CHILLED BLUE CHEESE SOUP WITH CAVIAR

**2 ounces blue cheese, crumbled (about ¼ cup)**
**½ cup milk**
**1 cup dairy sour cream**
**¼ teaspoon basil**
**¼ teaspoon chervil**
**¼ teaspoon oregano**
**¼ teaspoon pepper**
**1 4-ounce jar red caviar**

Put cheese and milk in blender container; cover and run on speed 3 (or low) until smooth. Add sour cream and seasonings; cover and run on speed 2 (or low) a few seconds. Check consistency and add more milk, if desired. Cover and chill 24 hours. Top each serving with a spoonful of caviar. *Makes 4–5 servings.*

### CLAM BISQUE

**2 cups cream**
**¼ teaspoon tarragon**
**4 drops Tabasco**
**1 teaspoon celery salt**
**2 7½-ounce cans minced clams, with liquid**

Put all ingredients in blender container; cover and run on speed 7 (or high) until clams are very finely cut. Serve cold or pour into saucepan and heat. *Makes 3–4 servings.*

### FROSTED CUCUMBER SOUP

**2 cucumbers, pared, seeded and cut up**
**1 envelope dry cream of leek soup mix**
**2½ cups milk**
**1 cup dairy sour cream**
**1 teaspoon lemon juice**
**Few drops green food coloring**
**4–6 sprigs mint**

Put cucumbers, soup mix, milk, ¾ cup sour cream, lemon juice and food coloring in blender container; cover and run on speed 3 (or low) a few seconds or until color is even. Chill several hours. Garnish each serving with a spoonful of sour cream and a mint sprig. *Makes 4–6 servings.*

### GAZPACHO

**5–7 slices fresh white bread, with crusts removed**
**4 large ripe tomatoes, peeled and cut into 1-inch pieces**
**1 clove garlic**
**1 quart water**
**3 tablespoons olive oil**
**3 tablespoons vinegar**
**2 teaspoons salt**
**⅛ teaspoon white pepper**
**1 green pepper, seeded and cut into 1-inch pieces**
**1 cucumber**
**1 onion**
**Croutons**

Break 1 slice bread into 4 pieces; drop into blender container. Cover container and run on speed 4 (or low) until finely crumbed. Empty into a large measuring cup. Repeat process with remaining bread until you have 3 cups crumbs; put in a large bowl. Put tomatoes, garlic, water, olive oil, vinegar, salt and white pepper in bowl with bread crumbs. Cover and let stand 2–3 hours. Put half the mixture in blender container; cover and run on speed 6 (or high) until smooth; empty into a container. Repeat process with remaining half. Refrigerate the soup for at least 2 hours.

Before serving, put green pepper in blender container; cover and run on speed 4 (or low) until pepper is coarsely chopped; empty into a small bowl. Repeat process with cucumber and onion, emptying each into its own bowl. Pass vegetables and croutons in individual bowls to spoon into soup. *Makes 8 servings.*

*Cold Cream of Avocado Soup (p. 67)*

*Blender Borscht (p. 66)*

## SUMMER GARDEN MADRILENE

**1 envelope (1 tablespoon) unflavored gelatin**
**½ cup boiling water**
**1 cup rosé wine**
**3 12½-ounce cans madrilene**
**½ medium green pepper, seeded and cut up**
**1 small carrot, cut up**
**½ medium cucumber, pared, seeded and cut up**
**Thin lime slices**
**Dairy sour cream**
**Fresh dill, snipped, or dill weed**

Put gelatin and boiling water in blender container; cover and run on speed 1 (or low) until gelatin is dissolved. Add wine; cover and run on speed 3 (or low) a few seconds. Add to madrilene and chill until mixture begins to thicken. Put a few pieces of green pepper in blender container; cover and run on speed 3 (or low) until chopped. Empty into a bowl. Repeat process until all green pepper is chopped. Repeat process with carrot and cucumber. Add to the slightly thickened mixture and chill until firm. To serve, break up mixture with a fork. Top each serving with a lime slice, a spoonful of sour cream and a sprinkling of dill. *Makes 8–10 servings.*

## COLD CREAM OF AVOCADO SOUP

**¾ cup chicken broth**
**1 cup whipping cream**
**1 very large avocado, pitted, peeled and cut up**
**⅓ cup dry white wine**
**2 teaspoons lemon juice**
**1 teaspoon salt**
**⅛ teaspoon pepper**
**Pinch cayenne**

Put broth, cream and avocado in blender container; cover and run on speed 2 (or low) for 15 seconds. Add wine, lemon juice, salt, pepper and cayenne; cover and run on speed 4 (or high) for 5 seconds, until smooth. Chill. *Makes 4–6 servings.*

***MENU FOR A HOT DAY***

*Chicken Curry Soup*
*Avocado stuffed with shrimp or crab*
*Green Goddess Dressing (p. 82)*
*Peachy Orange Sherbet (p. 143)*

## ICY BLACK BEAN SOUP

**½ cup chicken broth**
**¼ cup sherry**
**1 10½-ounce can condensed black bean soup, undiluted**
**¾ cup milk**
**Dairy sour cream**
**4 green onions, with tops, cut up**

Put broth, sherry, soup and milk in blender container; cover and run on speed 1 (or low) for 30 seconds. Chill. Serve in cups or low glasses; top with sour cream. Put green onion "swizzle stick" in each serving. *Makes 4 servings.*

## CHICKEN CURRY SOUP

**½ cup milk**
**1 10½-ounce can cream of chicken soup, undiluted**
**1 teaspoon curry powder**
**1 cup crushed ice**
**½ cup heavy cream**

Put milk, soup and curry powder in blender container. Cover and run on speed 4 (or low) about 15 seconds. Remove cover and add ice and cream. Cover and run on speed 6 (or high) until completely smooth. Serve cold; garnish with chopped chives and thin cucumber slices. *Makes 4 servings.*

## CHILLED CLAM-AVOCADO SOUP

**2 large ripe avocados, pitted, peeled and diced**
**1 cup light cream**
**1 cup chilled chicken stock**
**1 7½-ounce can minced clams, with liquid**
**½ teaspoon lemon juice**
**¼ teaspoon salt**
**⅛ teaspoon cayenne**
**Snipped chives**

Put all ingredients except chives in blender container; cover and run on speed 6 (or high) until smooth. Serve in chilled bowls with chives on top. *Makes 6 servings.*

## VICHYSOISSE

**2 cups chicken broth**
**3 tablespoons butter or margarine**
**½ teaspoon salt**
**¼ teaspoon white pepper**
**1 large onion, cubed**
**3 medium potatoes, pared, cooked and diced**
**1 cup milk**
**¾ cup heavy cream**

Put all ingredients except milk and cream in blender container in order listed; cover and run on speed 7 (or high) until perfectly smooth. Pour into saucepan and add milk. Simmer 20 minutes over low heat. Add cream. Chill; serve topped with cut chives. *Makes 6 servings.*

## CHILLED RASPBERRY SOUP

**1 cup water**
**2 10-ounce packages frozen raspberries, thawed**
**1 teaspoon lemon juice**
**Heavy cream**

Put all ingredients except cream in blender container in order listed; cover and run on speed 7 (or high) until smooth. Pour through a fine strainer to remove seeds. Chill. Pour into 4 sherbet glasses; carefully pour cream down side of glass so a thin layer floats on top of the soup. *Makes 4 servings.*

## CHILLED STRAWBERRY-RHUBARB SOUP

**1 1-pound package frozen rhubarb**
**½ cup water**
**⅓ cup sugar**
**Unsweetened pineapple juice**
**2 cups fresh strawberries, cleaned and hulled**
**1 tablespoon lemon juice**
**¼ teaspoon nutmeg**

Put rhubarb, water and sugar in saucepan and bring to a boil; cover and cook 3 minutes. Drain rhubarb; reserve juice. Add enough pineapple juice to rhubarb juice to make 4 cups. Put 1 cup of this liquid, the rhubarb, strawberries, lemon juice and nutmeg in blender container; cover and run on speed 5 (or high) until smooth. Add to remaining rhubarb and pineapple juice. Chill. *Makes 6 servings.*

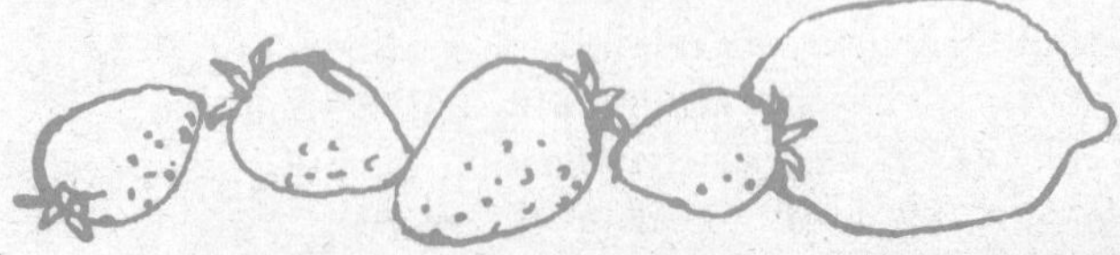

# All Kinds of Salads

*Considering the number of ingredients that may be used, it is possible to serve a different salad every day of the year, one more delicious than the other. To create salad excitement, try some of the delightful combinations suggested here, then go on to develop some of your own.*

*Whether the salad is to be a crisp, fresh touch added to your dinner or the principal dish at lunch or supper, consider the recipe as a basic pattern. Add a vegetable here, substitute a fruit there. Use fresh, frozen and canned products, sometimes in halves or slices, sometimes blender-chopped. Try different types of oil in your dressing. Experiment with vinegar or use lemon juice instead. Change the herb from basil to thyme or tarragon, or add a touch of nutmeg or allspice. Above all, use different greens.*

## Experiment with Salad Greens

*Leafy greens bring to the table considerable amounts of important vitamins and iron. (The deep green leaves are especially generous with vitamin A.) Buy several kinds. As soon as you get them home, wash, trim and drain thoroughly. Tuck greens into a tightly covered salad saver or into a large plastic bag.*

*Crisp, firm-headed iceberg lettuce is America's favorite salad ingredient. For variety, serve it in thick cross-wise slices or rafts; tear it into bite-size chunks; shred it. But don't limit yourself to this green alone. Use delicately-flavored, tender-textured Bibb and Boston lettuces, or leaf lettuce, green and ruffled. A cousin to the lettuces is romaine or Cos, which has long leaves, green and crisp and sweet. Escarole, a variety of endive, is slightly bitter. It has large, broad, jagged leaves of rich green and white. The flat head of narrow leaves with curly tips is also an endive, although it is commonly called chicory. True chicory leaves come in small cigar-shaped heads and are, perversely, called French or Belgian endive.*

*Good in combination with these greens are young and tender spinach leaves, young beet tops, cabbage, celery, dandelion greens, field salad, the half-bitter Italian "aruca" or "rugola" and, of course, watercress and parsley.*

*When making a tossed salad, contrast bright green with light, tender with firm, sharp or bitter with sweet for an appealing whole. Be sure to tear greens in preference to chopping them; the irregular pieces seem to pick up the dressing, and are easier to manage with a fork. Unless marinating is part of the plan, add dressing and toss salad just before serving to insure crispness.*

New Flavors for Molded Salads

*New and exciting gelatin flavors are appearing, adding greater variety to molded salads. Celery, Italian, mixed vegetables and seasoned tomato are compatible with any combination of vegetables. Try these new tastes as well as the classic flavors.*

## To Stand Alone

### MAIN DISH CHICKEN SALAD

**2 tablespoons sherry**
**1 teaspoon lemon juice**
**½ cup boiling chicken broth**
**1 envelope (1 tablespoon) unflavored gelatin**
**¼ cup mayonnaise**
**2 egg yolks**
**¼ teaspoon dry mustard**
**2 drops Tabasco**
**2 sprigs parsley**
**1 slice onion**
**Dash pepper**
**¼ green pepper, seeded**
**2 stalks celery, cut into 1-inch pieces**
**2 cups diced cooked chicken**
**1 cup cooked peas**

Put first 4 ingredients in blender container; cover and run on speed 1 (or low) until gelatin is dissolved. Put remaining ingredients except chicken and peas in container; cover and run on speed 4 (or low) just until vegetables are coarsely chopped. Add chicken to container; cover and run on speed 7 (or high) just until all chicken goes through blades. Pour into a 1½-quart mold or a loaf pan; stir in peas. Chill until set. *Makes 6 servings.*

### MOLDED SALMON LOAF

**1 1-pound can red salmon, drained, bones and skin removed**
**¼ cup cold water**
**1 envelope (1 tablespoon) unflavored gelatin**
**¼ cup boiling water**
**½ teaspoon salt**
**2 tablespoons lemon juice**
**2 tablespoons vinegar**
**1 tablespoon sugar**
**1 thin slice onion**
**½ cup Blender Mayonnaise (page 79)**
**½ cup pitted ripe olives**
**½ large stalk celery, cut into 1-inch pieces**

Flake salmon in bowl and set aside. Put cold water and gelatin in blender container; add boiling water. Cover and run on speed 1 (or low) for a few seconds to dissolve gelatin. Add salt, lemon juice, vinegar, sugar and onion; cover and run on speed 3 (or low) until onion is grated. Empty into medium bowl and chill until consistency of unbeaten egg white.

Meanwhile, put mayonnaise, olives and celery in blender container in order listed; cover and run on speed 4 (or low) until olives and celery are chopped. Add mayonnaise mixture to salmon and mix. Fold salmon mixture into chilled gelatin. Turn into a 9x5x3-inch loaf pan and chill until firm. Turn onto a platter. *Makes 5–6 servings.*

## MOLDED CRAB MEAT SALAD

1 envelope (1 tablespoon) unflavored gelatin
¼ cup cold water
½ pint dairy sour cream
3 tablespoons vinegar
1 teaspoon salt
1 cup cooked crab meat, bony tissue removed
1 cup pared cucumber, cut into 1-inch cubes
¼ small onion

Sprinkle gelatin over cold water; let stand until moistened. Place over boiling water and stir to dissolve gelatin. Put in blender container with sour cream, vinegar and salt; cover and run on speed 1 (or low) about 30 seconds. Add crab meat, cucumber and onion; cover and run on speed 4 (or low) just until vegetables are chopped. Pour into a 1-quart mold; chill until firm. Unmold and garnish with cucumber and radish slices. *Makes 6 servings.*

## TUNA SALAD DE LUXE

½ cup Blender Mayonnaise (page 79)
½ cup pickle relish
½ small onion, quartered
1 stalk celery, cut into 2-inch pieces
1 4-ounce can tuna fish, drained
½ cup cubed Cheddar cheese
2 cups cooked macaroni, drained and cooled

Put mayonnaise, pickle relish, onion and celery in blender container; cover and run on speed 4 (or low) until vegetables are chopped. Add tuna and cheese; cover and run on speed 5 (or high) until chopped. Pour over macaroni in mixing bowl; mix well. Serve in lettuce cups or in tomato halves which have had the pulp scooped out. *Makes 4–6 servings.*

*Molded Crab Meat Salad*

## To Go with Dinner

### DEVILED EGGS

**6 hard-cooked eggs, shelled**
**3 tablespoons mayonnaise**
**3 tablespoons chili sauce**
**1 thin slice onion**
**½ teaspoon salt**
**¼ teaspoon pepper**
**½ teaspoon dry mustard**

Cut eggs in half lengthwise; separate yolks from whites. Put egg yolks and remaining ingredients in blender container; cover and run on speed 6 (or high) until smooth. If necessary, stop blender during processing and push ingredients toward blades with rubber spatula. Fill egg whites with blended mixture. Chill. *Makes 6 servings.*

### AVOCADO-STUFFED TOMATOES

**6 medium tomatoes**
**Salt**
**1 teaspoon lemon juice**
**2 tablespoons mayonnaise**
**1 thin slice onion**
**2 small avocados, peeled, seeded and cubed**
**2 canned green chili peppers**
**Dairy sour cream**

Peel tomatoes and scoop out centers, leaving a ¼-inch shell. Sprinkle insides with salt and turn upside down to drain. Put remaining ingredients except chili peppers and sour cream in blender container in order listed; cover and run on speed 6 (or high) until smooth. If necessary, stop blender during processing and push ingredients toward blades with rubber spatula. Add chili peppers; cover container and run on speed 4 (or high) until peppers are finely chopped. Fill tomatoes with avocado mixture; top with sour cream and serve on lettuce leaves. *Makes 6 servings.*

***SALAD SUPPER***

*White Bean Salad*
*Sliced salami*
*Sliced brick cheese*
*French bread*
*Pecan Crunch Cake (p. 157)*

### WHITE BEAN SALAD

**5 tablespoons salad oil**
**5 tablespoons vinegar**
**3 tablespoons sugar**
**5 tablespoons catsup**
**½ teaspoon salt**
**½ teaspoon garlic salt**
**½ teaspoon onion salt**
**¾ teaspoon celery salt**
**¼ teaspoon Worcestershire**
**¼ green pepper, seeded**
**4 sprigs parsley**
**3 tablespoons cut chives**
**4 cups cooked white beans, chilled**

Put salad oil, vinegar, sugar, catsup, salt, garlic salt, onion salt, celery salt, and Worcestershire in blender container; cover and run on speed 6 (or high) until smooth. Add green pepper, parsley and chives; cover and run on speed 4 (or low) just until vegetables are chopped. Mix dressing with chilled beans; serve in a bowl lined with romaine. *Makes 8 servings.*

### KIDNEY BEAN SALAD

**1 small head cabbage (5–6 inches), cored and sliced coarsely**
**½ green pepper, seeded and cut up**
**2 stalks celery, cut up**
**½ medium onion, cut up**
**1 17-ounce can red kidney beans, drained**
**½ cup Blender Mayonnaise (page 79)**
**1 teaspoon salt**
**½ teaspoon pepper**
**2 tablespoons vinegar**
**6 slices bacon, fried crisp and crumbled**

Fill blender container to top cup marking with cabbage, green pepper, celery and onion and add cold water just to cover. Cover container and run on speed 7 (or high) for 5 seconds, just until vegetables are coarsely chopped. Drain in a colander or sieve. Repeat process until all vegetables are chopped. Empty well-drained vegetables onto paper toweling to absorb excess moisture. Combine vegetables and drained kidney beans.

Put mayonnaise, salt, pepper and vinegar in blender container; cover and run on speed 2 (or low) until mixed. Toss with vegetables and chill thoroughly. Just before serving, arrange bean mixture in a lettuce-lined bowl and sprinkle top with crumbled bacon. *Makes 6 servings.*

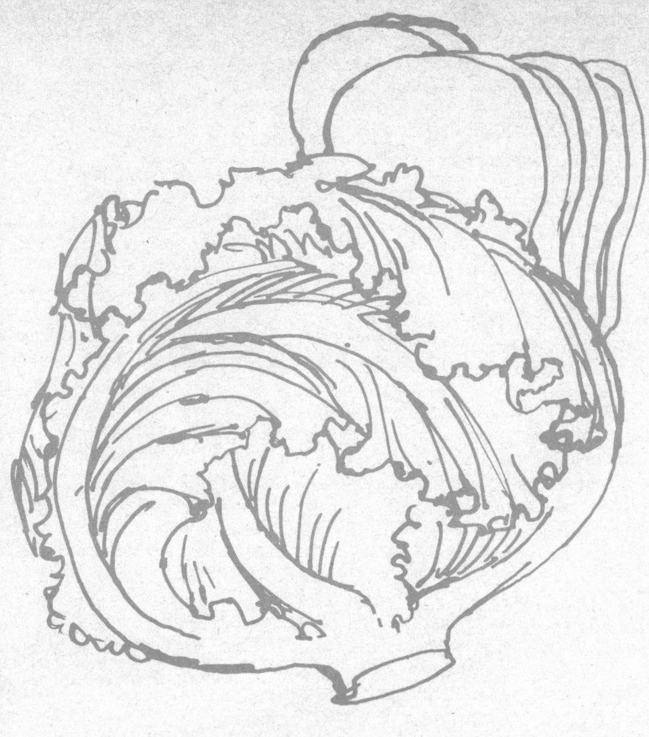

## MUSHROOM SALAD

**1 pound fresh mushrooms**
**¼ cup vinegar**
**¾ cup salad oil**
**1½ teaspoons salt**
**¼ teaspoon pepper**
**¼ teaspoon paprika**
**¼ teaspoon sugar**
**1 thin slice onion**
**1½ teaspoons tarragon**
**½ clove garlic**
**3 cups torn Belgian endive or mixed salad greens**

Clean and stem mushrooms. Put mushroom caps in a shallow bowl (save stems for use in cooked dishes). Put remaining ingredients except endive in blender container; cover and run on speed 7 (or high) until garlic is liquefied. Pour contents of blender container over mushroom caps. Refrigerate for 1 hour. Drain mushroom caps, saving the dressing. Toss mushroom caps with endive and ½ cup reserved dressing. *Makes 8 servings.*

## SOUR CREAM LETTUCE

**2 slices dry bread or toast**
**2 tablespoons butter or margarine, melted**
**1 large head lettuce, cored**
**3 tablespoons butter or margarine**
**½ cup hot chicken broth**
**2 teaspoons lemon juice**
**½ teaspoon salt**
**Dash pepper**
**3–4 slices dry bread or toast**
**½ cup dairy sour cream**

Break 2 slices dry bread into blender container; cover and run on speed 3 (or low) until crumbed. Empty into a bowl and mix with melted butter; set aside.

Coarsely cut lettuce into blender container to top cup marking; add water to cover. Cover and run on speed 7 (or high) about 5 seconds or until lettuce is chopped. Drain in a colander or sieve. Repeat until you have 3 cups chopped lettuce. Put lettuce in frypan with 3 tablespoons butter. Cover and cook, stirring occasionally, until tender but still crisp, about 10 minutes.

Put chicken broth, lemon juice and seasonings in blender container; cover and run on speed 5 (or high). While blender is running, break dry bread into container. Stop blender to check consistency and stop adding bread when mixture is thick enough for a sauce. (You will probably need 3–4 slices). Stir into lettuce with sour cream. Sprinkle with buttered crumbs. *Makes 4 servings.*

## MEXICAN POTATO SALAD

**1 clove garlic, cut in half**
**1 cup bread cubes**
**1 tablespoon salad oil**
**2 stalks celery, cut up**
**1 medium onion, cut up**
**1 medium carrot, cut up**
**¼ green pepper, seeded**
**¼ cup salad oil**
**3 tablespoons vinegar**
**1 teaspoon salt**
**1 teaspoon chili powder**
**1 canned pimiento**
**2 cups (3 medium) diced cooked potatoes**
**1 head lettuce, broken into chunks**

Sauté garlic and bread cubes in 1 tablespoon salad oil until bread is golden. Remove garlic and discard. Set bread cubes aside. Put cut-up vegetables in blender container and cover with water. Cover container and run on speed 4 (or high) just until vegetables are coarsely chopped. Drain vegetables in colander or sieve; empty into a bowl. Put ¼ cup salad oil, vinegar, seasonings and pimiento in blender container; cover and run on speed 2 (or low) just until pimiento is chopped. Pour over chopped vegetables; mix well. Add potatoes and toss lightly. Let stand 1 hour to marinate. At serving time, add lettuce and bread cubes; toss lightly. *Makes 6–8 servings.*

*Vegetable Slaw (p. 75)*

## CABBAGE SLAW

**1 head cabbage, cored and sliced coarsely**
**Sour Cream Dressing (page 84)**

Fill blender container to top cup marking with cabbage; add water just to cover cabbage. Cover container and run on speed 7 (or high) just until cabbage is chopped, about 5 seconds. Drain thoroughly in a colander or sieve; empty onto a paper towel to absorb excess moisture. Repeat process with any additional cabbage. Mix chopped cabbage with Sour Cream Dressing in a bowl. *Makes 2½ cups chopped cabbage from each containerful.*

### VEGETABLE SLAW

Put ½ seeded green pepper, ½ small onion and 1 carrot (cut into 1-inch pieces) in blender container with cabbage. Prepare slaw as directed above.

## ASPARAGUS EGG MOLD

**1 10-ounce package frozen cut asparagus OR 1 pound fresh asparagus, trimmed and cut into 1½-inch pieces**
**1 envelope (1 tablespoon) unflavored gelatin**
**1 slice onion**
**½ teaspoon salt**
**1 canned pimiento**
**1 tablespoon lemon juice**
**1 cup Blender Mayonnaise (page 79)**
**3 hard-cooked eggs, shelled and quartered**

Cook frozen asparagus according to package directions. If fresh asparagus is used, cook in covered saucepan with 1 teaspoon salt and 1 cup water just until tender-crisp. Measure cooking liquid; if necessary, add water or boil down to measure 1¼ cups. Cool liquid and asparagus.

Put ¼ cup cooled liquid in blender container with gelatin. Heat remaining liquid to boiling and add to gelatin. Cover and run on speed 1 (or low) until gelatin is dissolved. Cool. Add remaining ingredients except eggs and asparagus; cover container and run on speed 4 (or low) just until mixed and pimiento is chopped. Add eggs; cover container and run on speed 4 (or low) just until eggs are coarsely chopped. Pour into a bowl and chill until about the consistency of unbeaten egg white; stir in cooked asparagus. Pour into a 1½-quart mold; chill until set. *Makes 6 servings.*

## AVOCADO MOLD

**3 envelopes (3 tablespoons) unflavored gelatin**
**1 cup cold water**
**¼ cup lemon juice**
**3 avocados, peeled, pitted and cut up**
**1 cup dairy sour cream**
**1 cup Blender Mayonnaise (page 79)**
**¼ medium onion**
**⅛ green pepper, seeded**
**1 teaspoon salt**
**⅛ teaspoon pepper**
**Salad greens**

Soften gelatin in cold water; set over hot water to dissolve. Put all ingredients except gelatin and salad greens in blender container. Cover and run on speed 6 (or high) until smooth. Add gelatin and run on speed 6 (or high) until blended. Pour into 5½-cup ring mold that has been rinsed in cold water. Press waxed paper or plastic wrap against surface and refrigerate until set (about 3 hours). To serve, turn out on serving dish. Surround with salad greens. Fill with a seafood salad. *Makes 8 servings.*

**Note:** Avocado mold will discolor if stored in refrigerator longer than 1½ hours after it has been unmolded.

## GREEN VELVET MOLD

**1 envelope (1 tablespoon) unflavored gelatin**
**¼ cup cold water**
**¾ cup Blender Mayonnaise (page 79)**
**1 tablespoon prepared horseradish**
**1 thin slice onion**
**⅛ teaspoon green food coloring**
**½ teaspoon salt**
**Dash white pepper**
**3½ medium cucumbers, pared, seeded and cubed**
**½ cup whipping cream, whipped**

Oil a fancy 1-quart mold with salad oil. Set upside down to drain. Soften gelatin in cold water in a small bowl until moistened; then set bowl in hot water to dissolve gelatin.

Put mayonnaise, horseradish, onion, food coloring, salt and pepper in blender container; cover and run on speed 6 (or high). While blender is running, add cubed cucumbers; run until smooth. Add dissolved gelatin; cover container and run on speed 6 (or high) until thoroughly blended. Pour into a large bowl; chill until mixture is the consistency of unbeaten egg white. Fold in whipped cream. Turn into prepared mold and chill until firm. To serve, unmold and garnish with salad greens and cucumber slices. *Makes 4 servings.*

## MOLDED BEET SALAD

1 cup boiling beet juice
1 3-ounce package lemon-flavored gelatin
¼ lemon, peeled and seeded
1 teaspoon salt
¼ small onion
1 tablespoon prepared horseradish
2 carrots, cut into 1-inch pieces
1½ cups cooked, sliced beets

Add water, if necessary, to beet juice to make 1 cup. Put boiling beet juice and gelatin in blender container; cover and run on speed 1 (or low) until gelatin is dissolved. Add lemon, salt, onion and horseradish; cover container and run on speed 6 (or high) until smooth. Add carrots; cover and run on speed 4 (or low) just until carrots are coarsely chopped. Add beets; cover container and run on speed 4 (or low) just until all beets are chopped. Pour into a 1-quart mold. Chill until set. Serve on salad greens with mayonnaise. *Makes 6 servings.*

## FRESH TOMATO ASPIC

6 medium tomatoes, scalded, peeled and quartered
1 clove garlic
1 bay leaf
1 small onion, quartered
1½ teaspoons salt
2 envelopes (2 tablespoons) unflavored gelatin
½ cup cold water
2 tablespoons vinegar
1 teaspoon sugar

Put tomatoes, garlic, bay leaf, onion and salt in blender container; cover and run on speed 6 (or high) until smooth. Strain into a bowl. Soften gelatin in cold water and set over hot water until dissolved; add to tomato mixture. Stir in vinegar and sugar. Pour into two refrigerator trays and freeze until firm. Cut into squares and serve on lettuce leaves. *Makes 12 servings.*

## PERFECTION SALAD

1 cup boiling water
1 3-ounce package lemon-flavored gelatin
1 cup pineapple juice
1 tablespoon lemon juice
1 cup cabbage, coarsely sliced
2 medium carrots, cut into 1-inch pieces

Put water and gelatin in blender container; cover and run on speed 1 (or low) until gelatin is dissolved. Stop blender; add remaining ingredients in order listed; cover container and run on speed 4 (or low) just until vegetables are coarsely chopped. Empty into a bowl; chill until partially set, then stir and pour into six 4-ounce molds or a 1-quart mold. *Makes 6 servings.*

## JELLIED TOMATO RING

½ cup hot chicken broth
1½ tablespoons lemon juice
1 thin slice onion
2 envelopes (2 tablespoons) unflavored gelatin
2 drops Tabasco
1 tablespoon Worcestershire
½ teaspoon celery salt
2 cups tomato juice
1 cup crushed ice

Put first 4 ingredients in blender container; cover and run on speed 1 (or low) until gelatin is completely dissolved. Add remaining ingredients; cover container and run on speed 7 (or high) until completely smooth. Pour into a 5-cup ring mold; chill until set. Turn out onto serving plate and fill center with a cooked vegetable or seafood salad. *Makes 6-8 servings.*

### PREPARE QUICK-SETTING GELATIN DESSERTS OR SALADS

Put hot water and gelatin in blender container; cover and run on speed 1 (or low) until gelatin is dissolved. Substitute crushed ice for part of the cold water. Add ice and water; cover container and run on speed 7 (or high) until ice is liquefied. Pour into a bowl or mold; chill until firm.

## CREAMY PINEAPPLE SALAD

**1 No. 2½ can (3½ cups) crushed pineapple**
**2 envelopes (2 tablespoons) unflavored gelatin**
**½ cup sugar**
**½ teaspoon salt**
**1 cup unsweetened pineapple juice**
**1 cup orange juice**
**Rind of ½ lemon (colored portion only)**
**3 tablespoons lemon juice**
**1 8-ounce package cream cheese, cubed**

Drain pineapple, reserving syrup. If necessary, add enough water to make 1½ cups. Heat syrup to boiling. Put pineapple syrup and gelatin in blender container; cover and run on speed 1 (or low) until gelatin is dissolved. Add remaining ingredients except pineapple; cover and run on speed 6 (or high) until smooth. Pour into bowl and chill until the consistency of unbeaten egg white; stir in drained pineapple. Pour into a 2-quart mold and chill until set. *Makes 10 servings.*

## GOLDEN GLOW SALAD

**1 No. 2 can (2½ cups) crushed pineapple**
**1 3-ounce package orange-flavored gelatin**
**½ teaspoon salt**
**¼ cup lemon juice**
**4 raw carrots, cut into 2-inch pieces**
**½ cup cubed Cheddar cheese**

Drain pineapple, reserving syrup. If necessary, add enough water to syrup to make 1¼ cups. Heat ½ cup syrup and put in blender container with gelatin. Cover container and run on speed 1 (or low) until gelatin is dissolved. Add remaining syrup, salt, lemon juice, carrots and cheese; cover container and run on speed 4 (or low) until carrots and cheese are chopped. Pour into a 1-quart mold; chill until partially set. Stir in drained pineapple; chill until firmly set. Serve on salad greens; garnish with mayonnaise. *Makes 6 servings.*

## APPLE SNOW SALAD

**3 ½-inch pieces lemon rind**
**3 tablespoons lemon juice**
**1 8-ounce can (1 cup) crushed pineapple**
**2 eggs**
**½ cup sugar**
**Dash salt**
**2 medium red apples, cored and cut up**
**½ cup diced celery**
**1 cup whipping cream, Blender whipped (page 139)**

Put lemon rind and juice in blender container; cover and run on speed 3 (or low) about 45 seconds. Drain pineapple, reserving syrup. If necessary, add enough water to syrup to make ½ cup. Add syrup, eggs, sugar and salt; cover and run on speed 6 (or high) for 10 seconds. Empty into a saucepan and cook over low heat, stirring constantly, until mixture thickens. Cool.

Meanwhile, put a few pieces of apple in blender container; cover and run on speed 3 (or low) until finely chopped. Empty into a mixing bowl with pineapple, mixing to prevent darkening. Repeat process until all apples are chopped. If necessary, stop blender during processing and push apples toward blades with rubber spatula. Add cooked mixture and celery to apples. Fold in whipped cream. Pour into 2 refrigerator trays and freeze until firm. Cut into rectangles to serve. *Makes 10–12 servings.*

## LIME-WALNUT SALAD

**1 cup boiling water**
**1 3-ounce package lime-flavored gelatin**
**1 8-ounce can (1 cup) crushed pineapple with syrup**
**1 12-ounce carton creamed cottage cheese**
**2 stalks celery, cut into 1-inch pieces**
**½ cup walnuts**

Put boiling water and gelatin in blender container; cover and run on speed 1 (or low) until gelatin is dissolved. Add remaining ingredients except walnuts; cover container and run on speed 6 (or high) just until celery is chopped. Add walnuts; cover container and run on speed 7 (or high) just until all nuts go through the blades. Pour into a 9x9x2-inch pan. Chill until set. *Makes 6 servings.*

***SUNDAY SUPPER***

*Creamy Pineapple Salad*
*and Blender Mayonnaise (p. 79)*
*garnished with strawberries*
*Sliced ham in tiny soft rolls*
*Graham Nut Torte (p. 162)*

*Cranberry-Orange Mold*

## PEACHY-ORANGE RING

**1 1-pound can (1½ cups) sliced peaches**
**1 3-ounce package orange-flavored gelatin**
**Dash salt**
**½ 6-ounce can frozen orange juice concentrate, thawed**
**1 tablespoon lemon juice**
**½ 7-ounce bottle lemon-lime carbonated beverage, chilled**

Drain peaches, reserving syrup. If necessary, add enough water to syrup to make ¾ cup. Heat syrup. Put orange-flavored gelatin in blender container and add hot syrup; cover and run on speed 1 (or low) for 1 minute or until gelatin is dissolved. Add peaches, salt, frozen orange juice concentrate and lemon juice; cover and run on speed 5 (or high) for 1 minute until peaches are puréed. Slowly pour carbonated beverage down sides of blender container; mix gently with rubber spatula. Pour into a 1-quart mold. Chill until firm. *Makes 5–6 servings.*

## PEACH ASPIC

**1 envelope (1 tablespoon) unflavored gelatin**
**½ cup boiling water**
**1 1-pound can sliced peaches, well drained**
**2 tablespoons sugar**
**¼ cup vinegar**
**½ cup chili sauce**
**3 tablespoons lemon juice**
**½ teaspoon salt**
**½ thin slice onion**

Put boiling water and gelatin in blender container; cover and run on speed 1 (or low) until gelatin is dissolved. Add remaining ingredients; cover container and run on speed 7 (or high) until completely smooth. Pour into 9x5x3-inch loaf pan; chill until firm. Cut into slices. *Makes 8 servings.*

## CRANBERRY-ORANGE MOLD

**1¼ cups boiling water**
**1 3-ounce package raspberry-flavored gelatin**
**1 orange, seeded and diced**
**Rind of 1 orange (colored portion only)**
**1 1-pound can whole cranberry sauce**

Put boiling water and gelatin in blender container; cover and run on speed 1 (or low) until gelatin is dissolved. Add remaining ingredients; cover container and run on speed 6 (or high) until orange rind is very fine. Pour into a 1½-quart mold. Chill until set. *Makes 6 servings.*

## FROZEN FRUIT AND NUT SALAD

**1 1-pound can jellied cranberry sauce**
**1 cup creamed cottage cheese**
**¼ cup mayonnaise**
**½ cup pitted dates**
**¼ cup blanched almonds**
**½ cup maraschino cherries, drained**
**1 8-ounce can (1 cup) crushed pineapple, drained**
**1 cup miniature marshmallows**
**1 cup whipping cream, Blender whipped (page 139)**

Put cranberry sauce, cottage cheese and mayonnaise in blender container; cover and run on speed 6 (or high) until smooth. Add dates, almonds and cherries; cover and run on speed 4 (or low) just until fruits and nuts are chopped. Pour into bowl; add pineapple and marshmallows. Fold in whipped cream. Pour into two refrigerator trays and freeze until firm. Slice and serve on lettuce leaves. *Makes 12 servings.*

## Salad Dressings

*Salad dressing made in the blender yields a marvelously smooth product, with all ingredients well blended. A flick of the switch converts a simple French dressing into a restaurant delicacy. Blender dressings can be made more efficiently, too. Recipes that call for all ingredients to be combined and processed at the same time may be prepared and stored in the same jar—if your blender has a removable cutting assembly. Simply use a Mason jar about ½ cup larger than the promised yield of the recipe.*

Choose Your Dressing with Care

*Crucial to salad is the dressing. In a tossed salad, it should "marry" the flavors of the other elements rather than call attention to itself; it should enhance the stronger flavor of molded salads.*

### BLENDER MAYONNAISE

**1 egg**
**2 tablespoons vinegar or lemon juice**
**¾ teaspoon salt**
**½ teaspoon dry mustard**
**¼ teaspoon paprika**
**⅛ teaspoon ground white pepper**
**½ teaspoon salad herbs (optional)**
**1 cup salad oil**

Have all ingredients room temperature. Put egg, 1 tablespoon vinegar, salt, dry mustard, paprika, pepper and salad herbs in blender container; cover and run on speed 2 (or low). While blender is running, slowly pour in ½ cup salad oil. When more power is required, run on speed 7 (or high). If necessary, stop blender during processing and push ingredients toward blades with rubber spatula. Add remaining 1 tablespoon vinegar and slowly pour in remaining salad oil while blender is running on speed 7 (or high). *Makes about 1 cup.*

#### MAYONNAISE VARIATIONS

• Add 2 sprigs parsley, stems removed, after oil is incorporated. Run until parsley is minced.

• Add lemon juice instead of vinegar and a small piece of lemon rind. Nice for fruits and seafood.

• Add ½ clove of garlic.

#### IF MAYONNAISE SHOULD SEPARATE

There are several reasons why mayonnaise may separate or be thin. If all ingredients are not room temperature or the oil is added rapidly, then the emulsion may break and the mayonnaise become unusable. However, you can easily salvage the ingredients.

Pour the broken emulsion into a pitcher or 2-cup measure. Wash and dry blender container. Break one egg into container; cover and run on speed 2 (or low). While blender is running, slowly add the broken emulsion. When blender blades are covered, run on speed 7 (or high), continuing to add remaining ingredients slowly.

## MAYONNAISE CHAUD FROID

**1 envelope (1 tablespoon) unflavored gelatin**
**¼ cup water**
**1 cup Blender Mayonnaise (page 79)**

Soften gelatin in water in small bowl until moistened. Set bowl in boiling water until gelatin is dissolved. Blend into mayonnaise after all oil is incorporated on speed 7 (or high) about 15 seconds. Use to coat eggs, chicken, fish or any Chaud Froid recipe.

## ROCOCO DRESSING

**½ cup Blender Mayonnaise (page 79)**
**3 tablespoons chili sauce**
**¼ green pepper, seeded**
**2 green onions with tops, cut up**
**4 stuffed green olives**

Put all ingredients in blender container; cover and run on speed 3 (or low) about 45 seconds or until vegetables are chopped. Serve on lettuce wedges or with meat and fish salads. *Makes about 1 cup.*

## COOKED DRESSING

**1 cup water**
**2 eggs**
**½ cup vinegar**
**1½ teaspoons dry mustard**
**½ teaspoon salt**
**3 tablespoons cornstarch**
**½ cup sugar**

Have all ingredients room temperature. Put ingredients in blender container in order listed; cover and run on speed 5 (or high) for 1½ minutes. Pour mixture into a 1-quart saucepan; cook over low heat, stirring frequently, until thick (about 20 minutes). *Makes 1½ cups.*

## OLIVE DRESSING

**½ cup Blender Mayonnaise (page 79)**
**½ teaspoon dry mustard**
**1 thin slice onion**
**½ canned pimiento**
**¼ cup pitted ripe olives**

Put all ingredients in blender container; cover and run on speed 4 (or high) just until olives are chopped. Chill. *Makes about ¾ cup.*

## THOUSAND ISLAND DRESSING

**1 cup Blender Mayonnaise (page 79)**
**¼ cup catsup**
**1 slice onion**
**1 stalk celery, cut into 2-inch pieces**
**2 small sweet pickles**
**3 sprigs parsley**
**1 slice green pepper, seeded**
**1 teaspoon canned pimiento**
**1 hard-cooked egg, shelled and quartered**

Put all ingredients except egg in blender container; cover and run on speed 4 (or low) just until vegetables are coarsely chopped. Add egg; cover container and run on speed 4 (or low) just until egg is chopped. *Makes 2 cups.*

## CHOPPED VEGETABLE DRESSING

**¾ cup vinegar**
**1 cup salad oil**
**¾ cup sugar**
**1 tablespoon salt**
**1 medium onion, diced**
**1 4-ounce can pimientos, drained**
**1 green pepper, seeded and cut up**

Put all ingredients in blender container in order listed; cover and run on speed 4 (or high) just until vegetables are chopped. Chill. Shake before using. *Makes about 3½ cups.*

## PARMESAN DRESSING

2 eggs
1½ cups salad oil
½ cup dry white wine
⅓ cup vinegar
⅓ cup grated Parmesan cheese
1½ teaspoons seasoned salt
½ teaspoon pepper
½ teaspoon paprika
½ clove garlic
2 green onions with tops, cut into 1-inch pieces

Put all ingredients except onions in blender container; cover and run on speed 7 (or high) until garlic is liquefied. Add onions; cover and run on speed 4 (or low) until onions are chopped. Chill. *Makes 3 cups.*

## COUNTRY-STYLE DRESSING

½ cup salad oil
2 tablespoons vinegar
½ teaspoon salt
⅛ teaspoon pepper
1 thin slice onion
2 sprigs parsley
2 hard-cooked eggs, shelled and quartered

Put all ingredients except parsley and eggs in blender container; cover and run on speed 7 (or high) until onion is liquefied. Add parsley and eggs; cover and run on speed 4 (or low) just until eggs are chopped. Chill. Serve on vegetable salads. *Makes about 1 cup.*

## CELERY SEED DRESSING

*Perfect for cole slaw.*

¼ cup vinegar
1 cup salad oil
½ cup sugar
1 teaspoon salt
½ teaspoon dry mustard
1 thin slice onion
1½ teaspoons celery seed
1 teaspoon paprika

Put all ingredients in blender container; cover and run on speed 7 (or high) until onion is liquefied. Chill. *Makes 1½ cups.*

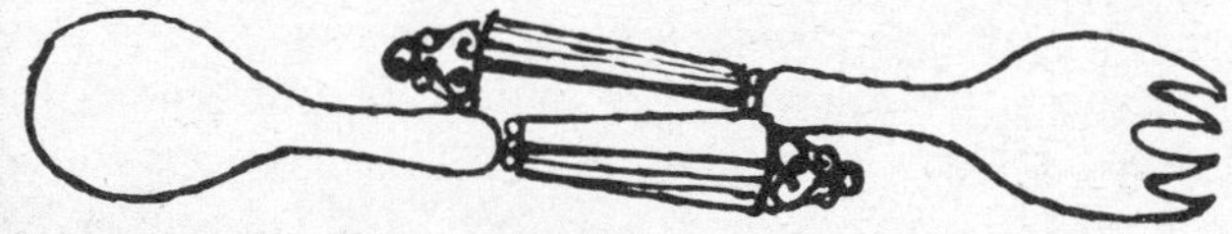

## ITALIAN DRESSING

3 cloves garlic
¾ cup salad oil
⅓ cup white vinegar
¼ canned pimiento

Put all ingredients except pimiento in blender container; cover and run on speed 6 (or high) until garlic is completely liquefied. Stop blender; add pimiento; cover and run on speed 3 (or low) until pimiento is chopped. *Makes 1 cup.*

## FRENCH DRESSING

¼ cup vinegar or lemon juice
¾ cup salad oil
1½ teaspoons salt
¼ teaspoon pepper
¼ teaspoon paprika
¼ teaspoon sugar
¼ small onion

Put all ingredients in blender container; cover and run on speed 5 (or high) about 30 seconds. *Makes 1 cup.*

## HONEY FRENCH DRESSING

¾ cup salad oil
¼ cup lemon juice
½ cup honey
½ teaspoon Worcestershire
¾ teaspoon salt
¼ teaspoon pepper
¼ teaspoon paprika
¼ teaspoon dry mustard
½ teaspoon celery seed
Small piece lemon rind (colored portion only)

Put all ingredients in blender container in order listed; cover and run on speed 6 (or high) about 30 seconds or until smooth. *Makes 1½ cups.*

***"TO GO WITH" DRESSINGS***

*Olive Dressing: With fried fish in place of tartar sauce or on broiled hamburgers*

*Chopped Vegetable Dressing: Pour over chilled cooked frozen broccoli; refrigerate 24 hours; serve as first course or with cold meats and cheeses*

## B.B.'S FRENCH DRESSING

**1½ cups salad oil**
**1½ cups vinegar**
**¾ cup sugar**
**1½ cups catsup**
**2¼ teaspoons salt**
**2¼ teaspoons garlic salt**
**2¼ teaspoons onion salt**
**1 tablespoon celery salt**
**1 teaspoon Worcestershire**

Put all ingredients in blender container; cover and run on speed 5 (or high) until mixed. Store in covered jars in refrigerator. *Makes 5½ cups.*

**Note:** If your blender has only a 4-cup capacity, cut recipe in half.

## GARLIC FRENCH DRESSING

**1½ cups salad oil**
**¾ cup vinegar**
**½ teaspoon sugar**
**1½ teaspoons salt**
**1 teaspoon paprika**
**½ teaspoon dry mustard**
**3 cloves garlic**

Put all ingredients in blender container; cover and run on speed 7 (or high) until garlic is liquefied. *Makes 2½ cups.*

## GREEN GODDESS SALAD DRESSING

**1 clove garlic**
**¼ teaspoon salt**
**¼ teaspoon dry mustard**
**2 tablespoons wine vinegar**
**1 tablespoon anchovy paste**
**½ teaspoon Worcestershire**
**4 large sprigs parsley**
**½ cup Blender Mayonnaise (page 79)**
**2 green onions with tops, cut up**
**¼ cup dairy sour cream**

Put first 9 ingredients in blender container; cover and run on speed 6 (or high) for 30 seconds. If necessary, stop blender during processing and push ingredients toward blades with rubber spatula. Add sour cream; cover and run on speed 1 (or low) for 5 seconds. Chill before serving. Serve over tossed salad greens. *Makes about 1 cup.*

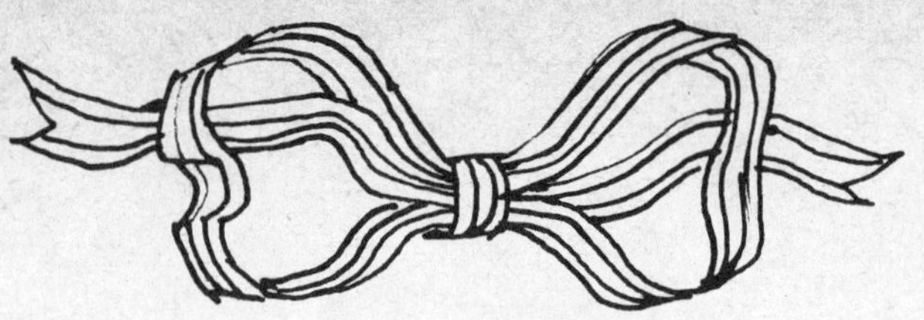

## BAVARIAN DRESSING

**¾ cup salad oil**
**½ cup vinegar**
**⅓ cup catsup**
**½ cup sugar**
**2 tablespoons lemon juice**
**½ teaspoon paprika**
**½ teaspoon celery salt**
**½ teaspoon salt**
**1 clove garlic**
**½ small onion, diced**

Put all ingredients in blender container in order listed; cover and run on speed 7 (or high) until perfectly smooth. Chill. *Makes 2¼ cups.*

## TOMATO HONEY DRESSING

**1 cup salad oil**
**½ cup catsup**
**⅓ cup vinegar**
**⅓ cup honey**
**1 teaspoon salt**
**1 teaspoon paprika**
**½ thin slice onion**
**¼ clove garlic**

Put all ingredients in blender container; cover and run on speed 7 (or high) until onion and garlic are liquefied. Chill. *Makes 2½ cups.*

## FRENCH-STYLE BLUE CHEESE DRESSING

**1 cup salad oil**
**3 tablespoons lemon juice or vinegar**
**1 teaspoon sugar**
**1 teaspoon salt**
**4 ounces blue cheese, crumbled (½ cup)**
**2 teaspoons paprika**
**1 slice onion**

Put all ingredients in blender container; cover and run on speed 4 (or low) until blue cheese and onion are chopped. *Makes about 1½ cups.*

## DILL SOUR CREAM DRESSING

**1½ teaspoons lemon juice**
**½ cup dairy sour cream**
**1 tablespoon mayonnaise**
**⅛ teaspoon dry mustard**
**Dash cayenne**
**Dash salt**
**2 sprigs fresh dill OR ½ teaspoon dill weed**

Put all ingredients in blender container in order listed; cover and run on speed 2 (or low) for 15 seconds. If necessary, stop blender during processing and push ingredients toward blades with rubber spatula. Chill before serving. Serve over sliced tomatoes, with cold canned or poached fish, or in seafood salad. *Makes about ½ cup.*

## GREEN GLORY DRESSING

**1 tablespoon lemon juice**
**1 tablespoon tarragon vinegar**
**1 cup Blender Mayonnaise (page 79)**
**½ clove garlic**
**3 green onions with tops, cut into 1-inch pieces**
**4 sprigs parsley**
**½ teaspoon salt**
**Dash pepper**
**½ cup dairy sour cream**

Put all ingredients except sour cream in blender container; cover and run on speed 4 (or high) until onions and parsley are finely chopped. Add sour cream; cover and run on speed 4 (or high) just until all ingredients are combined. *Makes 2 cups.*

*B.B.'s French Dressing (p. 82)*

## ITALIAN CHEESE DRESSING

**2 cups Blender Mayonnaise (page 79)**
**1 8-ounce can (1 cup) tomato sauce**
**¼ cup grated Parmesan cheese**
**1 ounce Gorgonzola or blue cheese, crumbled (2 tablespoons)**
**2 tablespoons cooking sherry**
**2 cloves garlic**
**1 teaspoon paprika**

Put all ingredients in blender container in order listed; cover and run on speed 4 (or high) for 30 seconds or until smooth. Serve over lettuce wedges or sliced tomatoes. *Makes about 3½ cups.*

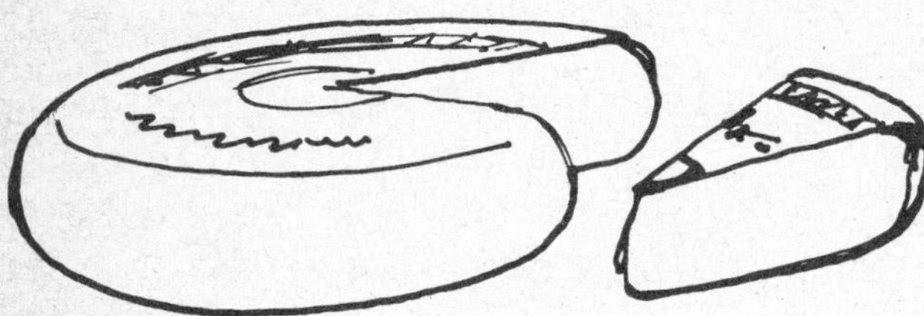

## TWO-CHEESE DRESSING

**¾ cup milk**
**1 8-ounce package cream cheese, cubed**
**1 4-ounce package blue cheese, crumbled (½ cup)**
**½ teaspoon tarragon**
**1 teaspoon salt**
**¼ teaspoon pepper**
**¼ clove garlic**

Put all ingredients in blender container; cover and run on speed 7 (or high) until smooth and garlic is liquefied. Chill. *Makes about 2 cups.*

## SULLIVAN SPECIAL

**1 cup buttermilk**
**2 cups Blender Mayonnaise (page 79)**
**¼ onion**
**1 tablespoon Worcestershire**
**¼ teaspoon garlic powder**
**8 ounces Roquefort or blue cheese, crumbled (1 cup)**

Put first 5 ingredients and half the cheese in blender container; cover and run on speed 6 (or high) until smooth. Stop blender and add remaining cheese in large chunks. Cover and run on speed 5 (or high) about 6 seconds or until coarsely chopped. (If a smooth dressing is preferred, run until smooth.) *Makes 1 quart.*

## BUTTERMILK DRESSING

**½ cup buttermilk**
**¼ cup lemon juice**
**½ cup creamed cottage cheese**
**1 teaspoon salt**
**½ teaspoon paprika**
**½ green pepper, seeded and cut up**

Put all ingredients except green pepper in blender container; cover and run on speed 6 (or high) until smooth. Add green pepper; cover and run on speed 3 (or low) just until pepper is chopped. Serve on vegetable salads. *Makes 1 cup.*

## HERBED SOUR CREAM DRESSING

**1 cup dairy sour cream**
**2 tablespoons red wine vinegar**
**1 teaspoon sugar**
**½ teaspoon salt**
**½ teaspoon celery seed**
**¼ teaspoon thyme**

Put all ingredients in blender container; cover and run on speed 3 (or low) until mixed. Chill. *Makes about 1 cup.*

## SOUR CREAM DRESSING

*A delightful cole slaw dressing.*

**1 cup dairy sour cream**
**¼ cup vinegar**
**3 tablespoons sugar**
**1½ teaspoons salt**
**1 teaspoon celery seed**

Put all ingredients in blender container; cover and run on speed 5 (or high) until smooth. *Makes 1¼ cups.*

### *"TO GO WITH" DRESSINGS*

*Green Goddess Dressing: Any seafood salad*

*Two Cheese Dressing: Chilled cooked vegetables, served separately or "en bouquet"*

*Sullivan Special: Any tossed vegetable combination; a dip for chilled cooked artichoke hearts served as a snack*

*Buttermilk Dressing: Sliced cucumbers and tomatoes with radish garnish*

## DOMINO DRESSING

½ cup Blender Mayonnaise (page 79)
1 cup dairy sour cream
½ cup parsley sprigs, stems removed
2 tablespoons vinegar
1 teaspoon Worcestershire
½ teaspoon salt
2–3 green onions with tops, cut up
1 cup pitted ripe olives, drained

Put all ingredients except olives in blender container; cover and run on speed 5 (or high) until smooth. Add olives; cover and run on speed 4 (or high) a few seconds or until chopped, but not minced. Serve on vegetable or potato salad. *Makes about 2 cups.*

## CHEESE AND LEMON DRESSING

4 ounces blue cheese, crumbled (½ cup)
1-inch square lemon rind (colored portion only)
¼ cup lemon juice
¾ cup salad oil
1 cup dairy sour cream
1 teaspoon salt
½ teaspoon monosodium glutamate

Put cheese, lemon rind and juice in blender container; cover and run on speed 4 (or high) about 30 seconds. Add remaining ingredients; cover and run on speed 3 (or low) for 15 seconds. Chill. Serve on salad greens. *Makes 2 cups.*

**Note:** Be careful. Sour cream thins exceptionally fast in blender processing.

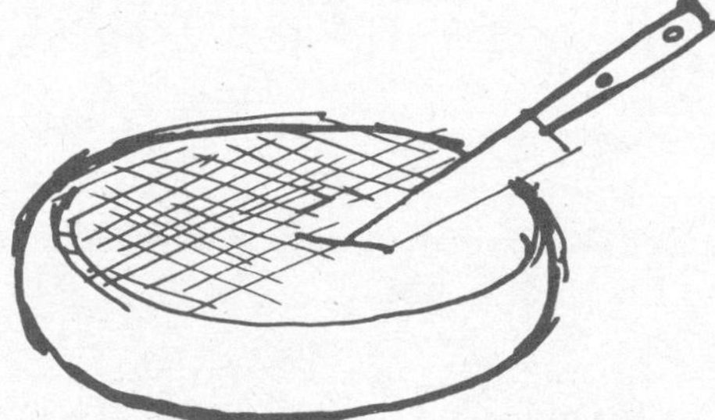

## GINGER CHEESE DRESSING

2 tablespoons milk
1 12-ounce carton creamed cottage cheese
½ cup Blender Mayonnaise (page 79)
¼ teaspoon salt
½ teaspoon ginger
2 tablespoons sugar

Put all ingredients in blender container; cover and run on speed 6 (or high) until smooth. Chill. *Makes about 2¼ cups.*

*Fruity Cream Cheese Dressing (p. 86) on Fruit Salad*

## CHIVE COTTAGE CHEESE DRESSING

**2 tablespoons lemon juice**
**2 tablespoons salad oil**
**½ teaspoon salt**
**2 tablespoons cut chives**
**1 cup creamed cottage cheese**

Put all ingredients in blender container in order listed; cover and run on speed 7 (or high) until smooth. Serve on fruit or vegetable salads. *Makes about 1¼ cups.*

## FRUITY CREAM CHEESE DRESSING

**¼ cup orange juice**
**2 teaspoons lemon juice**
**1 teaspoon sugar**
**¼ teaspoon salt**
**1 3-ounce package cream cheese, cubed**

Put all ingredients in blender container in order listed; cover and run on speed 5 (or high) until smooth. Serve on fruit salads. *Makes ¾ cup.*

## PINEAPPLE SALAD DRESSING

**1 cup Blender Mayonnaise (page 79)**
**1 8-ounce can (1 cup) crushed pineapple, drained**
**3 tablespoons light cream**
**3 tablespoons lemon juice**

Put all ingredients in blender container; cover and run on speed 5 (or high) until thoroughly mixed. Chill. Serve on plain or molded fruit salads. *Makes 2 cups.*

## LEMONADE DRESSING

**1 6-ounce can frozen lemonade concentrate, thawed**
**1 cup honey**
**1 cup salad oil**
**2 teaspoons celery seed**

Put all ingredients in blender container; cover and run on speed 6 (or high) until thoroughly mixed. Chill. Serve on fruit salads. *Makes 3 cups.*

## LIME HONEY DRESSING

**¼ cup sugar**
**1 teaspoon salt**
**1 teaspoon paprika**
**1 teaspoon dry mustard**
**⅓ cup lime juice**
**⅓ cup honey**
**⅔ cup salad oil**

Put all ingredients in blender container; cover and run on speed 6 (or high) for 15 seconds. Serve on citrus or avocado salad. *Makes 1½ cups.*

## GOLDEN SALAD DRESSING

**½ cup orange juice**
**2 tablespoons lemon juice**
**¼ cup mayonnaise**
**1 tablespoon sugar**
**½ cup creamed cottage cheese**
**⅓ cup walnuts**

Put all ingredients except walnuts in blender container in order listed; cover and run on speed 5 (or high) until smooth. Add walnuts; cover and run on speed 4 (or low) until walnuts are chopped. Serve on fruit salad. *Makes about 1½ cups.*

## ORANGE-HONEY FRUIT SALAD DRESSING

**½ cup orange juice**
**½ cup honey**
**1 12-ounce carton (1½ cups) creamed cottage cheese**

Put ingredients in blender container in order listed; cover and run on speed 7 (or high) just until smooth (with longer blending, dressing becomes thinner). Chill. Serve on fruit salads. *Makes 2½ cups.*

## NIPPY NECTAR DRESSING

**Rind from ¼ lemon (colored portion only)**
**2 tablespoons lemon juice**
**2 tablespoons honey**
**½ cup salad oil**
**¼ teaspoon salt**
**Dash cayenne**
**1 3-ounce package cream cheese, cubed**

Put all ingredients in blender container; cover and run on speed 5 (or high) until smooth. Chill. Serve over fruit salad. *Makes 1 cup.*

# Now for the Main Course

*Blender cooking can simplify the preparation of many familiar dishes and, at the same time, improve the finished product. In addition, it can put on your table dishes restricted, until now, to expensive restaurants — not after long, wearisome preparation, but in relaxed minutes. The blender does the time-consuming part of the work in seconds.*

Everyday Dishes Improve

*Such daily jobs as crumbing crackers and mixing seasonings for a meat loaf or crumbing bread for cutlets can be accomplished with ease and speed by the blender. You can change the flavor of many dishes by varying the crumbs. Try crumbing unsweetened ready-to-eat cereals, specialty crackers, pretzels, corn chips and potato chips. Use up dry bread, in the form of crumbs, and you can stretch a little meat to serve many or turn a roast into a masterpiece. For examples, look to Cheesy Meat Cups (page 90) or Crown Lamb Roast with Sherry Apple Dressing (page 99).*

Difficult Dishes Become Easy

*In German homes the potato pancake is often on the table. Sometimes it is the main dish, served with applesauce and bacon or sausage; on other occasions, it accompanies a richly gravied pot roast. American homemakers who know and like potato pancakes have avoided them, in general, because grating the potatoes is such a chore. With the blender, cubed potatoes can be grated simultaneously with the mixing of the batter — in a flick of the switch. Pour batter onto the griddle straight from the blender container. Nothing could be simpler. (See page 111.)*

*Gefüllte fish is another time-honored dish, the perfect base for a cold supper or, in small balls, an unusual snack. To make it the traditional way, one must be inspired by love; to make it the blender way (page 107) one need only be inspired by the desire for a delicately flavored, wholesome food.*

*These and other foreign specialties, like Beef Fondue (page 88) and Enchiladas (page 89) can easily fit into your family meal pattern, when the blender takes over the chopping and mixing chores.*

## Meat Takes a Star Role

### BEEF FONDUE

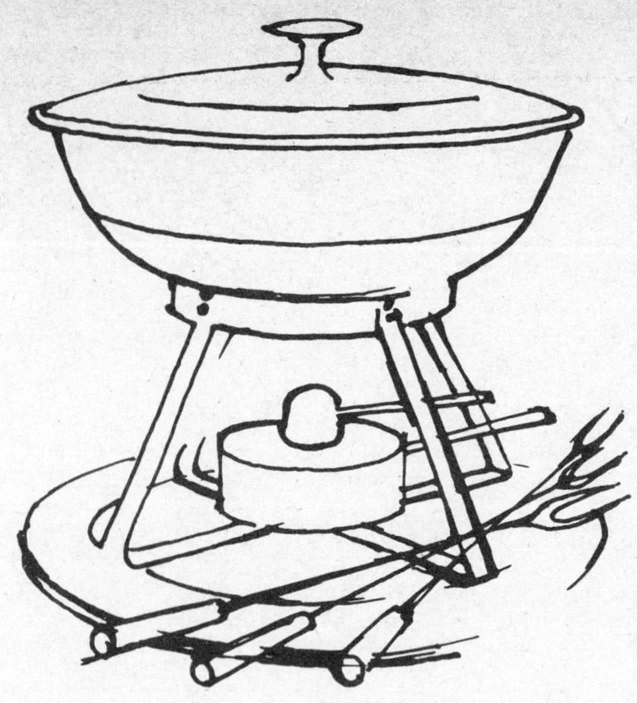

Cut 1-inch thick sirloin steak into bite-size cubes. Trim off all fat and connective tissue. Refrigerate until serving time.

Heat ½ pound (1 cup) butter or margarine and 2 cups salad oil together in a saucepan over medium heat. When it bubbles and begins to brown, pour into a 2-quart fondue dish or chafing dish and set over heating unit. (Hot fat should be not more than 2 inches deep.)

Each person spears a piece of meat on a fondue fork or disposable bamboo stick and cooks it in the hot oil and butter mixture for a few minutes, or until of the desired doneness, then dips into a sauce (see recipes below and right).

**Note:** Fondue may be served as an appetizer, too.

### BEEF FONDUE SAUCES

#### MUSTARD SAUCE

**1 cup Blender Mayonnaise (page 79)**
**2 tablespoons vinegar**
**1 tablespoon dry mustard**

Put all ingredients in blender container in order listed. Cover and run on speed 2 (or low) until thoroughly mixed. Chill. *Makes about 1 cup.*

#### CURRY SAUCE

**1 10½-ounce can beef gravy**
**½ clove garlic**
**1½ teaspoons lemon juice**
**2 teaspoons curry powder**

Put all ingredients in blender container; cover and run on speed 7 (or high) until garlic is liquefied. *Makes 1½ cups.*

#### SOUR CREAM-HORSERADISH SAUCE

**1 cup dairy sour cream**
**2 teaspoons prepared horseradish**
**Thin slice onion**
**⅛ teaspoon salt**
**¼ teaspoon paprika**

Put all ingredients in blender container; cover and run on speed 2 (or low) until well mixed. Chill. *Makes 1 cup.*

#### CUCUMBER CHEESE SAUCE

**2 tablespoons milk**
**2 3-ounce packages cream cheese, cubed**
**½ small cucumber, pared, seeded and cubed**
**½ thin slice onion**
**½ teaspoon salt**
**¼ teaspoon ground cumin**

Put all ingredients in blender container; cover and run on speed 6 (or high) until smooth. *Makes about 1½ cups.*

#### GARLIC BUTTER

**½ cup very soft butter or margarine**
**2 cloves garlic**
**½ teaspoon peppercorns**
**½ teaspoon salt**

Put all ingredients in blender container; cover and run on speed 4 (or high) until garlic is liquefied. If necessary, stop blender during processing and push ingredients toward blades with rubber spatula. *Makes ½ cup.*

#### ANCHOVY SAUCE

**1 cup Blender Mayonnaise (page 79)**
**4 anchovy fillets**
**1 teaspoon dill weed**

Put all ingredients in blender container; cover and run on speed 3 (or low) just until anchovies are chopped. Chill. *Makes 1 cup.*

## BEEF ENCHILADAS

**½ pound sharp American cheese, cubed (about 2 cups)**
**2 large onions, cut up**
**2 cloves garlic**
**2 8-ounce cans (2 cups) tomato sauce**
**2 tablespoons olive or salad oil**
**2 teaspoons sugar**
**1 teaspoon salt**
**1 fresh or canned green hot pepper**
**2 1-pound cans (4 cups) tomatoes**
**1 pound ground beef**
**1 clove garlic**
**2½ bunches (about 24) green onions with tops, cut up**
**15 pitted ripe olives**
**2¼ teaspoons chili powder**
**¾ teaspoon salt**
**18 frozen or canned tortillas**

Put ¼ of the cheese in blender container; cover and run on speed 4 (or high) until grated. Remove cover and add a few pieces of cheese while blender is running. When half the cheese is grated, empty into a measuring cup and repeat process until you have 1¾ cups grated cheese. Set aside.

Preheat oven to 350°. Put onions, 2 cloves garlic, tomato sauce, olive oil, sugar and 1 teaspoon salt in blender container; cover and run on speed 3 (or low) about 15 seconds or until onions are chopped. Add half the hot pepper; cover and run on speed 3 (or low) a few seconds. Taste and add more hot pepper, if desired. Pour into a large frypan and add tomatoes; simmer, uncovered, 35–40 minutes.

Meanwhile, brown beef in another frypan, breaking it into pieces as it cooks. Put 1 clove garlic, half the green onions and half the ripe olives in blender container; cover and run on speed 4 (or low) until chopped. Empty into frypan with meat. Repeat process with remaining onions and olives. If necessary, stop blender during processing and push ingredients toward blades with rubber spatula. Add chili powder and ¾ teaspoon salt. Cook until onion is tender; add grated cheese.

Heat tortillas as directed on package or can. Place about 3 tablespoons filling on each tortilla; roll up and place, seam side down, on a heat-proof platter or in a 13x9x2-inch baking dish. Cover with tomato sauce and bake 25–30 minutes. *Makes 6–8 servings.*

**Note:** If tortillas are not available, substitute large, thin pancakes.

## HUNGARIAN STEAK

2 pounds round steak, ½-inch thick
1 clove garlic, cut in half
1 teaspoon salt
⅛ teaspoon pepper
2 tablespoons shortening
1 large onion, cut up
½ pound mushrooms
1 8-ounce can tomato sauce
1 cup water
1 green pepper, seeded and cut up

Cut meat into serving-size portions and rub with cut garlic. Sprinkle with salt and pepper. Brown in shortening in large frypan. Meanwhile, put onion, mushrooms, tomato sauce and ¾ cup water in blender container; cover and run on speed 3 (or low) until vegetables are chopped. Pour over browned meat; cover and cook 1½ hours or until meat is tender. Put remaining ¼ cup water and green pepper in blender container; cover and run on speed 3 (or low) until pepper is chopped. Add to meat and cook about 10 minutes longer. *Makes 4–6 servings.*

## TWO-MEAT LOAF

20 crisp soda crackers
1 pound ground beef
½ pound bulk pork sausage
1 cup milk
1 egg
1 small onion, quartered
5 sprigs parsley
1 teaspoon salt
⅛ teaspoon pepper
1 4-inch stalk celery, halved
¼ teaspoon sage

Preheat oven to 350°. Grease a 9x5x3-inch loaf pan. Break half the crackers into blender container; cover and run on speed 4 (or low) until finely crumbed. Empty into mixing bowl. Repeat process until you have 1 cup crumbs. Add ground meats to crumbs; mix. Put remaining ingredients in blender container; cover and run on speed 4 (or low) just until vegetables are chopped. Pour over meat mixture and mix thoroughly. Pack lightly into prepared pan; bake 1½ hours or until done. *Makes 8 servings.*

## CHEESY MEAT CUPS

16–18 rich cheese crackers
½ medium onion, cut up
¼ green pepper, seeded
¼ cup chili sauce
2–3 drops Tabasco
½ cup milk
2 eggs
¾ teaspoon salt
Dash pepper
1½ pounds ground beef

Preheat oven to 350°. Grease 8–10 custard or muffin cups. Break half the crackers into blender container; cover and run on speed 4 (or high) until crumbed. Empty into a measuring cup. Repeat process until you have ½ cup crumbs. Put remaining ingredients except ground beef in blender container; cover and run on speed 4 (or high) until vegetables are chopped. Pour into a mixing bowl with crumbs and ground beef; mix well. Spoon into prepared cups and bake 45 minutes. *Makes 8–10 servings.*

**Note:** May be baked in a 9x5x3-inch loaf pan for 1¼ hours.

## CORNED BEEF AND PANNED CABBAGE

1 small head cabbage, cut up
2 tablespoons butter or margarine
¼ cup water
½ teaspoon salt
⅛ teaspoon pepper
6–8 slices cooked corned beef OR one 12-ounce can corned beef, sliced

Fill blender container to top cup marking with cabbage; add enough water to cover cabbage. Cover container and run on speed 7 (or high) until cabbage is chopped. Drain in a colander or sieve. Repeat process until you have 4 cups chopped cabbage. Melt butter in a frypan. Add well-drained cabbage, water, salt and pepper. Cover and cook over low heat 5–10 minutes. Arrange slices of corned beef over top of cabbage. Cover and continue cooking until meat is hot and cabbage is cooked, 5–10 minutes. *Makes 3–4 servings.*

*Corned Beef and P*[illegible]

## LIVER AND BACON BURGERS

**1 pound beef liver, cut into 2-inch pieces**
**5 slices dry bread**
**1 pound bacon**
**2 large onions, cut up**
**1 egg**
**¼ cup chili sauce**
**1½ teaspoons seasoned salt**
**¼ teaspoon pepper**

Cook liver in boiling water for 3 minutes; drain and cool. Break 1 slice bread into blender container; cover and run on speed 4 (or high) until crumbed. Empty into bowl. Repeat process with remaining bread until you have 1 cup crumbs.

Reserve 5–6 slices bacon for wrapping patties; cut remainder into 1-inch pieces. Put half the onion and half the cut-up bacon in blender container; cover and run on speed 4 (or high) until chopped. If necessary, stop blender during processing and push ingredients toward blades with rubber spatula. Empty into a large frypan. Repeat process with remaining onion and cut-up bacon. Cook until onion is lightly browned. Turn out into large bowl.

Put egg, chili sauce, salt and pepper in blender container; cover and run on speed 3 (or low) until smooth. Pour out half of mixture and set aside. Add half the liver to mixture remaining in blender container; cover and run on speed 3 (or low) until smooth. Add to onion and bacon. Repeat with remaining liver and reserved chili sauce. Mix well with all but ½ cup bread crumbs and form into 5 or 6 patties. Coat patties with remaining ½ cup of bread crumbs.

Cook remaining bacon partially, being careful not to cook until crisp. Wrap around patties and fasten with toothpicks. Broil 3 inches from heat 3–5 minutes on each side. *Makes 5–6 servings.*

### CHOP RAW MEAT

Put ¼ slice white bread, torn into small pieces, in blender container; then add ½ cup cubed raw meat (with all gristle and heavy connective tissue removed). Cover container and run on speed 4 (or high) until meat is chopped. If necessary, start and stop blender to toss meat toward blades. Empty onto waxed paper; shape into 1 meat patty. Note: A small piece onion may be added with the meat.

## MEAT CROQUETTES

**4–5 slices dry bread**
**1 cup milk or meat stock**
**¼ cup soft butter or margarine**
**¼ cup flour**
**½ teaspoon salt**
**¼ teaspoon pepper**
**2 sprigs parsley**
**2½ cups cooked meat (chicken, ham, beef, etc.) cut into ¼-inch pieces**
**1 egg, slightly beaten**
**2 tablespoons water**

Break 1 slice bread into 6 pieces and drop into blender container; cover and run on speed 4 (or high) until very finely crumbed. Empty into a measuring cup. Repeat until you have 1 cup crumbs; set aside.

Combine milk, butter, flour, salt, pepper and parsley in blender container; cover and run on speed 6 (or high) until smooth. Empty into a saucepan and cook, stirring constantly, over low heat until very thick; stir in meat. Chill mixture 1 hour. When cool, shape meat mixture into 8 croquettes or patties and return to refrigerator for several hours or overnight.

About a half hour before they are ready to fry, dip croquettes in egg combined with water, then in the bread crumbs. Allow to dry. Fry in deep fat heated to 375° until browned. Do not touch croquettes while frying. Drain on absorbent paper. Serve plain or with a white sauce, cheese or tomato sauce. *Makes 8 croquettes, about 4 servings.*

## SPICY POT ROAST

**3 tablespoons shortening**
**3 pounds beef chuck roast**
**2 teaspoons salt**
**¼ teaspoon pepper**
**1 cup water**
**1 clove garlic**
**¼ cup chili sauce**
**¾ teaspoon Worcestershire**
**¼ small onion**

Preheat oven to 325°. Melt shortening in a Dutch oven and brown meat on both sides. Season with salt and pepper. Put remaining ingredients in blender container; cover and start on speed 1 (or low), then run on speed 4 (or high) until onion is chopped. Pour sauce over meat; cover and bake about 3 hours, basting with sauce occasionally. *Makes 5–6 servings.*

## ROAST VEAL IN CRUST

**1 4- to 6-pound rolled veal shoulder roast**
**1 clove garlic, cut**
**1½ cups chicken broth OR 2 chicken bouillon cubes dissolved in 1½ cups hot water**
**8 slices dry bread or toast**
**½ medium onion, cut up**
**10–12 sprigs parsley**
**1 clove garlic**
**1 cup grated Parmesan cheese**
**1 teaspoon salt**
**¼ teaspoon pepper**
**Dash basil**
**¼ cup butter or margarine, melted**

Preheat oven to 325°. Place meat in roasting pan; rub surface with cut garlic. Pour chicken broth around meat and roast until meat thermometer registers 180° (about 40 minutes per pound). Baste occasionally with broth.

Meanwhile, break 2 slices bread into blender container; add a few pieces of onion and parsley. Cover and run on speed 4 (or low) until bread is crumbed and onion and parsley are chopped. Empty into a mixing bowl. Repeat with remaining bread and vegetables, adding the garlic to last processing. Mix in Parmesan cheese and seasonings.

Remove roast from oven; cut and remove string. Brush roast generously with pan drippings; roll in crumb mixture. Mix remaining crumbs with melted butter and pat onto roast to cover completely. Pour off drippings and set aside for gravy. Raise oven temperature to 350°; return veal to oven and roast 20 minutes longer or until crust is golden. *Makes 12 servings.*

***AN ELEGANT DINNER***

*Roast Veal in Crust*
*Asparagus with Blender Hollandaise (p. 114)*
*Orange and onion slices on greens*
*with Lime-Honey Dressing (p. 86)*
*Poppy Seed Rolls (p. 132)*
*No-bake Fruit Cake (p. 156) with whipped cream*

## VEAL SCALOPPINE DE LUXE

**½ cup flour**
**½ teaspoon salt**
**⅛ teaspoon pepper**
**1 pound veal cutlet, cut into 1-inch pieces**
**¼ cup olive oil**
**¼ cup butter or margarine**
**2 4-ounce cans mushrooms, drained**
**1 medium onion, thinly sliced**
**1¾ cups cooked tomatoes**
**½ clove garlic**
**1 teaspoon salt**
**⅛ teaspoon pepper**
**2 sprigs parsley**
**¼ teaspoon oregano**
**¼ cup capers**

Put flour, ½ teaspoon salt and ⅛ teaspoon pepper in a paper bag; coat meat by shaking 3 or 4 pieces at a time in bag with flour mixture. Heat olive oil in a large frypan; add veal and slowly brown on both sides. While veal is browning, heat butter in another frypan; add mushrooms and onion. Cook until mushrooms are lightly browned and onion is transparent. Put remaining ingredients except capers in blender container; cover and run on speed 6 (or high) until smooth. Add mushrooms and onions, tomato mixture and capers to veal. Cover frypan and simmer about 25 minutes, or until veal is tender, stirring occasionally. *Makes 4 servings.*

***GOURMET DINNER***

*Marinated Leg of Lamb (p. 98)*
*Rice*
*Green beans with butter*
*Avocado slices and grapefruit sections*
*with Honey French Dressing (p. 81)*
*Chocolate Pots de Crème (p. 148)*

## HAM-BEEF LOAF WITH MUSTARD SAUCE

**6–7 slices dry bread or toast**
**1 pound ground beef**
**1 10½-ounce can condensed tomato soup, undiluted**
**⅓ cup milk**
**2 eggs**
**1 medium onion, quartered**
**1 pound cooked ham, cubed**
**1 tablespoon sugar**
**2 tablespoons prepared mustard**
**1 tablespoon vinegar**
**1 tablespoon butter or margarine**

Preheat oven to 350°. Break 2 slices bread into blender container; cover and run on speed 3 (or low) until crumbed. Empty into bowl with ground beef. Repeat process until all bread is crumbed. Put ½ can tomato soup, milk, 1 egg and onion in blender container; cover and run on speed 3 (or low) until onion is chopped. Empty into bowl with ground beef.

Add ¼ of the ham; cover and run on speed 3 (or low) until ham is chopped. Remove cover and add remaining ham slowly while blender is running. If necessary, stop blender during processing and push ham toward blades with rubber spatula; cover when restarting blender. When all ham is chopped, add to beef and mix well. Pack lightly into a 9x5x3-inch loaf pan. Bake 1¼ hours.

When loaf is almost done, put remainder of tomato soup, 1 egg, sugar, mustard, vinegar and butter in blender container; cover and run on speed 2 (or low) a few seconds. Pour into a saucepan and cook, stirring constantly, until mixture thickens. Pour off excess fat from meat loaf and let stand 5 minutes before serving with hot sauce. *Makes 8–10 servings.*

## HAM LOAF IN CHEESE CRUST

**50–55 rich cheese crackers**
**¼ cup butter or margarine, melted**
**⅔ cup evaporated milk**
**1 medium onion, quartered**
**½ medium green pepper, seeded and cut up**
**1 tablespoon prepared mustard**
**1 tablespoon prepared horseradish**
**¼ teaspoon salt**
**2 eggs**
**1 pound cooked or canned ham, cubed (about 4 cups)**

Preheat oven to 350°. Put 10 crackers in blender container; cover and run on speed 3 (or low) until crumbed. Empty into a measuring cup; repeat process until you have 1½ cups crumbs. Mix crumbs with melted butter; set aside 2 tablespoons for top of loaf. Press remaining crumbs onto bottom and sides of a 9-inch pie pan. Bake 10 minutes.

Meanwhile, put half each of the milk, onion, green pepper, mustard, horseradish and salt in blender container; cover and run on speed 3 (or low) until vegetables are chopped. Add 1 egg and half the ham; cover and run on speed 6 (or high) until ham is chopped. If necessary, stop blender during processing and push ingredients toward blades with rubber spatula. Pour into a bowl. Repeat entire process and mix thoroughly. Pour into baked crust; top with reserved crumbs. Return to oven and bake 45–50 minutes or until firm in center. Let stand 5 minutes before serving. Cut into wedges to serve. *Makes 6 servings.*

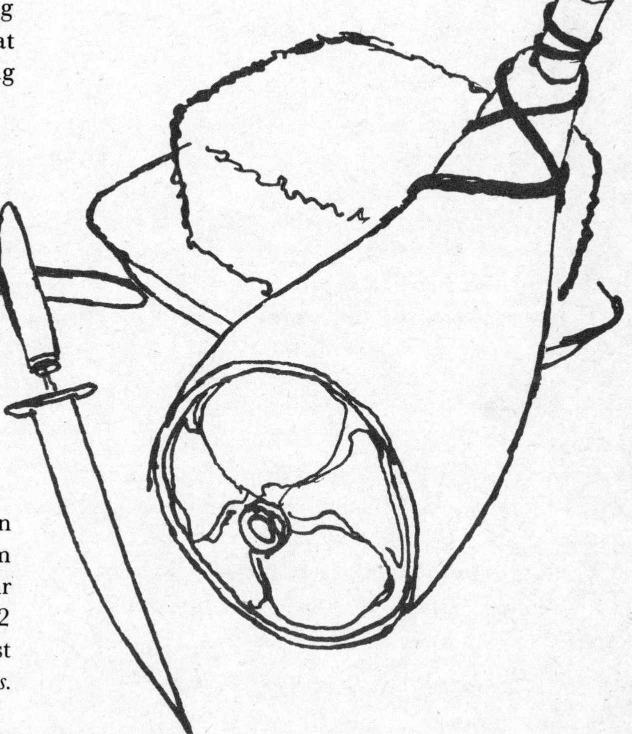

## BAKED HONEY-ORANGE HAM SLICE

**1 ham slice, 1½-2 inches thick**
**½ cup Honey-Orange Ham Glaze (page 118)**

Preheat oven to 325°. Cut fat edge of ham slice in several places with scissors or knife to keep it from curling. Put ham slice in a shallow baking dish; pour on Honey-Orange Ham Glaze. Cover; bake 1½–2 hours or until ham is fork-tender. Uncover during last 15 minutes of baking to brown. *Makes 3–4 servings.*

*m-Beef Loaf with Mustard Sauce*

## PORK CHOPS WITH ORANGE DRESSING

**4 pork chops, cut 1-inch thick**
**2 tablespoons flour**
**1 teaspoon salt**
**½ teaspoon paprika**
**⅛ teaspoon pepper**
**1 tablespoon shortening**
**6 slices fresh white bread, with crusts removed**
**Rind of 1 orange (colored portion only*)**
**1 large stalk celery, cut into 1-inch pieces**
**1 small onion, cut up**
**1 tablespoon sugar**
**1 teaspoon salt**
**¼ teaspoon thyme**
**⅛ teaspoon pepper**
**½ cup orange juice**

Preheat oven to 350°. Lightly grease a 2-quart casserole with a tight-fitting cover. Wipe pork chops with a clean, damp cloth; coat both sides with a mixture of the flour, salt, paprika and pepper. Heat shortening in large, heavy frypan over medium heat and brown chops on both sides.

While chops are browning, prepare dressing. Break 1 slice bread into 6 pieces and drop into blender container with orange rind; cover and run on speed 4 (or low) until bread is crumbed and orange rind is grated. Empty into a bowl. Repeat process with remaining bread (without rind). Put celery in blender container; cover and run on speed 4 (or low) until chopped. Add with sugar and spices to bread crumbs; mix lightly.

Arrange browned chops in the prepared casserole. Heap ¼ of the dressing onto each chop. Pour the orange juice into skillet and stir to dissolve any brown residue; pour liquid around chops. Cover and bake 45 minutes. Remove cover and bake 15 minutes longer. *Makes 4 servings.*

*Use a vegetable parer to remove colored portion of rind.

## STUFFED PORK TENDERLOIN

**2 pork tenderloins, split lengthwise and flattened**
**Lemon juice**
**8 slices bread**
**2–3 tart apples, pared, cored and quartered**
**¾ cup salted peanuts**
**2 tablespoons dark corn syrup**
**1 teaspoon dry mustard**
**¼ teaspoon salt**

Preheat oven to 325°. Rub meat with lemon juice. Tear 1 slice bread into blender container; cover and run on speed 4 (or low) until crumbed. Empty into mixing bowl. Repeat process with remaining bread. Put 4 apple quarters in blender container; cover and run on speed 3 (or low) until finely chopped. Empty into a measuring cup. Repeat until you have 1 cup and add to crumbs. Put half the peanuts in blender container; cover and run on speed 3 (or low) until chopped. Empty into a measuring cup. Repeat process until you have ½ cup chopped nuts. If necessary, stop blender during processing and push apples or peanuts toward blades with rubber spatula. Combine peanuts, corn syrup and seasonings with bread crumbs and apples; mound this stuffing on one piece of pork. Cover with remaining piece and tie securely. Place on rack in shallow baking pan. Roast 1½ hours or until done. *Makes 8 servings.*

## SWEET-SOUR PORK OR BEEF

**10 gingersnaps**
**2 medium onions, quartered**
**2 tablespoons shortening**
**⅓ cup vinegar**
**2 cups water**
**1 tablespoon sugar**
**1½ teaspoons salt**
**½ cup drained pineapple tidbits**
**⅓ cup raisins**
**2 cups cubed cooked pork or beef**

Break 3 or 4 gingersnaps into blender container; cover and run on speed 3 (or low) until crumbed. Repeat process until all gingersnaps are crumbed; set aside. Put 1 onion in blender container; cover and run on speed 4 (or high) until chopped. Empty into a large frypan. Repeat process with remaining onion. Sauté onion in shortening until lightly browned. Add gingersnap crumbs. Add vinegar, water, sugar and salt to mixture in frypan and cook, stirring occasionally, until thick and smooth. Add remaining ingredients and simmer 15 minutes. *Makes 4–6 servings.*

*SUNDAY DINNER*

*Applesauce-stuffed Spareribs*
*Baked sweet potatoes*
*Chilled cooked broccoli with sliced tomatoes*
*French Dressing (p. 81)*
*Pecan Pie (p. 180) with vanilla ice cream*

## APPLESAUCE-STUFFED SPARERIBS

**8 slices fresh bread**
**¼ cup water**
**1 tablespoon lemon juice**
**3 medium cooking apples, pared, cored and cubed**
**1 small onion, quartered**
**1 teaspoon caraway seed**
**¼ cup butter or margarine, melted**
**2 sections (each about 1 pound) spareribs**
**Salt and pepper**

Preheat oven to 350°. Tear 1 slice bread into 6 pieces and drop into blender container; cover and run on speed 4 (or low) just until coarsely crumbed. Empty into a large measuring cup. Repeat process until you have 4 cups crumbs. Put water and lemon juice in blender container; add 1 cubed apple. Cover and run on speed 2 (or low) until apple is puréed. While blender is running, gradually add remaining apples. Add onion and caraway seed and run on speed 6 (or high) just until onion is chopped. Toss together melted butter, bread crumbs and apple mixture.

Sprinkle both sides of sparerib sections with salt and pepper. Place 1 section on rack in shallow roasting pan; spread stuffing over it. Cover with second section. Fasten sections together with skewers. Roast for 1½ hours or until meat is tender when pierced with a fork. Remove skewers before serving. *Makes 4 servings.*

*QUICK DINNER*

*Thick chopped beef patties, broiled*
*Frozen French-fried potatoes heated in oven*
*Slices of tomato and avocado on ¾-inch slices of iceberg lettuce*
*Thousand Island Dressing (p. 80)*
*Fruit Chiffon (p. 143)*

## ZESTY BARBECUED SPARERIBS

**2 pounds spareribs**
**1 recipe Zesty Barbecue Sauce (page 115)**

Preheat oven to 325°. Put spareribs in a shallow pan; cover with aluminum foil and roast 30 minutes. Pour off fat; cover and roast 30 minutes longer. Meanwhile, prepare Zesty Barbecue Sauce. Pour off excess fat from pan; cover ribs with sauce. Increase oven temperature to 375°; bake ribs, uncovered, about 1 hour longer or until tender and browned. Baste frequently with sauce. *Makes 3 servings.*

## LUAU RIBS

**4 pounds spareribs**
**1 1-pound can sliced peaches, drained**
**½ cup firmly packed brown sugar**
**⅓ cup catsup**
**⅓ cup vinegar**
**2 tablespoons soy sauce**
**2 cloves garlic**
**2 teaspoons ginger**
**1 teaspoon salt**
**Dash pepper**

Preheat oven to 450°. Place spareribs, meat side up, in a shallow baking pan. Bake for 45 minutes; pour off fat. Put remaining ingredients in blender container; cover and run on speed 5 (or high) until smooth. Spoon sauce over ribs. Lower oven temperature to 350° and bake 1½ hours or until done, basting ribs with sauce every 15 minutes. Cut into serving-size pieces. *Makes 4 servings.*

# Carving Cues

### CHICKEN OR TURKEY

Place roast bird with legs to the right. Grasp a leg and gently pull away while cutting through meat and joint between thigh and body. Cut thigh from drumstick at the joint. Slice meat from drumstick and thigh parallel to bone.

With fork astride breastbone, cut wing from body. To slice breast, start just above where wing was removed; cut thin slices parallel to the breastbone. Turn bird and repeat procedure.

### STANDING RIB ROAST

Ask butcher to cut backbone from ribs when you buy the roast, to make carving easier.

Put roast on platter with larger cut surface down and rib side to the left. Insert carving fork between two top ribs. Starting at right outside edge, slice across face of roast toward rib side, making slices about ¼ inch thick. To release each slice, cut along rib bone with end of knife.

### LOIN OF PORK

To make carving easier, ask the butcher to saw across the base of the ribs, close and parallel to backbone, to loosen backbone. Place the roasted loin with rib side up on cutting board. With fork astride the rib bones, cut along backbone, close and parallel to it; remove backbone. Set roast on the surface from which backbone has been removed. Steadying roast with a carving fork, carve downward between the ribs. For thin slices, cut near the rib bone, leaving the meat between.

### LEG OF LAMB

Place leg of lamb with shank to your right and thinner, less meaty side facing you. Insert carving fork in large end and cut 2 or 3 thin slices from side facing you. Turn leg so it rests on cut surface. Use carving fork to steady roast. Close to shank end, make a cut straight down to leg bone. Continue to cut parallel slices about ¼ inch thick. Run knife along leg bone, to release slices. For additional slices, turn and slice thick side parallel to big bone.

### CORNED BEEF BRISKET

Place cooked meat on cutting board with fat side up. Look at the lean side of the brisket to determine the direction of the grain of the meat. Steady the meat with a carving fork. Cut thin slices at a slight angle across the grain of the meat. Turn the piece as the direction of the fibers change, always cutting across the grain.

### POT ROAST OF BEEF

*Bladebone Shoulder Roast of Beef.* Use a carving fork to steady the roast. Cut around bladebone and small piece of backbone and remove. Always cut the meat across the grain. If necessary, loosen some of the muscles from the roast and turn so that they may be sliced across the grain. Using a carving fork to steady the piece of meat being carved, cut ¾ to 1 inch thick slices. To carve the muscles with the grain running parallel to the carving board, steady roast with a carving fork and slice across the muscles from one side of the roast to the other.

## MARINATED LEG OF LAMB

**5–6 pound leg of lamb**
**1 cup dry red wine**
**½ cup orange juice**
**¼ cup chili sauce**
**¼ cup water**
**1 teaspoon chili powder**
**2 tablespoons olive oil**
**1 medium onion, cubed**
**2 cloves garlic**
**¾ teaspoon oregano**
**1 teaspoon cumin seed**
**1 tablespoon brown sugar**
**½ teaspoon salt**
**¼ teaspoon pepper**

Place meat in a deep glass or enamel pan. Put all remaining ingredients in blender container; cover and run on speed 4 (or high) until onion is finely chopped. Pour over meat; refrigerate at least 24 hours, turning occasionally. Lift meat from marinade and let drain; place on rack in baking pan. Roast in oven preheated to 450° for 15 minutes; reduce temperature to 350°. Pour marinade over meat and roast 2½ hours or until meat is tender, basting frequently. Add a few tablespoons boiling water to pan if juices tend to cook down quickly. *Makes 8–10 servings.*

## CROWN LAMB ROAST WITH SHERRY APPLE STUFFING

**10–16 rib crown lamb roast**
**Salt and pepper**
**1 loaf dry, sliced bread**
**1 medium onion, cut up**
**1 large stalk celery with leaves, cut up**
**½ cup butter or margarine, melted**
**4–5 medium apples, pared, quartered and cored**
**1 cup grated coconut**
**½ cup cooking sherry**
**2 eggs**

Preheat oven to 325°. Wrap rib ends of roast with foil to prevent charring; season meat with salt and pepper. Place roast, bone ends up, on rack in roasting pan. Break 2 slices bread into blender container with onion; cover and run on speed 3 (or low) until bread is crumbed and onion chopped. Stop and start blender to toss ingredients toward blades. Empty into frypan. Put celery in blender container; cover and run on speed 3 (or low) until chopped. Add to mixture in frypan and sauté in melted butter until vegetables are tender. Break 2 slices of the remaining bread into blender container; cover and run on speed 3 (or low) until crumbed. Empty into a large measuring cup; repeat until you have 4 cups bread crumbs. Empty into a large mixing bowl; set aside.

Put 4 apple quarters in blender container; cover and run on speed 3 (or low) until chopped. Empty into a large measuring cup; repeat until you have 2 cups. Add to crumbs in mixing bowl. Then add coconut, sherry, eggs and vegetables from frypan; mix well. Fill lamb roast with stuffing and roast until meat thermometer registers 180°, or 30–35 minutes per pound. *Makes 6–8 servings.*

## Poultry in Fancy Dress

### STUFFED CORNISH GAME HENS

1 loaf (approximately) day-old bread
1 medium onion, cut into 6 pieces
2 stalks celery, cut into 2-inch pieces
6 sprigs parsley
1½ teaspoons poultry seasoning
¼ teaspoon pepper
½ teaspoon salt
1 3-ounce can mushrooms, drained
½ cup butter or margarine, melted
4 Rock Cornish game hens (about 1 pound each)
2 teaspoons salt
¼ teaspoon monosodium glutamate
¼ cup butter or margarine, melted

To make stuffing, break 1 slice bread into 6 pieces and drop into blender container; cover and run on speed 4 (or low) just until coarsely crumbed, about 3 seconds. Empty into a 1-quart measure. Repeat process until you have 2 quarts coarse crumbs. Empty crumbs into a large bowl.

Put onion in blender container; cover and run on speed 4 (or low) until coarsely chopped. Add to crumbs. Put celery in blender container; cover and run on speed 4 (or low) until chopped. Add to crumbs. Put parsley in blender container; cover and run on speed 3 (or low) until finely chopped. Add to bread crumbs along with poultry seasoning, pepper, ½ teaspoon salt and mushrooms; mix well. Add ½ cup melted butter and mix until ingredients are moistened. Set aside.

Rinse the game hens and pat dry with absorbent paper. Rub cavities of the hens with a mixture of the 2 teaspoons salt and monosodium glutamate. Lightly fill body cavities with the stuffing. To close body cavities, sew or skewer and lace with cord. Fasten neck skin to backs and wings to bodies with poultry pins. Put game hens, breast side up, on rack in roasting pan; brush with ¼ cup melted butter. Roast uncovered at 350° about 1½ hours or until hens test done. Remove pins before serving. Serve on heated platter. *Makes 4 servings.*

**Note:** To add a crisp texture to stuffing, add an 8-ounce can sliced water chestnuts, drained.

### CASHEW-STUFFED BRAISED CHICKEN

1 cup cashew nuts
3 tablespoons butter or margarine, melted
3 tablespoons cooking sherry
1 clove garlic
½ medium onion, cubed
2 stalks celery, cut into 1-inch pieces
4 sprigs parsley
½ teaspoon pepper
¼ teaspoon ginger
¼ teaspoon mace
⅛ teaspoon thyme
2 cups steamed brown rice
2 2-pound frying chickens
Flour
Salt and pepper
½ cup butter or margarine
1½ cups dry white wine or chicken broth

Put cashew nuts in blender container; cover and run on speed 4 (or low) until chopped. Empty into a bowl. Put melted butter, sherry and garlic in blender container; cover and run on speed 7 (or high) until garlic is liquefied. Add onion, celery and parsley; cover and run on speed 4 (or low) just until vegetables are chopped. Add to chopped nuts. Add seasonings and cooked rice; toss together lightly.

Stuff the chickens lightly with this mixture; skewer the openings closed and truss and tie the legs. Dust with flour seasoned with salt and pepper. Melt ½ cup butter in a large Dutch oven; brown chickens on all sides; add ½ cup of the wine. Cover and simmer about 1 hour or until tender. Baste occasionally, adding remaining wine or broth as needed. Remove chickens to a hot platter. Remove skewers and string. Thicken liquid if desired. *Makes 4–6 servings.*

## CHICKEN NORMANDY

**2 1½- to 2-pound broiling chickens, cut up**
**½ cup butter or margarine**
**¼ cup brandy**
**1 medium onion, cut up**
**2 stalks celery, cut up**
**2 tart apples, pared, quartered and cored**
**8 sprigs parsley**
**⅓ cup cooking sherry**
**Salt and pepper**
**⅓ cup whipping cream**

In a frypan brown chicken in butter; pour brandy over chicken and ignite. Let flame burn out. Remove chicken and keep warm. Put onion in blender container; cover and run on speed 3 (or low) until chopped. Empty into frypan. Repeat process with celery, then with apples. If necessary, stop blender during processing and push ingredients toward blades with rubber spatula. Sauté onion, celery and apples in pan drippings about 5 minutes. Put parsley and sherry in blender container; cover and run on speed 3 (or low) a few seconds. Add to mixture in frypan. Season with salt and pepper. Return chicken to pan, spooning sauce over it. Simmer 35 minutes or until chicken is tender. Do not let mixture boil. Stir in cream. Heat. *Makes 4–6 servings.*

## CHEESY-BAKED CHICKEN

**5 slices slightly dry bread**
**4 ounces sharp Cheddar cheese, cubed**
**4 sprigs parsley**
**2 teaspoons salt**
**⅛ teaspoon pepper**
**1 teaspoon monosodium glutamate**
**½ teaspoon garlic salt**
**2½- to 3-pound frying chicken, cut up**
**¾ cup butter or margarine, melted**

Preheat oven to 350°. Break 1 slice bread into 6 pieces and drop into blender container; add ¼ of the cheese. Cover container; run on speed 3 (or low) until bread and cheese are fine. Empty into a bowl. Repeat process, using 1 slice bread and ¼ of the cheese each time. Add the parsley to blender container with the fifth slice of bread; crumb. Add seasonings to crumb-cheese mixture; mix well.

Dip chicken pieces in butter, then into crumb mixture, coating thoroughly. Arrange in an uncrowded single layer in a shallow baking pan. Bake, uncovered, about 1 hour or until thickest pieces are tender. *Makes 4–5 servings.*

## BAKED CHICKEN HASH

**2 cups cut-up cooked chicken**
**2 cups chicken gravy OR one 10½-ounce can condensed cream of chicken soup plus ½ cup milk**
**2 medium raw potatoes, pared and cut up**
**2–3 medium carrots, cut up**
**½ small onion, cut up**
**6 sprigs parsley**
**1 canned pimiento**
**½ teaspoon salt**
**½ teaspoon poultry seasoning**

Preheat oven to 350°. Put chicken and gravy in blender container; cover and run on speed 4 (or high) until chicken is chopped. Empty into a saucepan and heat to boiling.

Meanwhile, put a few pieces of potato in blender container; cover and run on speed 3 (or low) until chopped. Empty into measuring cup and repeat process until you have 1 cup chopped potato. Repeat process with carrots until you have 1 cup chopped carrot. Put onion, parsley, pimiento and seasonings in blender container; cover and run on speed 4 (or high) until vegetables are chopped. If necessary, stop blender during processing and push vegetables toward blades with rubber spatula. Add with chopped potato and carrot to chicken mixture; pour into a buttered 1½-quart casserole. Bake for 45 minutes.

Meanwhile, if crumb topping is desired, break 1 slice bread into blender container; cover and run on speed 3 (or low) until crumbed. Repeat process with 2 additional slices. Mix with 3 tablespoons melted butter. Sprinkle crumbs over baked casserole and bake 15 minutes longer. *Makes 6 servings.*

*Glazed Salmon Steaks with Sauce Verte (p. 103)*

## Fish Dishes to Enjoy

### GLAZED SALMON STEAKS WITH SAUCE VERTE

**4 ¾-pound salmon steaks**
**2 cups hot water**
**1 cup dry white wine**
**2 sprigs parsley**
**1 medium onion, quartered**
**1 bay leaf**
**1 teaspoon salt**
**1 egg white and shell**
**1 envelope (1 tablespoon) unflavored gelatin**
**Sliced olives**
**4 stalks chives**
**1 cup Blender Mayonnaise (page 79)**
**2 tablespoons tarragon vinegar**
**¾ cup firmly packed spinach leaves**
**7 sprigs parsley**
**6–8 sprigs watercress**
**12–15 stalks chive**

Wrap each salmon steak in double layer of cheesecloth. Combine hot water, wine and parsley in a large frypan. Put onion in blender container; cover and run on speed 3 (or low) until chopped. Add to mixture in frypan with bay leaf and salt. Arrange salmon steaks in frypan and simmer 15–20 minutes. Carefully remove salmon with a large spatula and allow to cool on a wire rack.

Add egg white and shell to fish broth in frypan and bring to a boil. Allow to stand 5 minutes and strain through a double layer of cheesecloth. Soften gelatin in ¼ cup cold water in blender container. Measure 1 cup of cleared fish broth and pour over softened gelatin; cover and run on speed 1 (or low) until gelatin is dissolved. Refrigerate until gelatin is the consistency of unbeaten egg white.

Remove cheesecloth from salmon and arrange on wire rack in a jelly roll pan. Brush gelatin over top and sides of salmon. Make a flower on top of each salmon steak, using sliced olives for petals and a stalk of chive for the stem. Spoon remaining gelatin over top and sides of salmon. Refrigerate at least 1 hour.

Meanwhile, put mayonnaise, vinegar, spinach and parsley in blender container, pushing spinach toward blades with a rubber spatula; cover and run on speed 3 (or low) until vegetables are finely chopped. Add half the watercress and chives; cover and run on speed 3 (or low) until chopped. Add remaining watercress and chives to taste. Serve with glazed salmon steaks. *Makes 4 servings.*

### ROCK LOBSTER THERMIDOR

**6 8-ounce rock lobster tails**
**1½ cups milk**
**3 tablespoons soft butter or margarine**
**3 tablespoons flour**
**3 tablespoons butter or margarine**
**1 3-ounce can mushrooms, drained**
**1 medium onion, quartered**
**3 tablespoons light cream**
**2 tablespoons white wine**
**2 sprigs parsley**
**½ teaspoon Worcestershire**
**½ teaspoon dry mustard**
**¼ teaspoon salt**
**⅛ teaspoon cayenne**
**1 egg yolk, slightly beaten**
**Grated Parmesan cheese**

Fill a kettle about ⅔ full of water; add 1 teaspoon salt per quart of water and bring to a boil. Add lobster tails; cover and return rapidly to a boil. Reduce heat and simmer about 11 minutes; drain. Rinse tails under cold water until cool enough to handle. Place on a cutting board, shell side down, and remove soft membrane on underside of each tail. Take care not to break shells. Carefully remove the meat and cut into ½-inch cubes; set aside. Reserve shells.

Put milk, 3 tablespoons butter and flour in blender container; cover and run on speed 4 (or low) until smooth. Empty into a saucepan and cook, stirring constantly, over low heat until thickened. Pour half of this white sauce into top part of double boiler; set aside.

Melt 3 tablespoons butter in a small frypan; add mushrooms. Put onion in blender container; cover and run on speed 4 (or low) until chopped. Sauté with mushrooms until onion is transparent. Add to sauce remaining in saucepan. Put cream, wine, parsley, Worcestershire, mustard, salt and cayenne in blender container; cover and run on speed 4 (or low) until parsley is finely chopped. Add to onion-mushroom mixture in saucepan; add lobster. Stir over low heat just until heated. Place lobster shells in a shallow baking pan; fill shells with lobster mixture.

Slowly stir slightly beaten egg yolk into sauce in double boiler; cook over hot water, stirring constantly, until very thick. Spread over filling in lobster shells; sprinkle generously with Parmesan cheese. Bake 25 minutes in oven preheated to 325°. *Makes 6 servings.*

## CRISPY SALMON STEAKS

**18–20 soda crackers**
**4 cups potato chips**
**½ cup butter or margarine, melted**
**1 teaspoon salt**
**⅛ teaspoon paprika**
**6 salmon steaks, ¾-inch thick**
**6 sprigs parsley (optional)**
**10 stalks chives (optional)**
**Lemon wedges**

Break 10 crackers into blender container; cover and run on speed 4 (or high) until crumbed. Empty into a measuring cup. Repeat process until you have 1 cup crumbs. Break half the potato chips into blender container and proceed as above. Mix cracker and potato chip crumbs in a pie pan. Combine butter, salt and paprika. Dip each salmon steak in butter and then in crumbs; place on lightly greased broiler pan rack. Drizzle with remaining butter. Broil 6 inches from heat 10 minutes on each side or until fish flakes when tested with a fork.

Meanwhile, put parsley and chives in blender container; cover and run on speed 4 (or high) until chopped. Arrange salmon on a warm serving platter; sprinkle with chopped parsley and chives. Garnish with lemon. *Makes 6 servings.*

*With Crispy Salmon Steaks,*
*serve Olive Dressing (p. 80) or Sauce Câpre (p. 114)*

## INDIVIDUAL DEVILED SALMON LOAVES

**6 thin slices lemon, with rind**
**1 1-pound can salmon**
**3 slices fresh bread**
**1 egg**
**1 cup canned, condensed tomato soup, undiluted**
**¼ medium onion**
**¼ medium green pepper, seeded**
**3 tablespoons soft butter**
**½ teaspoon salt**
**1 teaspoon prepared mustard**
**1 thin slice lemon, with rind**

Preheat oven to 350°. Grease six 3½-inch custard cups; place 1 slice lemon in bottom of each. Drain salmon; remove skin and bones and flake in a mixing bowl. Break 1 slice bread into 6 pieces; drop into blender container; cover and run on speed 4 (or low) until finely crumbed. Add to salmon. Repeat process with remaining bread. Lightly mix salmon and crumbs. Put all remaining ingredients in blender container in order listed; cover and run on speed 4 (or high) until onion and green pepper are finely chopped. Add to salmon mixture and mix well. Fill custard cups with this mixture and bake 35–40 minutes. Unmold to serve. *Makes 6 servings.*

## SHRIMP JAMBALAYA

**2½ cups canned tomatoes**
**½ medium onion, cut up**
**1 large stalk celery, cut into 1-inch pieces**
**¼ green pepper, seeded**
**1 clove garlic**
**1 bay leaf**
**1¼ teaspoons salt**
**½ teaspoon thyme**
**2 sprigs parsley**
**1½ cups uncooked rice**
**1½ cups water**
**1 cup diced cooked ham**
**1 pound raw shrimp, shelled and deveined**

Put first 9 ingredients in blender container; cover and run on speed 4 (or high) until vegetables are chopped. Pour into frypan. Add rice, water and ham; mix well. Arrange shrimp around outside edge of skillet; cover and cook 30 minutes. *Makes 6 servings.*

***FOR COMPANY ON FRIDAY***
*Fillet of Sole with Shrimp Sauce*
*Broccoli Crumble (p. 122)*
*Ginger Pecan Cream Pie (p. 180)*

## SHRIMP CURRY

**1½ pounds raw shrimp OR two 12-ounce packages frozen shrimp**
**6 cups boiling water**
**1 tablespoon salt**
**1 bay leaf**
**2 thin lemon slices**
**1 small onion, sliced**
**1 large onion, cut into 6 pieces**
**¼ cup butter or margarine**
**1–2 tablespoons curry powder***
**1 teaspoon salt**
**1 medium apple, cored and quartered**
**2 large stalks celery, cut into 2-inch pieces**
**3 tablespoons flour**
**1 cup raisins**

Shell and devein shrimp. Cook in boiling water with 1 tablespoon salt, bay leaf, lemon slices and sliced onion for 5 minutes; remove from heat. Drain shrimp, reserving 2½ cups shrimp stock; set aside.

Put cut-up onion in blender container; cover and run on speed 4 (or low) until chopped. Sauté in butter just until tender. Put reserved shrimp stock, sauteéd onion and remaining ingredients except shrimp in blender container; cover and run on speed 4 (or low) just until apple and celery are coarsely chopped, about 5 seconds. Pour into a saucepan and cook over low heat, stirring constantly, until sauce thickens. Continue to cook 10 minutes longer to blend flavors. Add shrimp to sauce and cook just until shrimp are hot, about 5 minutes. Serve with hot cooked rice and condiments such as chutney, pineapple, salted peanuts and grated coconut. *Makes 6 servings.*

*For a mild curry flavor, use 1 tablespoon curry powder; for stronger flavor, increase amount according to taste.

## FILLET OF SOLE WITH SHRIMP SAUCE

**4 large fillets of sole**
**Salt and pepper**
**¼ cup dry white wine**
**2¼ cups hot water**
**2 tablespoons lemon juice**
**1 tablespoon soft butter or margarine**
**3 slices fresh white bread**
**3 tablespoons flour**
**3 tablespoons butter or margarine**
**½ teaspoon Tabasco**
**1 green onion with top, cut into 1-inch pieces**
**¼ green pepper, seeded**
**2 tablespoons chervil**
**1 cup cooked shrimp, fresh or canned**

Sprinkle fillets with salt and pepper and marinate at least 4 hours in white wine. Transfer to a frypan; cover with hot water and lemon juice and simmer 10 minutes. Remove fish to a buttered flame-proof 13x9x2-inch baking dish; reserve cooking liquid.

Preheat oven to 350°. Spread 1 tablespoon butter evenly on the 3 slices of bread. Break 1 slice bread into 6 pieces and drop into blender container; cover and run on speed 4 (or low) until bread is crumbed. Empty into a bowl. Repeat process with remaining buttered bread. Put the liquid in which the fish was cooked, flour, 3 tablespoons butter, Tabasco, green onion, green pepper and chervil in blender container; cover and run on speed 4 (or low) until vegetables are chopped. Return to the frypan; add shrimp. Cook, stirring constantly, until thickened. Sprinkle half the crumbs over the fish; cover with sauce. Sprinkle remaining crumbs over all. Bake for 15 minutes; then set under broiler for a few seconds to brown top. *Makes 4 servings.*

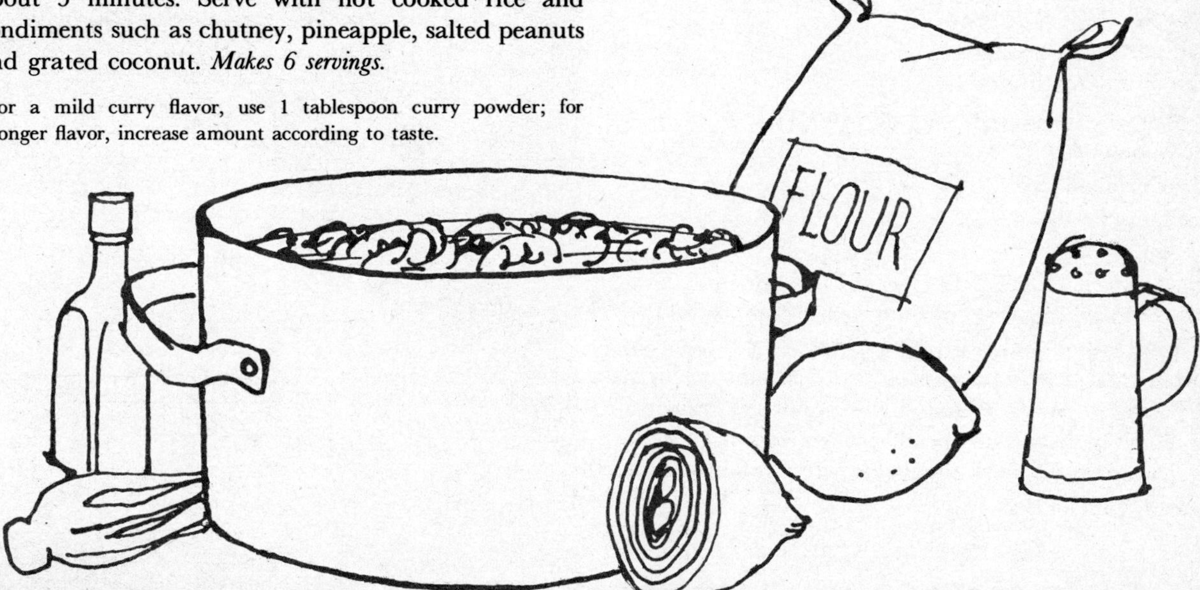

## STUFFED TROUT

**1 3- to 4-pound trout, cleaned and boned**
**Salt**
**1 tablespoon lemon juice**
**8 slices fresh bread**
**1 medium onion, quartered**
**2 stalks celery, cut up**
**1 3-ounce can chopped mushrooms, drained**
**¼ cup butter or margarine, melted**
**1 teaspoon salt**
**1 teaspoon poultry seasoning**
**⅛ teaspoon white pepper**
**Melted butter or margarine**

Preheat oven to 425°. Rub inside of trout with salt and sprinkle with lemon juice. Tear 1 slice of bread into blender container; cover and run on speed 4 (or low) until finely crumbed. Empty into a mixing bowl and repeat process until all bread is crumbed. Put onion and celery in blender container; cover and run on speed 3 (or low) until coarsely chopped. If necessary, stop blender during processing and push ingredients toward blades with rubber spatula. Add onion and celery, mushrooms, ¼ cup melted butter, 1 teaspoon salt, poultry seasoning and pepper to bread crumbs.

Fill trout with stuffing and fasten with skewers and string. Wrap in foil and bake in a shallow pan for 30 minutes. Open foil and bake 15 minutes longer. Baste with melted butter during last 15 minutes. *Makes 4 servings.*

**Note:** If trout is not available, substitute whitefish, striped bass or red snapper.

## RED SNAPPER PARMESAN

**2 1-pound packages frozen red snapper fillets, thawed**
**1 cup dairy sour cream**
**¼ cup grated Parmesan cheese**
**1 tablespoon lemon juice**
**½ small onion, cut up**
**1 hard-cooked egg, shelled and quartered**
**½ teaspoon salt**
**2–3 drops Tabasco**
**Paprika**

Preheat oven to 350°. Grease a 13x9x2-inch baking dish. Skin fillets and cut into serving-size portions. Place in a single layer in baking dish. Put remaining ingredients except paprika in blender container; cover and run on speed 4 (or high) about 10 seconds. Spoon over fish and sprinkle with paprika. Bake 25–30 minutes or until fish flakes when tested with a fork. *Makes 8 servings.*

*Stuffed Trout*

## GEFÜLLTE FISH

3 pounds mixed fish (whitefish, pike, carp)
1 quart water
1 medium onion
2 stalks celery
2 carrots
2 teaspoons salt
1 medium onion, quartered
2 eggs
4 slices bread, each broken into 6 pieces, OR ¾ cup matzo meal
1 teaspoon salt
¼ teaspoon pepper
1 cup cold water

Have fish headed, boned, skinned and cut into 1-inch cubes at market; save heads, bones and skin. Put 1 quart water, fish bones, skin and heads, 1 whole onion, celery, carrots and 2 teaspoons salt in a large saucepan; cook 30 minutes.

Meanwhile, put 1 cup of the cubed raw fish and the quartered onion in blender container; cover and run on speed 5 (or high) until finely chopped. If necessary, stop blender during processing and push ingredients toward blades with rubber spatula. Remove chopped fish to a large mixing bowl. Put ½ cup cold water, eggs, 2 slices bread (or half the matzo meal) and half the remaining cubed fish in blender container; cover and run on speed 7 (or high) until almost smooth. Add to chopped fish. Put another ½ cup water with remaining bread, cubed fish, salt and pepper in blender container; cover and run on speed 7 (or high) until almost smooth. Add to fish in bowl. Wet hands and form mixture into loose balls, each the size of an egg. Strain stock, reserving carrots. Return stock to saucepan and bring to boiling. Add fish balls to boiling stock. Cover and boil 30 minutes. Reduce heat and boil slowly 1 hour longer. Cool slightly; lift fish out with slotted spoon or pancake turner. Slice carrots for garnish. Strain stock; chill to jell. Serve fish with jelled stock and beet horseradish. *Makes 10 servings.*

## TUNA NOODLE CASSEROLE

1 6-ounce package medium noodles
½ cup Blender Mayonnaise (page 79)
1 10½-ounce can condensed cream of celery soup, undiluted
½ cup milk
⅔ medium onion, cut up
½ green pepper, seeded and cut up
1 canned pimiento
1 teaspoon salt
½ pound sharp American cheese, cubed (about 2 cups)
1 7-ounce can tuna, drained and flaked
4–5 potato- or vegetable-flavored crackers

Preheat oven to 425°. Grease a 1½-quart casserole. Cook noodles in boiling salted water until tender; drain. Meanwhile, put mayonnaise, soup, milk, vegetables and salt in blender container; cover and run on speed 4 (or high) until vegetables are chopped. Turn to speed 3 (or low); add cheese, a few cubes at a time, while blender is running. If necessary, stop blender and push cheese toward blades with rubber spatula; cover before restarting blender. Combine with noodles and tuna; pour into casserole. Bake 30 minutes or until hot. Meanwhile, put crackers in clean, dry blender container; cover and run on speed 3 (or low) until crumbed. Sprinkle over casserole and bake 10 minutes longer. *Makes 6 servings.*

## CHEESE-BAKED HALIBUT

**2½ pounds halibut steaks, ¾-inch thick**
**¼ cup lemon juice**
**½ teaspoon salt**
**⅛ teaspoon pepper**
**¼ teaspoon thyme**
**¼ pound Swiss cheese, cut into ½-inch cubes**
**3 slices dry white bread**
**¼ cup butter or margarine, melted**

Preheat oven to 375°. Lightly grease a large shallow baking dish. Wipe halibut with a damp cloth and place in baking dish. Pour lemon juice over fish, then sprinkle with salt, pepper and thyme; bake, uncovered, 20 minutes.

Meanwhile, break 1 slice bread into 6 pieces and drop into blender container; add ⅓ of the cubed cheese. Cover and run on speed 4 (or high) until bread is finely crumbed and cheese is grated. Empty into a bowl. Repeat process with remaining bread and cheese, using 1 slice bread and ⅓ of cheese each time. Sprinkle bread-cheese mixture over fish; then pour melted butter evenly over top. Bake 10 minutes longer or until fish flakes easily with fork. *Makes 6 servings.*

# Glamorized Cheese and Egg Dishes

## SCRAMBLED EGGS

**½ cup milk**
**9 eggs**
**1½ teaspoons salt**
**¼ teaspoon pepper**
**¼ cup butter or margarine**

Put milk, eggs, salt and pepper in blender container; cover and run on speed 3 (or low) about 5 seconds. Melt butter in a skillet; pour in egg mixture and cook slowly over low heat. With a spatula lift mixture from sides and bottom of pan as it thickens. Cook until all eggs are thick and creamy but still moist. *Makes 6 servings.*

### MEXICAN SCRAMBLE

Add ¼ seeded green pepper, ½ small onion and ⅛ teaspoon cayenne to Scrambled Eggs ingredients before blending; run on speed 3 (or low) until vegetables are finely chopped.

## EGG CROQUETTES

**40 soda crackers (approximately)**
**8 hard-cooked eggs, shelled and quartered**
**3 tablespoons soft butter or margarine**
**¼ cup flour**
**1 cup milk**
**½ teaspoon salt**
**½ teaspoon paprika**
**Dash nutmeg**
**¼ teaspoon pepper**
**Small piece onion**
**3 sprigs parsley**
**1 cup flour**
**2 eggs**
**¼ cup water**
**Salad oil or shortening for deep frying**

Break about 8 soda crackers into blender container; cover and run on speed 4 (or low) until finely crumbed. Empty into a 2-cup measure. Repeat process until you have 2 cups crumbs; set aside.

Put 8 pieces hard-cooked egg in blender container; cover and run on speed 4 (or low) until coarsely chopped. Empty into a bowl. Repeat process until all eggs are chopped. Put butter, ¼ cup flour, milk, salt, paprika, nutmeg, pepper, onion and parsley in blender container; cover and run on speed 5 (or high) until onion and parsley are chopped. Empty into a saucepan; cook, stirring constantly, until very thick. Remove from heat; stir in chopped eggs and ½ cup of the cracker crumbs. Chill about 1 hour or until ready to use.

Shape croquette mixture into eighteen 2-inch ovals. Roll lightly in flour, then roll in eggs which have been beaten with ¼ cup water. Roll in crumbs to coat completely.

In a deep skillet heat salad oil or shortening (at least 2 inches deep) to 385° on a deep-frying thermometer. Deep-fry croquettes, a few at a time, 3–4 minutes, or until golden brown. Drain thoroughly on absorbent paper. Serve hot. *Makes 6 servings.*

**Note:** Good with a white sauce, cheese sauce or deviled olive sauce.

*Cheese Omelet (p. 109) with Spanish Sauce (p. 1*

## CHEESE OMELET

**⅓ cup water**
**6 eggs**
**1 teaspoon salt**
**¼ teaspoon pepper**
**¼ teaspoon paprika**
**1 cup cubed Cheddar cheese**
**2 tablespoons shortening**

Preheat oven to 325°. Put all ingredients except shortening in blender container; cover and run on speed 6 (or high) until smooth. Melt shortening in oven-proof skillet or omelet pan; pour in egg mixture. Cook over low heat until puffed and delicately browned underneath; then bake in oven for 15 minutes or until top is browned. Turn onto heated serving platter. Spoon half of Spanish Sauce (page 116) over half the omelet, crease in center and fold over; pour remaining sauce over top. Serve immediately. *Makes 4 servings.*

### PUFFY CHEESE OMELET

Separate eggs in above recipe. Blend egg yolks with other ingredients; beat egg whites with an electric mixer until stiff but not dry and fold into egg yolk mixture. Complete as directed for Cheese Omelet.

## MACARONI AND CHEESE LOAF

**1–2 slices fresh white bread**
**1½ cups hot milk**
**2 tablespoons butter or margarine**
**1 4-ounce can deviled ham**
**½ pound Cheddar cheese, cut into 1-inch cubes**
**¼ teaspoon salt**
**3 eggs**
**1 canned pimiento**
**¼ small onion**
**8 ounces macaroni, cooked and drained**

Preheat oven to 325°. Break 1 slice bread into 6 pieces and drop into blender container; cover and run on speed 4 (or low) until finely crumbed. Empty into a measuring cup. Repeat process until you have 1 cup crumbs; set aside.

Put hot milk, butter, ham, cheese and salt in blender container; cover and run on speed 6 (or high) until smooth. While blender is running, add eggs, one at a time. Stop blender. Add pimiento and onion; cover and run on speed 4 (or low) just until pimiento and onion are chopped. Add cheese mixture and bread crumbs to cooked macaroni. Pour into a buttered 9x5x3-inch loaf pan. Bake 1 hour or until firm and browned. Cool 10 minutes in pan. Unmold and serve hot. *Makes 6–8 servings.*

## SWISS CHEESE AND HAM SOUFFLÉ

1 cup milk
4 eggs, separated
3 tablespoons soft butter or margarine
¼ cup flour
¾ teaspoon salt
⅛ teaspoon dry mustard
6 ounces Swiss cheese, cubed
½ cup cubed cooked ham

Preheat oven to 300°. Put milk, egg yolks, butter, flour, salt, mustard and cheese in blender container; cover and run on speed 7 (or high) until completely smooth. Add ham; cover and run on speed 5 (or high) until ham is finely chopped. Pour into a saucepan; cook over low heat, stirring often, until very thick. Cool slightly. Beat egg whites in a medium bowl with electric mixer until stiff but not dry; carefully fold into cheese mixture. Pour into an ungreased 2-quart casserole or soufflé dish until ¼ inch from the top. (Bake any extra in a small ungreased casserole.) Bake 1¼ hours. *Don't open oven door while baking!* Serve at once. *Makes 4 servings.*

## WELSH RAREBIT

2¼ cups hot milk
2 eggs
¾ teaspoon salt
¾ teaspoon dry mustard
¾ teaspoon Worcestershire
3 tablespoons flour
¾ pound Cheddar cheese, cubed
Paprika

Put all ingredients except paprika in blender container in order listed; cover and run on speed 5 (or high) until smooth. Pour into top of a double boiler; stir constantly over hot water until thick. Serve over buttered toasted English muffins or toast. Sprinkle with paprika. *Makes 6 servings.*

## CHEESE AND BACON PIE

30 soda crackers
¼ cup butter or margarine, melted
½ pound bacon, fried crisp
1¾ cups light cream
½ medium onion, cut up
3 eggs
1 teaspoon Worcestershire
½ teaspoon salt
Dash cayenne
¾ pound Swiss or Gruyère cheese, cubed (about 3 cups)
¼ cup grated Parmesan cheese

Preheat oven to 350°. Break 4 or 5 crackers into blender container; cover and run on speed 3 (or low) until crumbed. Empty into a measuring cup and repeat until you have 1½ cups crumbs. Mix crumbs with butter; reserve 2 tablespoons for topping. Press remaining crumbs onto bottom and sides of a 9-inch pie pan. Bake 10 minutes; remove.

Reduce oven temperature to 325°. Crumble bacon over bottom of baked pie shell. Put cream, onion, eggs, Worcestershire, salt and cayenne in blender container; cover and run on speed 6 (or high) until smooth. Slowly add cubed cheese while blender is running; run until smooth. Pour into pie shell; sprinkle with Parmesan cheese and remaining crumbs. Bake 50 minutes or until pie is set in center. Let stand 10 minutes before serving. Cut in wedges. *Makes 6–8 servings.*

*Cheese and Bacon Pie*

## POTATO PANCAKES

¼ cup milk
2 eggs
3 cups diced raw potatoes
1 small onion, quartered
3 tablespoons flour
1 teaspoon salt
¼ teaspoon baking powder

Put all ingredients in blender container in order listed; cover and run on speed 7 (or high) just until all potatoes go through blades, about 10 seconds. (Do not overblend or potatoes will be liquefied.) Pour small amounts onto a hot, greased griddle or frypan. Fry until brown on both sides, turning once. *Makes 18 pancakes.*

## SPAGHETTI WITH MEAT SAUCE

1 medium onion, quartered
1 clove garlic
2 tablespoons olive oil
1 3-ounce can mushrooms, drained
1 pound ground beef
1 No. 2½ can (3½ cups) tomatoes
1 6-ounce can tomato paste
1 teaspoon salt
¼ teaspoon pepper
¼ teaspoon oregano
12 ounces uncooked spaghetti
4 quarts water, boiling
1½ tablespoons salt

Put onion and garlic in blender container; cover and run on speed 4 (or low) until onion is coarsely chopped. Heat olive oil in a large saucepan; add chopped onion and garlic. Put mushrooms in blender container; cover and run on speed 4 (or low) until chopped. Add to onion and sauté in olive oil until onion is transparent. Add beef and cook 10 minutes, stirring frequently. Drain off excess fat. Put tomatoes, tomato paste, salt, pepper and oregano in blender container; cover and run on speed 5 (or high) until smooth. Pour over ingredients in saucepan; simmer, covered, over low heat for 2 hours. Cook spaghetti in boiling, salted water 10–15 minutes or until tender; drain in a large colander or sieve and rinse with hot water. Serve with meat sauce. *Makes 6 servings.*

## Sauces for Every Taste

*There is no question but that a great sauce can make a great dish. Among the recipes that follow you will find many that you are preparing now by traditional methods, with some degree of success. Note how you can reduce preparation time with the blender and easily produce sauces equal to those made by a trained saucier.*

*You will also find sauces that have been restricted to outstanding restaurants or to homes where a highly skilled cook was employed. Using your own blender-made mayonnaise or Hollandaise as a base, you can move easily, with the aid of the blender, to a dozen or more of these exquisite chef's sauces. Add one to a boiled or broiled meat (even a hamburger), chicken or fish, an omelet or a vegetable—and a routine dinner becomes a banquet.*

*One word of caution: when a rich or highly seasoned sauce is offered, let the rest of the meal provide a neutral background for it. A meal composed entirely of dishes with sauces and/or exotic seasonings can result in a race for the medicine cabinet. And the conflict of flavors will spoil the effect of each dish.*

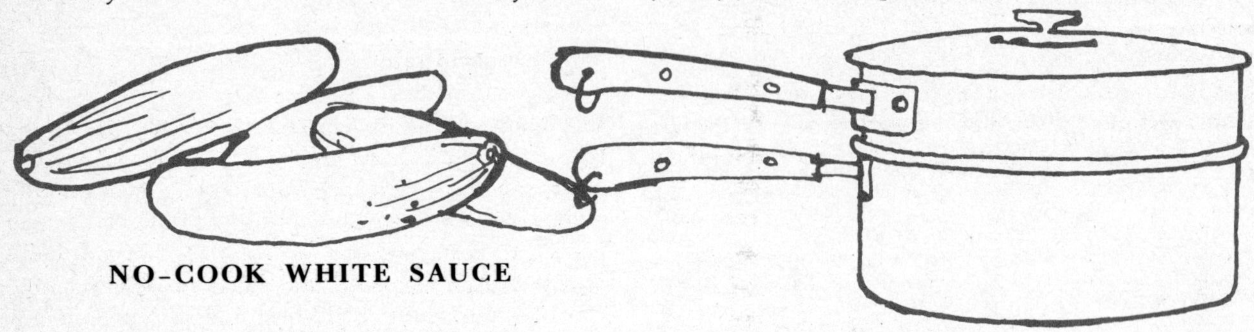

### NO-COOK WHITE SAUCE

### THIN WHITE SAUCE

**1 cup hot milk**
**2 tablespoons butter or margarine**
**½ teaspoon salt**
**Dash pepper**
**2–3 slices white bread, with crusts removed**

Put all ingredients except bread in blender container; cover and run on speed 5 (or high). While blender is running, break each slice bread into 6 pieces and add slowly. (Bread varies in composition and size of slices, so stop blender at intervals as bread is added to check consistency.) Serve immediately or keep warm over hot water. *Makes 1¼ cups.*

#### MEDIUM WHITE SAUCE

Use 5–7 slices white bread, with crusts removed, in above recipe. Add bread slowly, checking consistency frequently. *Makes about 1¼ cups.*

#### THICK WHITE SAUCE

Use 8–10 slices white bread, with crusts removed, in above recipe. Add bread slowly, checking consistency frequently. *Makes about 1¼ cups.*

#### QUICK CHEESE SAUCE

Add ½ cup cubed Cheddar cheese to Medium White Sauce after bread is added. Blend until smooth. *Makes 1½ cups.*

### DEVILED OLIVE SAUCE

**1 cup Medium White Sauce**
**½ cup stuffed green olives**
**1 canned pimiento**
**¼ teaspoon Worcestershire**
**⅛ teaspoon celery salt**

Put all ingredients in blender container; cover and run on speed 4 (or high) for 15 seconds. If necessary, stop blender during processing and push ingredients toward blades with rubber spatula. Heat to serving temperature. Serve over salmon or tuna loaf or soufflé. *Makes 1½ cups.*

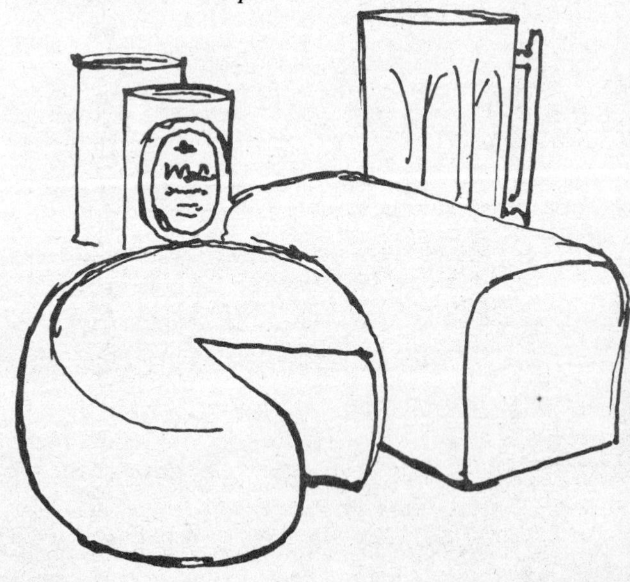

## MOCK SOUR CREAM

*An excellent sauce—low-calorie, too.*

**¼ cup water**
**1 tablespoon lemon juice**
**1 cup creamed cottage cheese**
**¼ teaspoon salt (optional)**

Put ingredients in blender container; cover and run on speed 6 (or high) until completely smooth, about 10 seconds. *Makes 1 cup.*

**Note:** Use as you would cold sour cream.

## SOUR CREAM HERB SAUCE

**½ cup milk**
**1 cup dairy sour cream**
**½ teaspoon salt**
**⅛ teaspoon paprika**
**2 slices white bread, with crusts removed**
**1 green onion with top, cut into 1-inch pieces**
**2 sprigs parsley**

Put all ingredients except onion and parsley in blender container; cover and run on speed 6 (or high) until smooth. Add parsley and onion; cover and run on speed 4 (or low) until parsley and onion are finely chopped. Pour into top of a double boiler and heat over boiling water, stirring frequently, until hot and slightly thickened. Serve over hot vegetables, omelets or fish. *Makes 1½ cups.*

## SOUR CREAM CUCUMBER SAUCE

**3 1-inch slices cucumber, pared**
**2 green onions with tops, cut up**
**½ cup dairy sour cream**
**½ teaspoon salt**

Put all ingredients in blender container; cover and run on speed 4 (or high) a few seconds, until vegetables are chopped. Chill. Serve with fish. *Makes ⅔ cup.*

*Serve Horseradish Cream with cold roast beef or ham and lime-flavor gelatin molded with cucumber and pitted ripe olives, blender chopped.*

## SAUCE REMOULADE

**1 recipe Blender Mayonnaise (page 79)**
**½ teaspoon dry mustard**
**½ teaspoon garlic salt**
**2 teaspoons anchovy paste**
**1 sprig parsley**
**½ dill pickle OR 4 stuffed green olives**
**1 teaspoon dried chervil**
**Salt and pepper to taste**

Make mayonnaise; add remaining ingredients to blender container. Cover and run on speed 7 (or high) until mixed. Serve with shrimp or other seafood cocktails. *Makes 1¼ cups.*

### SAUCE RUSSE

Add 3 tablespoons prepared horseradish to Sauce Remoulade. Serve with shellfish, fish or meat.

## TARTAR SAUCE

**3 tablespoons lemon juice**
**1 cup Blender Mayonnaise (page 79)**
**1 large dill pickle, cut into 1-inch pieces**
**1 small onion, quartered**
**1 tablespoon capers**
**1 tablespoon chives**
**1 hard-cooked egg, shelled and quartered**

Put lemon juice, mayonnaise, pickle and onion in blender container; cover and run on speed 4 (or low) until pickle and onion are chopped. Add capers, chives and hard-cooked egg; cover and run on speed 4 (or low) about 2 seconds, or just until egg is coarsely chopped. Serve with fish. *Makes about 2 cups.*

## HORSERADISH CREAM

**1 recipe Blender Mayonnaise (page 79)**
**3 tablespoons prepared horseradish**
**1 tablespoon tarragon vinegar**
**1 tablespoon lemon juice**
**¼ teaspoon prepared mustard**
**Few grains each cayenne, salt and sugar**
**1 cup chilled whipping cream**

Make mayonnaise; add remaining ingredients except whipping cream to blender container; cover and run on speed 7 (or high) until blended. Whip cream and fold into blender mixture. *Makes 3 cups.*

## BLENDER HOLLANDAISE SAUCE

*A never-fail recipe for this most important sauce.*

**½ cup butter or margarine**
**3 egg yolks**
**2 tablespoons lemon juice**
**¼ teaspoon salt**
**Dash white pepper**
**½ teaspoon prepared mustard**

Heat butter in a small saucepan until bubbly but not browned. Put egg yolks, lemon juice, salt, white pepper and mustard in blender container; cover and run on speed 2 (or low) about 5 seconds. While continuing to run on same speed, add butter in a slow, steady stream until blades are covered; turn to speed 6 (or high) and add remaining butter slowly. Serve immediately on cooked vegetables, fish or Eggs Benedict. *Makes about 1 cup.*

### ALMOND HOLLANDAISE

Omit mustard in Blender Hollandaise Sauce. Add ¼ cup blanched almonds to finished sauce; cover container and run on speed 4 (or high) until almonds are finely chopped. Serve with vegetables or fish.

### MALTAISE SAUCE

Omit mustard in Blender Hollandaise Sauce. Add 2 tablespoons orange juice and ½ teaspoon grated orange rind to finished sauce. Cover container and run on speed 4 (or high) for 5 seconds. Serve with asparagus, artichokes or beets.

### SAUCE TOLSTOI

Add 1 teaspoon anchovy paste, ¼ cup cooked mushrooms, ¼ dill pickle and 2 tablespoons cooked diced beets to finished Blender Hollandaise Sauce; cover container and run on speed 4 (or high) until mushrooms, pickle and beets are chopped. Serve with fish or meat.

### SAUCE AUX OEUFS

Add 1 hard-cooked egg, shelled and quartered, to finished Blender Hollandaise Sauce; cover container and run on speed 4 (or high) until egg is finely chopped. Serve with vegetables or fish.

### SAUCE NOISETTE

Add ¼ cup hazelnuts or filberts to finished Blender Hollandaise Sauce; cover container and run on speed 4 (or high) until nuts are finely chopped. Serve with chicken or asparagus.

### SAUCE CÂPRE

Add 3 tablespoons whole, drained capers to finished Blender Hollandaise Sauce; cover container and run on speed 4 (or high) until capers are finely chopped. Serve with fish, poultry or cauliflower.

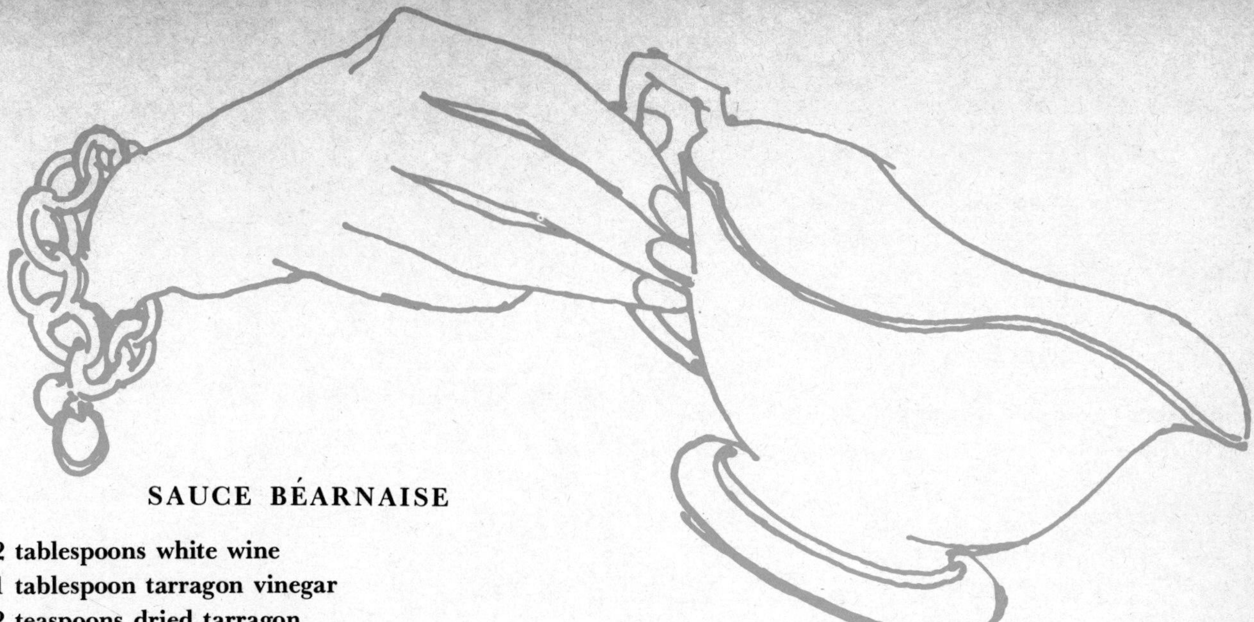

## SAUCE BÉARNAISE

**2 tablespoons white wine**
**1 tablespoon tarragon vinegar**
**2 teaspoons dried tarragon**
**2 teaspoons chopped shallots or onion**
**¼ teaspoon freshly ground black pepper**
**¼ teaspoon sugar**
**¾ cup Blender Hollandaise Sauce (page 114)**

Put all ingredients except Hollandaise Sauce in small saucepan. Cook rapidly over high heat until most of the liquid is gone. Pour mixture into Hollandaise Sauce in blender container; cover and run on speed 7 (or high) for 6 seconds. Serve with steak. *Makes about 1 cup.*

### SAUCE BEAUHARNAISE

Increase tarragon to 2 tablespoons in recipe for Sauce Béarnaise; add salt and pepper to taste. Serve with roast duck.

### SAUCE CHORON

Beat ¼ cup tomato purée into recipe for Sauce Béarnaise; add salt and pepper to taste.

## SPICY APPLE BARBECUE SAUCE

**½ cup red wine vinegar**
**½ clove garlic**
**¼ teaspoon rosemary**
**1 12-ounce bottle chili sauce**
**1 teaspoon salt**
**½ teaspoon pepper**
**2 teaspoons Worcestershire**
**¼ cup sugar**
**3 medium apples, cored and cubed**

Put all ingredients except apples in blender container; cover and run on speed 7 (or high) until smooth. While blender is running, add apples, a few pieces at a time; continue running on speed 7 (or high) until smooth. Use sauce to baste beef, pork, chicken or turkey as it cooks. *Makes 3½ cups.*

## GOLDEN BARBECUE SAUCE

**¾ cup molasses**
**½ cup prepared mustard**
**½ clove garlic**
**1 slice onion**
**¾ cup vinegar**
**1 teaspoon Tabasco**
**⅛ teaspoon marjoram**
**⅛ teaspoon oregano**

Put all ingredients in blender container; cover and run on speed 5 (or high) until smooth. Store covered in refrigerator. Use to prepare barbecued frankfurters, spareribs, hamburgers, bologna or canned luncheon meat. *Makes about 2 cups.*

## ZESTY BARBECUE SAUCE

**1 12-ounce bottle chili sauce**
**¼ cup water**
**1 medium onion, diced**
**1 clove garlic**
**½ teaspoon thyme**
**½ lemon, thinly sliced, with rind**
**5 drops Tabasco**
**¼ cup soft butter or margarine**

Put all ingredients except butter in blender container in order listed; cover and run on speed 5 (or high) until smooth. Pour into saucepan and simmer 15 minutes; add butter and stir over low heat to melt. Serve with beef, lamb or pork. *Makes about 1½ cups.*

BLEND LUMPY GRAVY SMOOTH

Put gravy which has lumps in blender container; cover and run on speed 7 (or high) until smooth.

## TOMATO SAUCE

**1 tablespoon butter or margarine**
**½ clove garlic**
**¼ onion, sliced**
**2 sprigs parsley**
**1 cup canned whole tomatoes**
**1 6-ounce can tomato paste**
**¼ teaspoon oregano**
**Pinch basil**
**½ teaspoon salt**
**⅛ teaspoon pepper**

Put all ingredients in blender container; cover and run on speed 6 (or high) until mixture is smooth. Pour into a saucepan; cover and simmer 30 minutes. Serve over spaghetti, hamburgers or veal cutlets. *Makes 1½ cups.*

## SPANISH SAUCE

**1½ cups canned tomatoes**
**1 teaspoon sugar**
**2 tablespoons flour**
**1 small onion, cut up**
**¼ green pepper, seeded**
**1½ teaspoons salt**
**Dash pepper**

Put all ingredients in blender container in order listed; cover and run on speed 4 (or low) until onion and pepper are chopped. Pour into a saucepan; stir over low heat until thickened. *Makes about 1 cup.*

**Note:** Serve this with Cheese Omelet (page 109).

## SNAPPY STEAK SAUCE

**¼ cup catsup**
**¼ cup lemon juice**
**Rind of ¼ lemon (colored portion only)**
**2 tablespoons soft butter or margarine**
**2 tablespoons prepared mustard**
**½ teaspoon Worcestershire**

Put all ingredients in blender container; cover and run on speed 3 (or low) until lemon rind is very finely chopped. *Makes ½ cup.*

## BEEF-MUSHROOM GRAVY

**¼ cup roast beef drippings**
**¼ cup flour**
**½ teaspoon salt**
**⅛ teaspoon pepper**
**2 cups beef stock or canned beef bouillon**
**¼ cup dry red wine**
**1 6-ounce can sliced mushrooms, drained**

Put all ingredients except wine and mushrooms in blender container; cover and run on speed 5 (or high) until smooth. Pour into a saucepan; cook over moderate heat, stirring constantly, until thickened. Stir in wine and mushrooms. Serve immediately. *Makes about 3 cups.*

## SAUCE CHIVRY

**2½ cups chicken broth**
**¼ cup butter or margarine**
**¼ cup flour**
**1 cup fresh spinach**
**¼ teaspoon tarragon**
**¼ teaspoon chervil**
**3 tablespoons chives**
**¼ cup water**

Put chicken broth, butter and flour in blender container; cover and run on speed 5 (or high) until smooth. Pour into a saucepan; bring to a boil, stirring constantly. Cook over low heat, stirring frequently, for 20 minutes. Put remaining ingredients in another saucepan; cover and cook 10 minutes. Drain. Put cooked sauce and drained spinach in blender container; cover and run on speed 4 (or low) until spinach is finely chopped. Return to saucepan; cook 2 minutes. Serve with chicken, eggs or fish. *Makes about 2 cups.*

## VINAIGRETTE SAUCE

¾ cup olive oil
½ cup tarragon vinegar
¾ teaspoon salt
¼ teaspoon pepper
⅛ teaspoon dried chervil
2 teaspoons capers
1 hard-cooked egg, shelled and quartered

Put all ingredients except egg in blender container; cover and run on speed 4 (or high) until capers are finely chopped. Add hard-cooked egg; cover and run on speed 3 (or low) until egg is finely chopped. Serve with vegetables, salads or boiled meats. *Makes 1 cup.*

## CALYPSO SHRIMP SAUCE

½ cup chili sauce
2 tablespoons molasses
1 teaspoon Worcestershire
2 tablespoons vinegar
¼ cup salad oil
½ clove garlic
½ teaspoon salt
¼ teaspoon pepper

Put all ingredients in blender container; cover and run on speed 6 (or high) until completely smooth. Brush on fresh uncooked shrimp; broil over charcoal 8-10 minutes. Sauce can also be heated and served as a hot dipping sauce for cooked shrimp. *Makes 1 cup.*

## ALMOND BUTTER SAUCE

½ cup butter or margarine, melted
¾ cup blanched almonds
1 teaspoon lemon juice
½ teaspoon salt
⅛ teaspoon white pepper

Put all ingredients in blender container in order listed; cover and run on speed 4 (or low) until almonds are chopped. Serve hot over fish or seafood. *Makes 1 cup.*

## AÏOLI SAUCE
### (Garlic Sauce)

2 egg yolks
3 cloves garlic
¾ teaspoon salt
¼ teaspoon black pepper
2 teaspoons lemon juice
½ cup olive or salad oil

Put egg yolks, garlic, salt, pepper and 1 teaspoon lemon juice in blender container; cover and run on speed 2 (or low) until garlic is crushed. Slowly add ¼ cup oil while blender is running; add the remaining lemon juice. Increase speed to 7 (or high) and slowly add remaining oil while blender is running. Serve with lamb, boiled beef or fish. *Makes ¾ cup sauce.*

## PARSLEY SAUCE

½ cup salad oil
3 tablespoons vinegar
½ teaspoon salt
½ cup parsley sprigs
¼ cup blanched almonds

Put all ingredients in blender container; cover and run on speed 4 (or low) until parsley and almonds are finely chopped. Chill. Serve on cold meats, cold or hot fish, or cooked vegetable salad. *Makes ¾ cup.*

## CRANBERRY SAUCE

2 cups fresh or frozen cranberries, thawed
½ cup honey
¼ teaspoon cloves
¼ teaspoon nutmeg

Put 1 cup cranberries in blender container; cover and run on speed 3 (or low) until chopped. If necessary, stop blender during processing and push cranberries toward blades with rubber spatula. Empty into a bowl. Repeat with remaining cranberries; add remaining ingredients to chopped cranberries in container. Cover and run on speed 4 (or high) until mixed. Stir into chopped cranberries in bowl. Serve over or cook with pork, steaks or chops. *Makes about 1½ cups.*

## CUMBERLAND SAUCE

**Rind from ¼ orange (colored portion only)**
**Rind from ¼ lemon (colored portion only)**
**¼ cup red currant jelly**
**2 tablespoons red wine**
**¼ cup orange juice**
**1½ teaspoons prepared mustard**
**1½ teaspoons paprika**
**1 teaspoon ginger**

Cover orange and lemon rinds with water and bring to a boil; drain. Put fruit rinds and remaining ingredients in blender container; cover and run on speed 4 (or high) for 1 minute or until rinds are chopped. Serve cold with roast duck. *Makes ¾ cup.*

## HONEY-ORANGE HAM GLAZE

**½ cup orange juice**
**½ cup honey**
**1 cup firmly packed brown sugar**
**Rind of ¼ orange (colored portion only)**

Put all ingredients in blender container; cover and run on speed 6 (or high) until orange rind is finely cut. *Makes 1½ cups, enough to glaze a whole ham.*

## SAVORY RAISIN SAUCE

**½ cup raisins**
**¼ medium onion, cut up**
**1 small clove garlic**
**½ cup catsup**
**½ cup bouillon**
**3 tablespoons salad oil**
**2 tablespoons vinegar**
**1 tablespoon brown sugar**
**1 teaspoon prepared mustard**
**½ teaspoon salt**
**2 sprigs fresh dill OR ⅛ teaspoon dill weed**

Put raisins, onion, garlic, catsup and bouillon in blender container; cover and run on speed 4 (or high) for 1 minute or until finely chopped. Add remaining ingredients; cover and run on speed 2 (or low) for 15 seconds. Use to baste spareribs or as sauce for a pot roast. *Makes about 2 cups.*

*Honey-Orange Ham Glaze on Ham Steak*

# Vegetable Varieties

*Vegetables, when well-cooked and presented with imagination, can be the most attractive part of a meal.*

*Americans, however, have been less appreciative of vegetables than the people of other lands. French restaurants present proudly a cold first course of a "bouquet" of perfectly cooked vegetables-in-season. Each guest makes his choice, then seasons his selection with salt, pepper, oil and vinegar. In Spain a similar presentation is made, but the vegetables are hot and follow the meat course. Southern Italians cook some vegetables in tomato sauce. Zucchini, green beans and peas are especially good this way. Green vegetables like broccoli, endive, escarole and beans are cooked quickly, then sautéed with olive oil, garlic, salt and pepper.*

*No matter how they are to be seasoned or served, vegetables should be carefully cooked to preserve flavor. When tenderly treated, they are treasure houses of the vitamins and minerals essential to growth and good health. Cut vegetables immediately before cooking, cook quickly and serve promptly to retain maximum nutritive value.*

*Most vegetables should be steamed, or cooked in a minimum of water as quickly as possible. If they are oven-steamed or cooked with care in heavy-bottomed saucepans, the liquid can be reduced to nothing. Carrots cooked in such a fashion are a new taste experience.*

*Vegetables that cause a strong odor, including cabbage, Brussels sprouts, turnips and onions, should be dropped into just enough rapidly boiling water to cover them completely and cooked over high heat, without a cover, until barely tender.*

### Add Sauce for a Change

*Cream sauce and cheese sauce are relatively common on the American table. The sauces on pages 112 to 118 may suggest other delicious combinations. Serve cabbage, Brussels sprouts, cauliflower or broccoli with Mustard Sauce (page 88). Try green beans, zucchini, small onions, eggplant, or potatoes in Tomato Sauce (page 116). Asparagus and broccoli with Hollandaise (page 114) are great combinations that may now, thanks to the blender, be found on any table.*

### Use Crumbs for Greater Interest

*If you serve vegetables with a white sauce or butter, a crumb topping can make your dish more attractive and add an appealing texture contrast. Use buttered bread or toast and follow the crumbing directions on page 11. (Vary the flavor by adding with each slice of bread a half teaspoonful of instant minced onion or half a dozen almonds; herbs may be added, too.) And cheese crumbs make a wonderful topping.*

### Vegetables in Broth—Delicious!

*Certain vegetables are enriched by cooking in broth. Arrange split bunches of celery, Belgian endive, cabbage, Chinese cabbage or wedges of lettuce in a skillet. Cover with chicken, beef or lamb broth and simmer just until tender. Drain. Pour Vinaigrette Sauce (page 117) over the vegetable and chill for 24 hours before serving as a salad or appetizer.*

### Cooked Vegetables As Salad

*Remember that any cold cooked vegetable may be marinated in a French-type dressing or garnished lightly with a dressing based on mayonnaise; serve in lettuce cups or on beds of salad greens. Good marinating vegetables include asparagus, broccoli, Brussels sprouts, cabbage, green beans, peas, beets, zucchini, cauliflower, Belgian endive, endive, diced or sliced potatoes and gently steamed leaf lettuces—or any combination of these.*

## ALMOND-TOPPED ARTICHOKE HEARTS

**2 10-ounce packages frozen artichoke hearts**
**3 slices dry white bread**
**½ cup blanched almonds**
**¼ cup butter or margarine**
**1 teaspoon seasoned salt**

Cook artichoke hearts according to package directions; drain. Meanwhile, break 1 slice bread into 6 pieces and drop into blender container; cover and run on speed 4 (or low) until bread is finely crumbed. Empty into bowl. Repeat process with remaining bread. Put almonds in blender container; cover and run on speed 4 (or low) until chopped. Add to bread crumbs. Melt butter in frypan; add crumb-almond mixture and seasoned salt. Cook over low heat, stirring constantly, until crumbs are browned. Add to artichoke hearts and toss lightly. *Makes 6 servings.*

## CRUMB-TOPPED ASPARAGUS

**4–5 slices dry white bread**
**2 hard-cooked eggs, shelled and quartered**
**½ cup butter or margarine**
**1 teaspoon salt**
**¼ teaspoon pepper**
**½ teaspoon dry mustard**
**2 pounds cooked asparagus spears**

Break 1 slice bread into 6 pieces and drop into blender container; cover and run on speed 4 (or low) until bread is finely crumbed. Empty into a 1-cup measure. Repeat process with remaining bread until you have 1 cup crumbs; set aside. Put eggs in blender container; cover and run on speed 4 (or low) until finely chopped. Melt butter in frypan; add bread crumbs, salt, pepper and dry mustard. Cook over low heat, stirring constantly, until crumbs are golden brown. Stir in chopped eggs. Serve hot over hot cooked asparagus. *Makes 6 servings.*

## ASPARAGUS-STUFFED ONIONS IN SAUCE

**4 medium onions**
**1 pound fresh asparagus**
**1 cup milk**
**1 egg yolk**
**½ teaspoon salt**
**½ teaspoon Worcestershire**
**2 tablespoons flour**
**2 tablespoons soft butter or margarine**
**Paprika**

Cook whole onions in boiling salted water about 30 minutes or just until tender. Cool. Slice top off each onion and remove center. Cook fresh asparagus in boiling salted water just until tender, about 15 minutes. Cut off tips about 2 inches in length; cut remaining stalks into 1-inch pieces; set aside. Stand asparagus tips up in onion shells in serving dish. Put all remaining ingredients except paprika in blender container; cover and run on speed 6 (or high) until smooth. Add cooked asparagus stalks and onion centers; cover and run on speed 4 (or low) just until vegetables are chopped. Pour into saucepan and cook, stirring constantly, until sauce is thickened. Pour sauce over asparagus-stuffed onions. Sprinkle with paprika; serve immediately. *Makes 4 servings.*

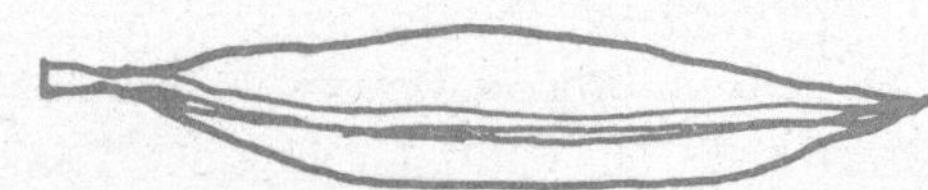

## GREEN BEANS VINAIGRETTE

**2 10-ounce packages frozen French-style green beans**
**1 cup French Dressing (page 81)**
**6 sprigs parsley**
**2–3 small sweet pickles**
**3 green onions with tops**
**1 hard-cooked egg, shelled and quartered**
**2 teaspoons capers**

Cook green beans according to package directions; drain. Put all remaining ingredients in blender container; cover and run on speed 2 (or low) about 30 seconds or until vegetables are chopped. Combine hot cooked beans with this mixture; spoon into serving dish.

If crumb topping is desired, break 2 slices dry bread into clean, dry blender container; cover and run on speed 3 (or low) until crumbed. Empty into small frypan and repeat with 2 more slices bread. Add 2 tablespoons butter or margarine to crumbs and sauté until crumbs are golden brown. Sprinkle beans with buttered crumbs and serve immediately. *Makes 6–8 servings.*

## TRIPLE BEAN BAKE

**1 10-ounce package frozen cut green beans**
**1 10-ounce package frozen Lima beans**
**1 1-pound can kidney beans, drained**
**1 cup Blender Mayonnaise (page 79)**
**2 hard-cooked eggs, shelled and quartered**
**5 green onions with tops**
**3 tablespoons lemon juice**
**1 teaspoon Worcestershire**
**1 teaspoon prepared mustard**
**¼ teaspoon garlic salt**
**Dash Tabasco**

Preheat oven to 350°. Cook green and Lima beans separately according to directions on packages; drain. Meanwhile, put all remaining ingredients in blender container; cover and run on speed 5 (or high) until smooth. Scatter ⅓ of each type of bean in 1½-quart casserole; cover with ⅓ of the sauce. Repeat until all beans and sauce are used.

If crumb topping is desired, break 2 slices dry bread into clean, dry blender container; cover and run on speed 3 (or low) until finely crumbed. Repeat process with 1 or 2 more slices. Mix crumbs with 2 tablespoons melted butter or margarine; sprinkle over beans. Bake for 30–40 minutes or until hot and bubbly. *Makes 8–10 servings.*

## LIMA BEANS SUPREME

**2 10-ounce packages frozen Lima beans**
**1 tablespoon soft butter or margarine**
**2 slices fresh white bread**
**½ teaspoon rosemary**
**½ teaspoon oregano**
**3 slices bacon, fried crisp**
**2 tablespoons butter or margarine**
**¼ clove garlic**
**2 tablespoons flour**
**¾ cup cubed Cheddar cheese**
**¾ teaspoon salt**
**¾ teaspoon dry mustard**
**1 cup milk**
**¼ small onion**
**1 canned pimiento**

Preheat oven to 350°. Cook Lima beans according to package directions; drain. Meanwhile, spread 1 tablespoon soft butter on bread. Break 1 slice into 6 pieces and drop into blender container; cover and run on speed 4 (or low) until finely crumbed. Empty into small bowl. Repeat process with second slice. Add rosemary and oregano to buttered crumbs and mix; set aside.

Put remaining ingredients except onion and pimiento in blender container; cover and run on speed 7 (or high) until mixture is perfectly smooth. Add onion and pimiento; cover and run on speed 4 (or low) until vegetables are chopped. Pour into a saucepan; cook over low heat, stirring constantly, until thick.

Put cooked Lima beans in 2-quart casserole; pour sauce over beans and mix. Top with buttered crumbs. Bake 30–35 minutes. *Makes 6 servings.*

## BEETS WITH APRICOTS

**2 bunches beets, pared and quartered**
**¼ cup butter or margarine**
**20 dried apricot halves, cut in half**
**½ cup boiling water**
**½ cup firmly packed light brown sugar**
**¼ teaspoon salt**

Put 4 pieces beets in blender container; cover and run on speed 3 (or low) until chopped. Empty into large frypan; repeat process until all beets are chopped. Add butter to beets. Put remaining ingredients in blender container; cover and run on speed 5 (or start on low, then move to high) until apricots are puréed. Add to beets in frypan; cover and cook over medium heat until beets are tender, about 30 minutes. *Makes 6 servings.*

## BROCCOLI CRUMBLE

**1 bunch broccoli, cut in spears**
**8 slices dry bread**
**¼ medium onion**
**½ cup butter or margarine, melted**
**2 hard-cooked eggs, shelled and quartered**
**1 teaspoon salt**
**½ teaspoon dry mustard**
**¼ teaspoon pepper**

Cook broccoli in boiling salted water until tender. Meanwhile, break 2 slices dry bread into blender container; cover and run on speed 3 (or low) until crumbed. Empty into frypan and repeat process until all bread is crumbed, adding the onion with the last 2 slices of bread. Sauté crumbs and onion in butter until golden brown. Put eggs in blender container; cover and run on speed 3 (or low) until chopped. If necessary, stop blender during processing and push egg toward blades with rubber spatula. Add eggs and seasonings to buttered crumb mixture. Drain broccoli. Roll hot cooked broccoli spears in crumbs. *Makes 6–8 servings.*

## BROCCOLI SOUFFLE

**1¾ cups cooked broccoli**
**1½ cups hot milk**
**¾ teaspoon salt**
**¼ teaspoon pepper**
**⅛ teaspoon nutmeg**
**¼ cup soft butter or margarine**
**3 tablespoons flour**
**6 eggs, separated**

Preheat oven to 350°. Butter a 2-quart casserole or soufflé dish. Put cooked broccoli in blender container; cover and run on speed 6 (or high) until smooth; empty into saucepan. Put milk, salt, pepper, nutmeg, butter, flour and egg yolks in blender container; cover and run on speed 2 (or low) until smooth. Add to broccoli; cook over low heat, stirring constantly, until thick. Cool slightly. Beat egg whites with an electric mixer until stiff but not dry; fold carefully and slowly into broccoli mixture. Pour into prepared casserole; bake 25 minutes or until browned and puffed. Serve immediately. *Makes 6–8 servings.*

## SCALLOPED CABBAGE

**1 small head cabbage**
**1 slice white bread, buttered**
**1¼ cups Medium No-Cook White Sauce (page 112)**

Preheat oven to 350°. Grease a 1½-quart casserole. Cut cleaned cabbage into 12–14 wedges; cook in boiling salted water 4 minutes or just until tender. Meanwhile, break buttered bread into 6 pieces and drop into blender container; cover and run on speed 4 (or low) until finely crumbed. Empty onto waxed paper. Drain cabbage and put in casserole; pour White Sauce over cabbage and top with buttered crumbs. Bake 20 minutes. *Makes 6 servings.*

## SWEET AND SOUR RED CABBAGE

**½ head cabbage, coarsely cut**
**1 apple, cored and diced**
**1 medium onion, diced**
**6 tablespoons sugar**
**½ cup water**
**1 cup red wine vinegar**

Fill blender container to top cup marking with cut cabbage, apple and onion; add cold water just to cover. Cover container and run on speed 7 (or high) just until contents go through the blades once (do not run too long or they will be liquefied). Drain in a colander or sieve; empty into saucepan. Repeat process until all are chopped. Add remaining ingredients to saucepan; cover and simmer 1 hour. *Makes 4 servings.*

*Broccoli Soufflé (p. 122)*

## CARROT CUTLETS

**5 slices fresh white bread**
**1 egg**
**1½ cups cooked diced carrots, drained**
**1 slice onion**
**¼ cup cubed Cheddar cheese**
**¾ teaspoon salt**
**⅛ teaspoon pepper**
**2 tablespoons butter or margarine**

Break 1 slice bread into 6 pieces; drop into blender container. Cover container and run on speed 4 (or low) until bread is finely crumbed. Empty into bowl. Repeat process with remaining bread; set aside. Put remaining ingredients except butter in blender container; cover and run on speed 6 (or high) until mixture is smooth. Measure 2 cups bread crumbs; stir into carrot mixture. Shape mixture into 8 patties; roll each patty in remainder of bread crumbs. Fry in hot butter until heated through and browned, about 3 minutes on each side. *Makes 8 cutlets.*

## JIFFY CARROTS

**½ cup water**
**2 tablespoons butter or margarine**
**¾ teaspoon salt**
**¼ teaspoon pepper**
**¼ cup firmly packed brown sugar**
**1 tablespoon cornstarch**
**½ teaspoon sweet basil**
**2 cups sliced raw carrots**

Put all ingredients in blender container in order listed; cover and run on speed 4 (or low) until carrots are chopped. Pour into a saucepan and cook over moderate heat for 15 minutes, stirring constantly. *Makes 4 servings.*

## CANDIED CARROTS

**1 bunch carrots, sliced diagonally**
**¼ cup butter or margarine**
**¼ cup jellied cranberry sauce**
**1 2-inch square orange peel (colored portion only)**
**2 tablespoons brown sugar**
**½ teaspoon salt**

Cook carrots in boiling salted water until tender. Put in a shallow flame-proof casserole. Put remaining ingredients in blender container; cover and run on speed 4 (or high) until well blended. Spoon cranberry mixture over carrots; place under broiler and broil 4–5 minutes or until glazed. *Makes 6 servings.*

## CHEESE-FROSTED CAULIFLOWER

**1 medium head cauliflower**
**½ cup Blender Mayonnaise (page 79)**
**2 teaspoons prepared mustard**
**½ pound sharp American cheese, cubed (about 2 cups)**
**Paprika**

Cook whole cauliflower in boiling salted water until tender. Drain. Preheat oven to 375°. Meanwhile, put mayonnaise and mustard in blender container; cover and run on speed 2 (or low) a few seconds. Add cheese slowly, while blender is running. If necessary, stop blender during processing and push ingredients toward blades with rubber spatula. When all cheese is grated, spread mixture over the hot cauliflower. Bake for 10 minutes or until cheese melts. Sprinkle with paprika. *Makes 6 servings.*

## CORN FONDUE

**4 slices white bread**
**1 cup milk**
**Small piece green pepper**
**¼ small onion**
**2 eggs**
**¾ teaspoon salt**
**⅛ teaspoon pepper**
**2 tablespoons butter or margarine**
**1½ cups cooked whole-kernel corn OR 12-ounce can whole-kernel corn**

Preheat oven to 350°. Grease a 1-quart casserole. Break 1 slice bread into 6 pieces and drop into blender container; cover and run on speed 4 (or low) until finely crumbed. Empty into casserole. Repeat process with remaining bread. Put remaining ingredients except corn in blender container; cover and run on speed 3 (or low) until onion and pepper are chopped. Pour over crumbs; add corn and mix well. Bake about 1 hour or until a silver knife inserted in center comes out clean. *Makes 4 servings.*

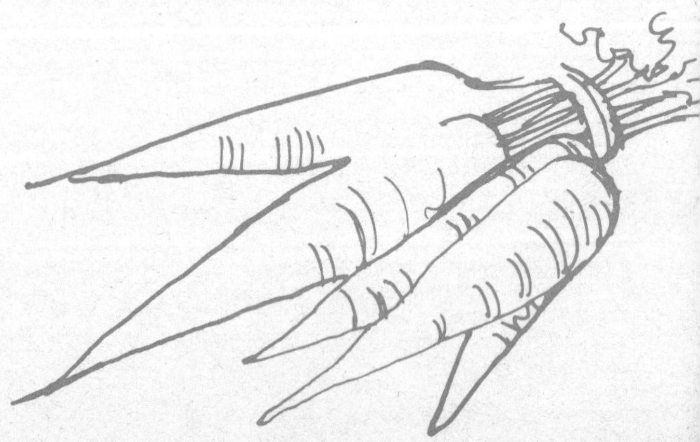

## SWISS-STYLE CORN

**2 12-ounce cans (3 cups) whole-kernel corn**
**½ cup milk**
**½ canned pimiento**
**2 sprigs parsley**
**1 green onion with top**
**3 tablespoons flour**
**¼ teaspoon salt**
**¼ teaspoon celery salt**
**⅛ teaspoon pepper**
**3 slices dry bread or toast**
**¼ pound brick cheese, cubed (about 1 cup)**

Preheat oven to 350°. Drain corn, reserving ¼ cup of the liquid. Put corn in a 1-quart casserole. Put corn liquid, milk, pimiento, parsley, green onion, flour and seasonings in blender container; cover and run on speed 3 (or low) until smooth. Pour over corn; stir to blend. Break 1 slice dry bread into clean, dry blender container; cover and run on speed 3 (or low) until finely crumbed; empty into small bowl. Repeat process until all bread is crumbed.

Put a few cubes of cheese in blender container; cover and run on speed 3 (or low) until grated. Remove cover and slowly add remaining cheese while blender is running. If necessary, stop blender during processing and push ingredients toward blades with rubber spatula. Empty into bowl with crumbs; mix well. Sprinkle crumbs and cheese over corn mixture in casserole. Bake for 30 minutes or until hot and bubbly. *Makes 4–6 servings.*

## ITALIAN EGGPLANT

**1 9-ounce can (1 cup) tomato sauce**
**1 medium onion, quartered**
**½ large green pepper, seeded and cut up**
**1 clove garlic**
**3 tablespoons butter or margarine**
**½ teaspoon oregano**
**¼ pound Mozzarella cheese, cubed (about 1 cup)**
**8 slices dry bread**
**¼ cup milk**
**1 egg**
**1 medium eggplant, pared and sliced**
**Flour**
**Fat or salad oil**
**Grated Parmesan cheese**

Put tomato sauce, onion, green pepper, garlic, butter and oregano in blender container; cover and run on speed 3 (or low) until smooth. Empty into saucepan; heat to boiling and simmer for 15 minutes.

Put a few cubes of Mozzarella cheese in clean, dry blender container; cover and run on speed 2 (or low) until cheese is grated. Remove cover and slowly add remaining Mozzarella cheese while blender is running. If necessary, stop blender during processing and push cheese toward blades with rubber spatula. Empty into small bowl; set aside.

Break 2 slices bread into blender container; cover and run on speed 3 (or low) until crumbed. Empty into a shallow bowl or pie pan. Repeat until all bread is crumbed. Put milk and egg in blender container; cover and run on speed 2 (or low) a few seconds. Pour into another shallow bowl or pie pan. Dip eggplant slices into flour, then into egg–milk mixture and finally into crumbs. Fry in shallow hot fat until tender and lightly browned on both sides. Arrange browned eggplant slices in a 13x9½x2-inch flame-proof baking dish. Cover with hot tomato sauce; sprinkle with grated Mozzarella cheese and grated Parmesan cheese. Place under broiler 3–5 minutes or until cheese melts. *Makes 6–8 servings.*

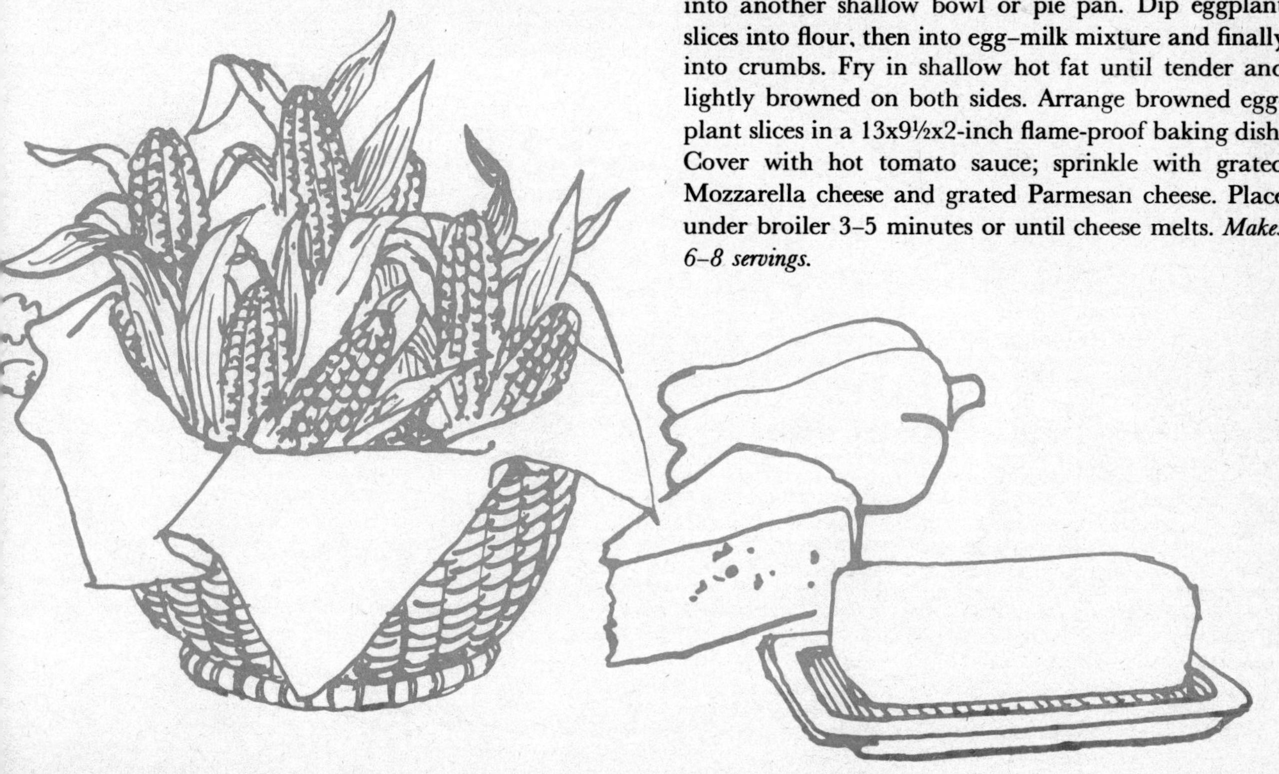

*Candied Carrots (p. 124)*

*Grated Potato Casserole (p. 127)*

*Cheese-frosted Cauliflower (p. 121)*

## MUSHROOMS IN SPINACH SAUCE

**½ pound fresh mushrooms, sliced**
**4 tablespoons butter or margarine**
**1 clove garlic**
**3 tablespoons flour**
**1 cup light cream**
**½ teaspoon salt**
**⅛ teaspoon white pepper**
**2 pounds spinach, washed**

Sauté mushrooms in 2 tablespoons butter for 5 minutes; set aside. Put remaining 2 tablespoons butter, garlic, flour, cream, salt and pepper in blender container; cover and run on speed 6 (or high) until smooth. Pour into saucepan; cook over low heat, stirring constantly, until thickened. Cook spinach (in a pan with a tightly fitting cover) just in water which clings to the leaves after washing. Cook until wilted but still bright green. Drain. Put cream sauce and spinach in blender container; cover and run on speed 4 (or low) just until all spinach goes through the blades once. Combine with mushrooms; serve immediately. *Makes 6 servings.*

## PEAS AND ONIONS IN MUSTARD SAUCE

**2 10-ounce packages frozen peas**
**1 1-pound can (2 cups) small white onions, drained**
**Double recipe Medium No-Cook White Sauce (page 112)**
**2 tablespoons white vinegar**
**2 tablespoons lemon juice**
**½ teaspoon dry mustard**

Cook peas according to package directions; add onions during last 8 minutes of cooking. Make Medium No-Cook White Sauce, adding vinegar, lemon juice, dry mustard (and a pinch of saffron, if desired) before adding bread. Pour hot sauce over drained cooked vegetables. Serve immediately. *Makes 8 servings.*

### PREPARE INSTANT MASHED POTATOES

Heat the milk and butter for four servings of instant mashed potato almost to boiling; put in blender container with salt. While running blender on speed 7 (or high) add instant mashed potatoes. Run just until potatoes are thickened. Empty into a bowl; serve immediately.

## GRATED POTATO CASSEROLE

**1 cup milk**
**3 eggs**
**1½ teaspoons salt**
**⅛ teaspoon pepper**
**1 cup cubed Cheddar cheese**
**2 tablespoons soft butter or margarine**
**½ green pepper, seeded and cut up**
**1 small onion, quartered**
**4 medium potatoes, pared and cubed**

Preheat oven to 350°. Grease 1½-quart casserole. Put all ingredients in blender container in order listed; cover and run on speed 6 (or high) just until all potatoes go through the blades (do not overblend). Pour into casserole and bake 1 hour. *Makes 6 servings.*

## SAVORY SCALLOPED POTATOES

**3 slices white bread, buttered**
**6 medium potatoes, pared and sliced thinly**
**Salt and pepper**
**Onion salt**
**1¾ cups milk**

Preheat oven to 350°. Grease 1½-quart casserole. Break 1 slice buttered bread into 6 pieces and drop into blender container; cover and run on speed 4 (or low) until finely crumbed. Empty onto waxed paper. Repeat process with remaining bread. Put ⅓ of the potato slices into casserole; sprinkle with salt, pepper and onion salt, then with ⅓ of buttered crumbs. Repeat process twice, ending with buttered crumbs. Add milk, pouring carefully down the side. Cover and bake 30 minutes; uncover and bake 30 minutes longer. *Makes 6 servings.*

#### CHEESE SCALLOPED POTATOES

Cube ½ cup sharp Cheddar cheese. Follow directions for Savory Scalloped Potatoes, but put ⅓ of the cubed cheese in blender container with each slice buttered bread; cover and run on speed 4 (or low) until bread is crumbed and cheese is grated. Complete as above.

## ROSY SAUERKRAUT-CHEESE BAKE

**15–18 soda crackers**
**¼ pound sharp Cheddar cheese, cubed (about 1 cup)**
**1 small onion, quartered**
**1½ cups canned tomatoes**
**1 teaspoon salt**
**⅛ teaspoon pepper**
**1 1-pound 11-ounce can (3½ cups) sauerkraut**
**2 tablespoons butter or margarine**

Preheat oven to 350°. Break 4 or 5 crackers into blender container; cover and run on speed 3 (or low) until crumbed. Empty into measuring cup or bowl. Repeat until you have 1 cup crumbs. Put a few cubes of cheese in blender container; cover and run on speed 3 (or low) until grated. Remove cover and slowly add remaining cheese while blender is running. If necessary, stop blender during processing and push cheese toward blades with rubber spatula. Empty into mixing bowl and set aside ¼ cup grated cheese. Put onion, tomatoes and seasonings in blender container; cover and run on speed 4 (or high) about 10 seconds or until onion is chopped. Add with cracker crumbs and sauerkraut to cheese in mixing bowl; mix well. Pour into a 2-quart casserole; dot with butter and sprinkle with reserved cheese. Bake 45 minutes or until hot. *Makes 6–8 servings.*

## VEGETABLE SOUFFLE

*A wonderful leftover idea for any vegetable.*

**¾ cup milk**
**¼ cup soft butter**
**4 eggs, separated**
**¼ cup flour**
**1 slice onion**
**1 teaspoon salt**
**⅛ teaspoon pepper**
**½ cup diced cheese (Cheddar or American)**
**2 cups packed washed raw spinach OR 1½ cups diced raw carrot**
**Paprika**

Preheat oven to 350°. Grease a 2-quart casserole. Put all ingredients except egg whites in blender container; cover and run on speed 4 (or low) until spinach is cut fine. Pour into saucepan and cook over moderate heat, stirring until thickened. Cool slightly.

Beat egg whites with an electric mixer until stiff. Fold spinach mixture into egg whites. Turn into casserole, sprinkle with paprika and bake 50-60 minutes. Serve immediately. Good with Tomato or Mushroom Sauce. *Makes 4–6 servings.*

## SPINACH AU GRATIN

**1 cup corn flakes**
**¾ cup hot milk**
**2 tablespoons butter or margarine**
**1½ tablespoons flour**
**¼ teaspoon salt**
**½ teaspoon dry mustard**
**½ teaspoon monosodium glutamate**
**4 ounces Cheddar cheese, cubed (about 1 cup)**
**2½ cups cooked drained spinach**

Preheat oven to 375°. Put corn flakes in blender container; cover and run on speed 4 (or low) until finely crumbed. Empty onto waxed paper; set aside. Put remaining ingredients except spinach in blender container; cover and run on speed 6 (or high) until mixture is smooth. Empty into saucepan; cook over low heat, stirring constantly, until sauce is thickened. Add spinach; mix well. Pour into a 1½-quart casserole; sprinkle crumbs over top. Bake 25 minutes. *Makes 6 servings.*

## CRUSTY PECAN SQUASH

**1 medium butternut squash, pared, seeded and cut up**
**¾ cup pecans**
**⅓ cup sugar**
**½ teaspoon cinnamon**
**2 tablespoons maple syrup**

Cook squash in boiling salted water until tender. Drain. Meanwhile, put pecans in blender container; cover and run on speed 3 (or low) until coarsely chopped; empty into a small bowl; reserve. Put squash, sugar and cinnamon in blender container; cover and run on speed 3 (or low) until squash is puréed. Empty into 1-quart flame-proof casserole; top with chopped nuts and drizzle with syrup. Place under the broiler for 3–5 minutes or until glazed and browned. *Makes 4–6 servings.*

## BAKED ACORN SQUASH WITH APPLES

**4 medium acorn squash**
**6 large tart apples, pared, cored and quartered**
**2 tablespoons lemon juice**
**⅓ pound sharp Cheddar cheese, cubed (about 1½ cups)**
**½ cup firmly packed brown sugar**
**½ teaspoon cinnamon**
**Butter or margarine**

Preheat oven to 350°. Cut squash in half and remove seeds; place cut side down on shallow baking pan. Bake 30 minutes.

Meanwhile, put 4 pieces of apple in blender container; cover and run on speed 3 (or low) until chopped. Empty into a mixing bowl. Repeat process until all apples are chopped; sprinkle with lemon juice. Put a few cubes of cheese in clean, dry blender container; cover and run on speed 3 (or low) until cheese is grated. While blender is running, slowly add a few additional pieces of cheese at a time. If necessary, stop blender during processing and push cheese toward blades with rubber spatula. Add brown sugar and cinnamon to apple-cheese mixture; mix well. Turn squash over and fill with apple mixture; dot each half with butter. Return to oven for 30 minutes or until squash is tender and apples are cooked. *Makes 8 servings.*

## SOUTH-OF-THE-BORDER SUCCOTASH

**1 10-ounce package frozen baby Lima beans**
**1 10-ounce package frozen whole-kernel corn**
**2 eggs**
**2 tablespoons catsup**
**¼ cup water**
**1 slice onion**
**¼ green pepper, seeded**
**1 teaspoon salt**
**⅛ teaspoon pepper**
**½ teaspoon chili powder**
**3 tablespoons soft butter or margarine**

Preheat oven to 325°. Cook Lima beans and corn separately, according to directions on packages; drain. Put in buttered 1½-quart casserole.

Meanwhile, put all remaining ingredients in blender container; cover and run on speed 4 (or low) until green pepper and onion are chopped. Pour over Lima beans and corn; stir to mix. Bake uncovered 45 minutes. *Makes 4 servings.*

## ORANGE-BAKED SWEET POTATOES

**2 1-pound 2-ounce cans sweet potatoes, drained**
**¼ cup butter or margarine**
**1 small unpeeled orange, cut into chunks**
**⅓ cup firmly packed brown sugar**
**¼ teaspoon salt**
**Dash nutmeg**
**Dash ginger**

Preheat oven to 350°. Slice sweet potatoes into a 9x9x2-inch baking dish. Put remaining ingredients in blender container in order listed; cover and run on speed 2 (or low) until orange is finely chopped. If necessary, stop blender during processing and push ingredients toward blades with rubber spatula. Spoon over sweet potatoes. Bake for 30 minutes. *Makes 6–8 servings.*

## EGG-STUFFED TOMATOES

**6 large tomatoes**
**8 hard-cooked eggs, shelled and quartered**
**½ stalk celery, cut up**
**⅓ green pepper, seeded**
**¼ medium onion**
**¼ cup lemon juice**
**¼ cup mayonnaise**
**2 teaspoons prepared mustard**
**1 teaspoon salt**
**3 slices bread**
**2 tablespoons butter or margarine, melted**

Preheat oven to 425°. Cut stem ends from tomatoes and scoop out pulp; turn upside down on paper towels to drain. Put 2 eggs in blender container; cover and run on speed 3 (or low) until chopped. Empty into mixing bowl. Repeat process until all eggs are chopped.

Put celery, green pepper, onion, lemon juice, mayonnaise, mustard and salt in blender container; cover and run on speed 3 (or low) until smooth. Add to eggs in mixing bowl and mix well. Fill tomatoes with egg mixture; place in a 10x6x1½-inch baking dish.

Tear 1 slice bread into 6 pieces and put in blender container; cover and run on speed 3 (or low) until crumbed. Empty into a small bowl. Repeat process with remaining bread. Toss crumbs with melted butter; sprinkle over tops of stuffed tomatoes. Bake 10 minutes or until hot. *Makes 6 servings.*

## BAKED STUFFED TOMATOES

**6 medium tomatoes**
**3 slices white bread**
**1 slice white bread, buttered**
**¼ cup cubed Cheddar cheese**
**1 teaspoon prepared horseradish**
**1 tablespoon Worcestershire**
**1 teaspoon salt**
**1 4-ounce can mushrooms, drained**

Preheat oven to 350°. Wash tomatoes; cut off tops. Hollow out tomatoes, leaving a thick outer shell; reserve pulp. Put tomato shells in a 9x9x2-inch square pan; set aside. Break 1 slice white bread into 6 pieces and drop into blender container; cover and run on speed 4 (or high) until coarsely crumbed; empty into a medium bowl. Repeat with remaining slices of bread. Break the slice of buttered bread into 6 pieces and drop into blender container; add cheese; cover and run on speed 4 (or high) until bread is crumbed and cheese grated. Empty onto a piece of waxed paper; set aside. Put tomato pulp, horseradish, Worcestershire and salt in blender container; cover and run on speed 6 (or high) until smooth. Add mushrooms to bread crumbs in bowl; mix. Stuff tomato shells with crumb-tomato mixture. Sprinkle buttered cheese-crumbs over top of each. Bake 30 minutes. *Makes 6 servings.*

***SERVE-ALONGS***

*Rosy Sauerkraut Cheese Bake with roast bologna*
*Spinach au Gratin with broiled fish*
*Orange Baked Sweet Potatoes*
*with roast duck or chicken*

## TURNIP CASSEROLE

**3 slices fresh white bread**
**1 tablespoon soft butter or margarine**
**2 eggs**
**3 tablespoons soft butter or margarine**
**2 tablespoons sugar**
**1¼ teaspoons salt**
**⅛ teaspoon pepper**
**½ teaspoon dill**
**3 cups cooked cubed yellow or white turnip**

Preheat oven to 350°. Butter 1½-quart casserole. Break 1 slice bread into 6 pieces and drop into blender container; cover and run on speed 4 (or low) until crumbed. Empty into casserole. Repeat with another slice bread.

Spread 1 tablespoon butter on remaining slice bread; break into 6 pieces and drop into blender container. Cover and run on speed 4 (or low) until bread is crumbed; empty into small bowl and set aside. Put remaining ingredients in blender container in order listed; cover and run on speed 7 (or high) until perfectly smooth. Add turnip mixture to crumbs in casserole; mix well. Sprinkle buttered crumbs over top. Bake 35 minutes. *Makes 4 servings.*

## ROMAN ZUCCHINI

**4–5 medium tomatoes, quartered**
**1 medium onion, quartered**
**½ green pepper, seeded and cut up**
**1 stalk celery, cut up**
**1 clove garlic**
**½ teaspoon salt**
**5–6 cups sliced zucchini**
**2 tablespoons butter or margarine**

Put 4 tomatoes in blender container; cover and run on speed 5 (or high) until puréed. Measure. If necessary, add remaining tomato. You should have 1½ cups purée. Add onion, green pepper, celery, garlic and salt; cover and run on speed 5 (or high) until vegetables are chopped. Pour tomato mixture into large frypan; add zucchini and butter. Cook until squash is tender, stirring occasionally. *Makes 4–6 servings.*

*Baked Stuffed Tomatoes*

# Fill Up the Breadbasket

*The blender is a real time-saver when used in the preparation of quick breads and yeast breads. In fact, the beating time necessary for good yeast breads is only a matter of seconds with the blender. And best of all, the tedious task of kneading is completely unnecessary.*

*Smooth batters for pancakes can be made in an instant and poured right from the blender container onto the griddle. You can whip up popover batter, too, almost instantaneously. For coffee cakes, fruit breads and muffins, all the necessary chopping can be done by the blender and the chopped ingredients are often combined with the batter just as quickly—with the blender, of course. Only a few strokes with the spoon are left for the cook.*

## YEAST BREAD AND ROLLS
### (Basic Recipe)

**1 cup milk**
**1 package dry yeast**
**3 cups white flour**
**¼ cup cooking oil**
**1 egg**
**1 teaspoon salt**
**2 tablespoons sugar**

Heat milk to scalding; cool to lukewarm. Put lukewarm milk and yeast in blender container; let stand 5 minutes. Meanwhile, measure flour into a bowl. Cover container and run on speed 5 (or high) for 20 seconds. Add shortening, egg, salt and sugar; cover and run on speed 5 (or high) for 5 seconds. Pour into the bowl of flour; stir until thoroughly mixed. Cover and let rise 1½ hours or until double in bulk. Stir down. Turn out onto a lightly floured board. Shape into 1 loaf or 24 rolls (see instructions below and right). Let rise 45 minutes or until doubled in bulk. Bake in oven preheated to 375° as directed. Remove from pan and cool on wire rack.

**To make 1 loaf of bread:** Form dough into a smooth oval on floured board. Turn over; pinch a seam in center. Turn ends under and pinch seams. Put loaf in a greased 9x5x3-inch loaf pan, seam side down. After doubled in bulk, bake 45 minutes.

**To make clover-leaf rolls:** Divide dough into 24 equal pieces; divide each of these pieces into 3 parts and form into balls. Grease muffin tins; put 3 balls in each tin. After doubled in bulk, bake 25 minutes.

**To make dinner rolls:** Divide dough into 24 equal pieces; form each into a ball. Grease muffin tins; put one ball in each tin. After doubled in bulk, bake 25 minutes.

#### POPPY SEED ROLLS

Make dinner rolls. Before putting in muffin tins, dip top of each roll in melted butter or margarine, then in poppy seeds.

#### ONION BREAD

Use ½ cup condensed onion soup and ½ cup milk in place of 1 cup milk in basic recipe. Complete as directed for bread.

#### CINNAMON BREAD

Make basic recipe. After doubled in bulk the first time, turn out on a floured board and pat out into a 10x16-inch rectangle. Sprinkle surface with a mixture of 3 tablespoons sugar and 1 tablespoon cinnamon. Roll up, from narrow end, as for jelly roll. Pinch closed. Fold under ends; pinch closed. Complete as directed for bread.

#### RYE BREAD OR ROLLS

Use 1½ cups white flour and 1½ cups rye flour in place of 3 cups white flour in basic recipe. Complete as directed for basic recipe.

#### HERB BREAD OR ROLLS

Mix 1½ teaspoons basil OR 1½ teaspoons thyme with flour in bowl before adding blended ingredients. Complete as directed for basic recipe.

#### ORANGE RAISIN LOAF

Use 1 cup lukewarm orange juice in place of milk in basic recipe. Omit sugar; add rind of ¼ orange (colored portion only) and ½ cup raisins to contents of blender container with the shortening, egg and salt. Complete as directed for bread.

#### GRAHAM DATE LOAF

Use 1½ cups white flour and 1½ cups graham flour in place of 3 cups white flour in basic recipe. Add ½ cup pitted dates and ½ cup walnuts to blender container with shortening, sugar, eggs and salt. Complete as directed for bread.

## MUFFINS

**2 cups sifted flour**
**2½ teaspoons baking powder**
**½ teaspoon salt**
**2 tablespoons sugar**
**1 cup milk**
**1 egg**
**½ cup soft shortening**

Preheat oven to 400°. Grease 14 medium muffin tins. Sift together flour, baking powder, salt and sugar into a medium bowl. Put remaining ingredients in blender container; cover and run on speed 4 (or low) until well mixed. Add to dry ingredients in bowl and stir just until all flour is moistened. Fill tins ⅔ full. Bake 20-25 minutes or until done. *Makes 14 muffins.*

### DATE-NUT MUFFINS

Add ¾ cup pitted dates and ¼ cup walnuts to ingredients in blender container; cover and run on speed 4 (or low) until dates and nuts are finely chopped. Complete as directed for basic recipe.

### RAISIN MUFFINS

Add 1 cup seedless raisins to ingredients in blender container; cover and run on speed 4 (or low) until raisins are finely chopped. Complete as directed for basic recipe.

### CARROT MUFFINS

Add 1 raw carrot, scraped and cut into 1-inch pieces, to ingredients in blender container; cover and run on speed 4 (or low) until carrots are very finely chopped. Complete as directed for basic recipe.

### GRAHAM MUFFINS

Use 1 cup sifted flour in place of the 2 cups in basic recipe. After blending liquid ingredients, break 16 graham crackers into blender container with liquid ingredients; cover container and run on speed 6 (or high) until smooth. Add to dry ingredients and complete as directed.

### MIXING PANCAKES FROM PREPARED MIX

Using proportions recommended on the package, put liquid and eggs in blender container; add pancake mix. Cover container and run on speed 6 (or high) just until smooth. Bake as directed.

## QUICK PANCAKES

**1¾ cups milk**
**2 eggs**
**¼ cup soft shortening**
**2 cups sifted flour**
**2½ teaspoons baking powder**
**1 teaspoon salt**

Have all ingredients room temperature. Put all ingredients in blender container in order listed; cover and run on speed 5 (or high) just until ingredients are combined. Pour about ¼ cup batter on lightly greased preheated frypan or griddle. Brown on one side, turn and brown on other side. *Makes sixteen-eighteen 4-inch pancakes.*

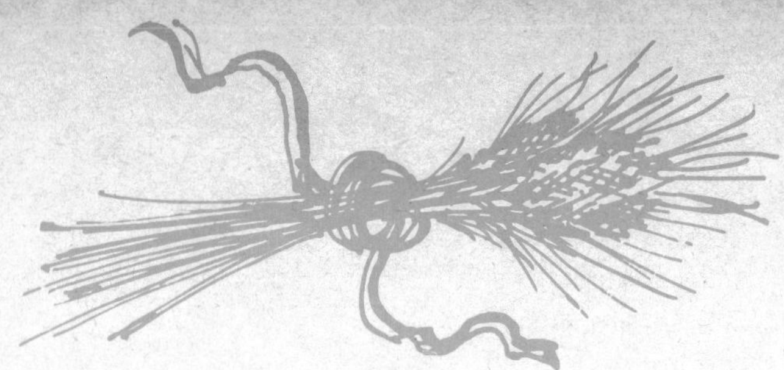

## COTTAGE CHEESE PANCAKES

**½ cup light cream**
**1 cup creamed cottage cheese**
**2 eggs**
**2 tablespoons sugar**
**3½ tablespoons flour**
**½ teaspoon salt**
**½ teaspoon baking powder**
**Butter or margarine**

Put cream, cottage cheese and eggs in blender container; cover and run on speed 7 (or high) until completely smooth. Add remaining ingredients except butter; cover and run on speed 5 (or high) just until mixed. Melt a small amount of butter in a frypan or on a griddle; for each pancake, spoon 1 tablespoon batter onto hot cooking surface. Brown on both sides, turning once. Serve immediately. Delicious when topped with sour cream and sweetened sliced strawberries. *Makes thirty 3-inch pancakes.*

*Quick Pancakes*

## DRIED BEEF GRIDDLE CAKES

**1¾ cups milk**
**1 egg**
**2 tablespoons soft shortening**
**½ teaspoon prepared mustard**
**2 cups pancake mix**
**1 cup dried beef**

Preheat griddle. Put milk, egg, shortening, mustard and pancake mix in blender container; cover and run on speed 5 (or high) until smooth. Add dried beef and run on speed 6 (or high) for 15 seconds or until finely chopped. Pour about ¼ cup batter on lightly greased griddle. Brown on one side, turn and brown on other side. If desired, serve with Deviled Olive Sauce (page112) or canned cream of mushroom soup, prepared as directed for sauce. *Makes sixteen-eighteen 4-inch pancakes.*

*For Sunday supper, serve Waffles with Strawberry Butter (p. 54) and grilled ham.*

## WAFFLES

**2 cups sifted flour**
**3 teaspoons baking powder**
**2 tablespoons sugar**
**¾ teaspoon salt**
**2 eggs, separated**
**1⅔ cups milk**
**½ cup soft shortening**

Have all ingredients room temperature. Preheat waffle baker. Sift flour, baking powder, sugar and salt together into a medium bowl. Put egg yolks, milk and shortening in blender container; cover and run on speed 5 (or high) until blended. Pour this mixture over dry ingredients and stir until smooth. Beat egg whites with an electric mixer until stiff but not dry; fold into batter. Bake according to manufacturer's directions or until baker stops steaming. *Makes 3 large square or six 7-inch waffles.*

### CHEESY WAFFLES

Add 1 cup diced Cheddar cheese to ingredients in blender container; cover and run on speed 5 (or high) until cheese is completely smooth. Complete batter as directed for waffles.

## POPOVERS

**2 cups milk**
**6 eggs**
**1 teaspoon salt**
**4 teaspoons butter or margarine**
**2 cups sifted flour**

Preheat oven to 450°. Grease 16 heat-resistant glass custard cups or popover pans thoroughly with shortening or cooking oil; preheat in oven for 15 minutes. Put all ingredients in blender container in order listed; cover and run on speed 6 (or high) until thoroughly combined. Fill preheated cups or pans ½ full. Bake 450° for 10 minutes; reduce temperature to 350° and bake 40 minutes longer. Serve immediately. *Makes 16 large popovers.*

**Note:** If a drier interior is desired, puncture top of each popover with a sharp-tined fork and allow steam to escape after baking; return to oven with the heat turned off and allow popovers to dry 10 minutes.

## APPLE FRITTERS

**1½ cups sifted flour**
**¼ cup sugar**
**⅛ teaspoon salt**
**2 teaspoons baking powder**
**½ cup milk**
**2 eggs**
**2 cooking apples, washed, cored and quartered**
**Powdered sugar**

Sift flour, sugar, salt and baking powder together into a medium bowl; set aside. Put milk, eggs and apples in blender container; cover and run on speed 4 (or low) just until apples go through the blades once (do not overblend or apples will be liquefied). Stir apple mixture into dry ingredients just until batter is smooth. Drop batter by teaspoonfuls into deep fat heated to 370°; fry until fritters are golden brown. Drain on absorbent paper; sprinkle with powdered sugar. *Makes about 30 fritters.*

## HOLIDAY ORANGE-BANANA BREAD

**2 cups sifted flour**
**3 teaspoons baking powder**
**½ teaspoon salt**
**1 cup mixed candied fruit**
**¾ cup walnuts**
**2 eggs**
**6 tablespoons soft shortening**
**1 small banana, peeled and quartered**
**1 small orange, quartered, peeled and seeded**
**½ cup sugar**

Preheat oven to 350°. Grease a 9x5x3-inch loaf pan; line with waxed paper. Sift flour, baking powder and salt together into a medium bowl. Add candied fruit and mix well. Put nuts in blender container; cover and run on speed 4 (or low) until coarsely chopped. Stir nuts into flour-fruit mixture. Put remaining ingredients in blender container in order listed; cover and run on speed 6 (or high) until completely smooth. Add to flour mixture in bowl and mix thoroughly. Pack batter into prepared pan and bake 1 hour or until done. Cool about 20 minutes before turning out on rack; remove paper. If desired, frost with confectioners' sugar icing and decorate with candied fruit. *Makes 1 loaf.*

## APRICOT AND BANANA BREAD

**1¼ cups sifted flour**
**1 teaspoon baking powder**
**½ teaspoon salt**
**½ teaspoon soda**
**1 cup whole bran**
**½ cup walnuts**
**2 eggs**
**⅓ cup shortening**
**⅔ cup sugar**
**¼ cup buttermilk**
**3 ripe bananas, peeled and cut up**
**1 cup dried apricots**

Preheat oven to 350°. Grease a 9x5x3-inch loaf pan. Sift together flour, baking powder, salt and soda into a medium bowl; add whole bran. Put nuts in blender container; cover and run on speed 4 (or low) until chopped; add to flour mixture. Put eggs, shortening, sugar and buttermilk in blender container; run on speed 6 (or high) to mix. Add bananas while blender is running; blend until completely liquefied. Stop blender and add apricots; run on speed 5 (or high) until all apricots are coarsely chopped. Add to dry ingredients; stir well and pour into prepared pan. Bake 45 minutes or until done. *Makes 1 loaf.*

## LEMON-NUT COFFEE CAKE

**Topping (below)**
**2 cups prepared biscuit mix**
**Chopped walnuts (from Topping)**
**½ cup milk**
**1 egg**
**½ cup firmly packed brown sugar**
**3 tablespoons butter or margarine, melted**
**1 tablespoon lemon juice**
**Rind of ½ lemon (colored portion only)**

Preheat oven to 400°. Have all ingredients room temperature. Grease an 8x8x2-inch pan. First, make Topping (below).

Measure biscuit mix into the medium bowl with reserved chopped walnuts. Put milk, egg, brown sugar, melted butter, lemon juice and rind in blender container; cover and run on speed 6 (or high) until lemon rind is finely cut. Add to biscuit mix; stir just until all dry ingredients are moistened. Pour batter into prepared pan; sprinkle evenly with Topping and bake 25 minutes or until coffee cake tests done. *Makes 9 servings.*

### TOPPING

**1 cup walnuts**
**1 cup cornflakes**
**¼ cup sugar**
**½ teaspoon cinnamon**
**¼ cup butter or shortening, melted**

Put walnuts in blender container; cover and run on speed 4 (or low) until nuts are finely chopped. Put half the nuts in small bowl; reserve remaining nuts in a medium bowl for use in coffee cake batter.

Put cornflakes in blender container; cover and run on speed 4 (or low) until flakes are crushed. Empty into the small bowl with nuts; add sugar, cinnamon and butter; stir well.

***LITTLE MEALS***

*For little meals with special appeal,*
*serve cream cheese or cottage cheese*
*with Holiday Orange-Banana Bread,*
*Apricot Banana Bread or Lemon Nut Coffee Cake.*

## SPICY ORANGE DROP DOUGHNUTS

**1½ cups sifted flour**
**2 teaspoons baking powder**
**½ teaspoon salt**
**½ teaspoon nutmeg**
**¼ teaspoon cinnamon**
**⅛ teaspoon cloves**
**½ cup milk**
**Rind of ½ orange (colored portion only)**
**1 egg**
**2 tablespoons fat, melted**
**½ cup sugar**

Sift the first 6 ingredients together into a bowl or onto waxed paper. Put remaining ingredients in blender container; cover and run on speed 4 (or low) until orange rind is finely chopped. Add half the dry ingredients to mixture in container; cover and run on speed 4 (or low) just until mixed, about 5 seconds. Add remaining dry ingredients; cover and run on speed 6 (or high) just until combined. If necessary, stop blender during processing and push batter toward blades with rubber spatula. Drop by teaspoonfuls into hot fat (365° on a deep-frying thermometer or when a 1-inch cube of bread browns in 60 seconds). Fry about 4 minutes or until browned on all sides. Drain on absorbent paper. Coat with granulated, confectioners' or powdered sugar. *Makes 24 doughnuts.*

### AT-HOME POWDERED SUGAR

You can make it easily and quickly with granulated sugar and your blender. Put about ½–1 cup granulated sugar in standard Mason jar and screw on cutting assembly. Run on speed 7 (or high) until pulverized.

# Happy Endings

*One of the most popular uses for the blender is the making of desserts. As you browse through the hundred-plus recipes in this chapter, the reason for this will become clear. How easily, and with what variety, table glamor is achieved when the blender is at work!*

*Note Fresh Applesauce, Fruit Chiffon, Peach Orange Sherbet and Chocolate Bavarian for evidence of the blender genius at work. The Chocolate Bavarian is especially exciting to make, since the blender does everything—including liquefying the chocolate.*

*Other desserts, if not immediately ready for the table, can be blender-prepared with a fraction of the time and effort needed for the traditional operation. Cheesecake, a popular dessert choice in restaurants, is seldom made at home. Who wants to spend a half hour pushing cottage cheese through a sieve, another half hour crumbing the graham crackers or zwieback, beating the eggs and putting everything together, then a third half hour cleaning sieves, spoons, spatulas, cups, bowls, board...and the kitchen floor? With the blender, the whole job can be accomplished in about 15 minutes, and there will be only the blender container, spatula and measuring cup to wash.*

## Eggs and Cream

*See page 139 for directions for blender-whipping cream. Never try to beat egg whites stiff in the blender—the impact of the blades breaks down the delicate foam faster than it can build up. Neither should you attempt, in the blender, recipes calling for egg yolks and sugar to be beaten to a pale, thick foam. Here again the electric mixer is needed. However, when egg yolks or whole eggs are to be incorporated in a mixture, the blender does an ideal job.*

## Chocolate

*The simplest means of liquefying chocolate is to blend it with a heated liquid. However, at speed 6 or 7 (or high) chocolate will become smoothly blended even with cool liquid ingredients.*

*So look forward to delicious meal finales in the days ahead—with these recipes, your reputation as a dessert-maker par excellence will be assured!*

## Puddings and Special Desserts

### BLENDER WHIPPED CREAM

Pour 1 cup chilled whipping cream into blender container; cover and run on speed 1 (or low). Remove cover during whipping so that you can watch it carefully; as soon as the cream thickens and begins to hold the shape of the blades, turn off blender. Watch carefully, as cream will be churned quickly to butter. If desired, add 1–2 tablespoons granulated sugar and ½ teaspoon vanilla to blender container.

**Note:** Blender whips 1–2 cups best. Do not whip more than 2 cups at one time.

#### COCOA WHIPPED CREAM

For each ½ pint (1 cup) whipping cream, put 2 tablespoons cocoa and 3 tablespoons confectioners' sugar in blender container with cream; whip as directed.

#### MOCHA WHIPPED CREAM

For each ½ pint (1 cup) whipping cream, put 2 tablespoons cocoa, ¼ cup confectioners' sugar and 1 teaspoon instant coffee in blender container with cream; whip as directed.

#### LEMON WHIPPED CREAM

For each ½ pint (1 cup) whipping cream, put ½ cup confectioners' sugar, 1 tablespoon lemon juice and a small piece lemon rind in blender container with cream; whip as directed. Perfect for gingerbread, spice cakes and other desserts.

#### PEPPERMINT WHIPPED CREAM

For each ½ pint (1 cup) whipping cream, put 3 tablespoons confectioners' sugar, ¼ teaspoon peppermint flavoring and a few drops green food coloring in blender container with cream; whip as directed. Good on chocolate cakes and desserts.

#### STRAWBERRY WHIPPED CREAM

For each ½ pint (1 cup) whipping cream, put 2 tablespoons strawberry jam and 2 drops red food coloring in blender container with cream; whip as directed. Wonderful for strawberry shortcakes and white cakes.

#### BUTTERSCOTCH WHIPPED CREAM

For each ½ pint (1 cup) whipping cream, put ¼ cup firmly packed brown sugar in blender container with cream; whip as directed. Delicious on cakes, peach shortcake and other desserts.

## CRÊPES DE CACAO

**4 eggs**
**2 cups milk**
**1½ cups sifted flour**
**2 tablespoons sugar**
**½ teaspoon salt**
**10–12 crisp macaroons**
**½ cup crème de cacao**
**½ cup sugar**
**¾ cup very soft butter or margarine**
**½ cup butter or margarine**
**2 cups whipping cream, Blender whipped (page 139)**
**Crème de cacao**

Put first 5 ingredients in blender container; cover and run on speed 6 (or high) until smooth. Chill 1 hour. Lightly butter a 6- to 8-inch omelet pan and set over medium heat. For each crêpe, pour 2 tablespoons batter onto pan. Bake until golden brown on both sides, turning once. Cool.

Break 5–6 macaroons into clean, dry blender container; cover and run on speed 4 (or low) until finely crumbed. Empty into a measuring cup. Repeat process until you have ½ cup crumbs. Put ½ cup crême de cacao, ½ cup sugar and ¾ cup soft butter in blender container; cover and run on speed 6 (or high) until smooth. Combine blended mixture and macaroon crumbs in a bowl. Spread each cooled crêpe with this mixture and roll. At serving time, melt ½ cup butter in a chafing dish or electric frypan; add filled crêpes and heat through. Top each with whipped cream and a drizzle of crème de cacao. *Makes 12 servings.*

## CHOCOLATE PUFF

**3–4 slices dry bread**
**¾ cup hot milk**
**2 tablespoons flour**
**2 tablespoons butter or margarine**
**5 eggs, separated**
**2 squares (2 ounces) unsweetened chocolate, cut up**
**½ cup sugar**
**1 teaspoon vanilla**
**¼ teaspoon salt**
**½ teaspoon cream of tartar**

Have all ingredients room temperature. Preheat oven to 300°. Grease a 2-quart casserole and coat inside with granulated sugar. Break 1 slice bread into 6 pieces and drop into blender container; cover and run on speed 4 (or high) until very finely crumbed. If necessary, switch blender on and off quickly during crumbing. Empty crumbs into measuring cup. Repeat process with remaining bread until you have ½ cup crumbs; set aside.

Put hot milk, flour, butter, egg yolks, chocolate and sugar in blender container; cover and run on speed 7 (or high) until smooth. Pour into a saucepan; stir over low heat until thickened and smooth; cool slightly. Stir in crumbs and vanilla.

Beat egg whites with salt and cream of tartar in a medium bowl with electric mixer until stiff but not dry. Carefully fold chocolate mixture into egg whites; pour into prepared casserole. Set in pan of hot water in oven and bake for 1¼–1½ hours, or until puffy and dry on surface. Serve plain or with whipped cream. *Makes 6 servings.*

*Crêpes de Cacao*

## SPICY CHOCOLATE BREAD PUDDING

**5–6 slices fresh white bread, with crusts removed**
**1 6-ounce package (1 cup) semisweet chocolate pieces**
**1½ cups hot milk**
**½ cup sugar**
**¼ teaspoon salt**
**½ teaspoon cinnamon**
**1 egg**
**¼ teaspoon vanilla**

Preheat oven to 400°. Grease six 6-ounce custard cups; set in a shallow pan. Break 1 slice bread into blender container; cover and run on speed 4 (or low) until finely crumbed. Empty crumbs into a measuring cup. Repeat process with remaining bread until you have 2½ cups crumbs; empty into a mixing bowl.

Put chocolate pieces and hot milk in blender container; cover and run on speed 7 (or high) until chocolate is liquefied. Add remaining ingredients; cover and run on speed 5 (or high) until smooth. Pour blended mixture over bread crumbs; mix. Pour into custard cups. Pour hot water in pan to depth of 1½ inches. Bake 25 minutes or until a silver knife inserted in center comes out clean. *Makes 6 servings.*

## DATE NUT COFFEE PUDDING

**1½ cups pecans**
**1 cup boiling water**
**⅔ cup pitted dates**
**½ cup butter or margarine**
**1 cup sugar**
**1 teaspoon instant coffee**
**½ teaspoon salt**
**2 medium apples, pared, quartered and cored**
**2 eggs, separated**
**1⅓ cups flour**
**2 teaspoons baking powder**

Preheat oven to 350°. Grease a 1½-quart mold. Put half the nuts in blender container; cover and run on speed 4 (or low) until chopped. Empty into a bowl and repeat process with remaining nuts. Put boiling water and dates in blender container; cover and run on speed 2 (or low) until smooth. While blender is running, add butter. sugar, instant coffee and salt and run on speed 2 (or low) until smooth.

Add 2 apple quarters and continue running in the same manner. Repeat until all apples have been added. Add egg yolks, flour and baking powder; cover and run on speed 2 (or low) until smooth. Pour into a bowl. Beat egg whites in a small bowl with an electric mixer until stiff peaks form. Fold into the first mixture along with the nuts. Pour into prepared mold and bake 45 minutes or until done. *Makes 10–12 servings.*

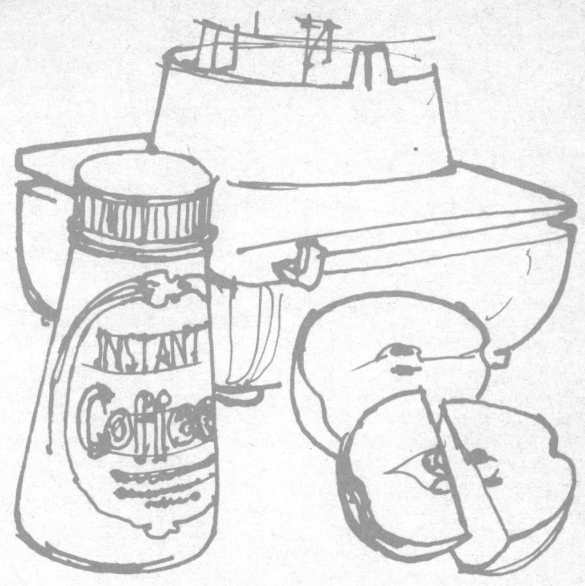


## STEAMED CARROT PUDDING

**1 cup sifted flour**
**1 teaspoon baking soda**
**1 cup sugar**
**1 teaspoon cloves**
**1 teaspoon cinnamon**
**1 teaspoon nutmeg**
**4 medium carrots, cut into 1-inch pieces**
**2 medium potatoes, cut in pieces**
**1 cup seedless raisins**
**1 cup walnuts**
**2 eggs**
**2 tablespoons soft butter**

Generously grease a 1½-quart mold; set aside. Sift dry ingredients together into a mixing bowl; set aside. Put a few pieces of carrot in blender container; cover and run on speed 3 (or low) until finely chopped. Empty into a measuring cup. Repeat until you have 1 cup firmly packed chopped carrots. Repeat process with potatoes until you have 1 cup firmly packed chopped potatoes.

Put half the raisins in blender container; cover and run on speed 4 (or high) until coarsely chopped; add to dry ingredients. Repeat process with remaining raisins. Put half the walnuts in blender container and proceed as with raisins. Put eggs and butter in blender container; cover and run on speed 1 (or low) about 10 seconds or until smooth. Stir into dry ingredients.

Stir carrots and potatoes into batter; pack into prepared mold. Cover mold tightly with waxed paper; place in steamer. Fill with hot water to the depth of half the mold. Steam, covered, for 1½–2 hours or until done. Serve with Hard Sauce (page 153) or Blender Whipped Cream (page 139). *Makes 8–10 servings.*

## CRANBERRY COTTAGE PUDDING

**½ cup milk**
**1 teaspoon vanilla**
**2 eggs**
**¼ cup butter**
**¾ cup sugar**
**½ teaspoon salt**
**1 cup cranberries**
**½ cup walnuts**
**2 cups biscuit mix**
**½ cup sugar**
**1 tablespoon cornstarch**
**¾ cup water**
**½ cup cranberries**
**1 tablespoon butter**

Preheat oven to 350°. Grease and flour 9x9x2-inch pan. Put milk, vanilla, eggs, ¼ cup butter, ¾ cup sugar and salt in blender container in order listed; cover and run on speed 6 (or high) until smooth. Add 1 cup cranberries and nuts; cover and run on speed 6 (or high) until fruit and nuts are coarsely chopped. Put biscuit mix in a mixing bowl; add cranberry mixture and mix well. Turn batter into prepared pan. Bake 25–30 minutes or until done.

Put ½ cup sugar and cornstarch in blender container; cover and run on speed 1 (or low) until well mixed. Add water and ½ cup cranberries; cover and run on speed 7 (or high) about 2 minutes or until cranberries are liquefied. Pour mixture into a saucepan and cook, stirring constantly, until mixture comes to a boil and thickens. Stir in 1 tablespoon butter. Cut cake into squares and serve warm with sauce. *Makes 9 servings.*

## FRESH APPLESAUCE

**2 large apples**
**¼ cup water**
**1 tablespoon lemon juice**
**1–3 tablespoons sugar**

Wash apples; core and cut into 1-inch cubes (if yellow apples, do not pare). Put in cold salted water to keep them from turning brown. Put ¼ cup water, lemon juice, sugar and half the apples in blender container; cover and run on speed 2 (or low) until puréed. Turn blender to speed 7 (or high); while blender is running, add remaining apples. Run until all sauce is of a fine consistency. Serve immediately. *Makes approximately 2 cups.*

### PINK APPLESAUCE

Add 1 tablespoon cinnamon candies to ingredients before processing.

### APPLE-Y APPLESAUCE

Substitute ¼ cup apple juice or cider for the water.

### ORANGE-APPLESAUCE

Substitute ¼ cup orange juice for water. Or add 1 tablespoon orange-flavored instant breakfast drink powder to water. Omit lemon juice.

### COOKED APPLESAUCE

Empty applesauce into saucepan; bring to a boil over moderate heat. Chill.

nberry Cottage Pudding (p. 142)



## PINK PINEAPPLE CREAM

**2 tablespoons lemon juice**
**¼ cup hot maraschino cherry juice**
**2 envelopes (2 tablespoons) unflavored gelatin**
**1 8-ounce can crushed pineapple**
**¼ cup sugar**
**½ cup whipping cream**
**20 maraschino cherries**
**Crushed ice**

Put lemon juice, hot cherry juice and gelatin in blender container; cover and run on speed 1 (or low) to dissolve gelatin, about 1 minute. Add pineapple (with juice) and sugar; cover and run on speed 5 (or high) until smooth. Add cream and 12 cherries, then fill container to 4-cup mark with crushed ice; cover and run on speed 7 (or high) until all ice is dissolved. Let set 1 minute; spoon into sherbet glasses and garnish with remaining cherries. *Makes 8 servings.*

## PEACHY-ORANGE SHERBET

**½ cup water**
**2 tablespoons orange-flavored instant breakfast drink powder**
**2 10-ounce packages frozen sliced peaches**
**Pinch salt**

Put water and orange drink powder in blender container. Break up frozen peaches with a fork and add with salt to blender container; cover and run on speed 7 (or high) until perfectly smooth and of sherbet texture. If necessary, stop blender during processing and push ingredients toward blades with rubber spatula. Serve immediately or store in refrigerator tray in freezing compartment of refrigerator. *Makes 4–6 servings.*

## FRUIT CHIFFON

**1 cup boiling water**
**2 3-ounce packages fruit-flavored gelatin**
**2 cups crushed ice**
**1 cup canned, fresh or frozen fruit pieces, well drained**

Put boiling water and gelatin in blender container; cover and run on speed 1 (or low) until gelatin is dissolved, about 2 minutes. Add ice; cover container and run on speed 6 (or high) until ice is liquefied and container is cool to touch. Immediately pour into a bowl and let set until it begins to thicken; fold in drained fruit. Let set 3–4 minutes or until thickened. Serve immediately or store in refrigerator. *Makes 6–8 servings.*

*Strawberry Fruit Chiffon*

## AVOCADO WHIP

**½ cup frozen limeade concentrate, thawed**
**2 tablespoons boiling water**
**1 envelope (1 tablespoon) unflavored gelatin**
**3 tablespoons sugar**
**2 ripe avocados, pitted, peeled and cubed**
**1 cup whipping cream, Blender whipped (page 139)**

Heat limeade concentrate almost to boiling point. Put boiling water, hot limeade and gelatin in blender container; cover and run on speed 1 (or low) about 1 minute or until gelatin is dissolved. Add sugar and avocados; cover and run on speed 6 (or high) until perfectly smooth. Cool. Fold whipped cream into avocado mixture. Spoon into sherbet glasses. Chill until set. *Makes 4 servings.*

## APRICOT WHIP

**1 cup dried apricots**
**1¼ cups milk**
**¼ lemon**
**½ cup sugar**
**2 egg whites**

Soak apricots in 1 cup milk for at least ½ hour or overnight. Put remaining ¼ cup milk, lemon, ¼ cup sugar and soaked apricot mixture in blender container; cover and run on speed 6 (or high) until smooth. Beat egg whites in a medium bowl with electric mixer until stiff but not dry. Gradually add ¼ cup sugar to egg whites, continuing to beat until they stand in soft peaks. Fold apricot mixture into beaten egg whites; chill. *Makes 6 servings.*

## PEACH MELBA CREAM

**2 envelopes (2 tablespoons) unflavored gelatin**
**3 tablespoons sugar**
**¼ cup boiling water**
**1 1-pound package frozen sliced peaches, partially thawed**
**1 tablespoon lemon juice**
**1 cup whipping cream, Blender whipped (page 139)**
**1 10-ounce package frozen raspberries, thawed and drained**
**40 vanilla wafers**

Put gelatin and sugar in blender container; cover and run on speed 1 (or low) until well mixed. Add boiling water; cover and run on speed 1 (or low) until gelatin is dissolved. Add peaches and lemon juice; cover and run on speed 4 (or high) until smooth. Pour into a bowl. Fold whipped cream into peach mixture. Fold in drained raspberries, reserving a few for garnish. Line a 1½-quart casserole or 9x5x3-inch loaf pan with vanilla wafers; cover with a layer of peach mixture. Repeat layers, ending with vanilla wafers. Garnish with raspberries. Chill until firm, about 4 hours. To serve, cut into slices or spoon out. *Makes 8–10 servings.*

## PEARS SUPREME

**1 cup water**
**2 cups sugar**
**6 pears, pared, cut in half lengthwise and cored**
**½ cup heavy cream, warm**
**2 tablespoons Cognac**
**1 6-ounce package (1 cup) semisweet chocolate pieces**
**1 ounce unsweetened chocolate, cut up**
**½ teaspoon instant coffee**
**1 quart vanilla ice cream**

Combine water and sugar in saucepan; bring to a boil. Add pears and simmer until tender; drain and chill. Put remaining ingredients except ice cream in blender container; cover and run on speed 7 (or high) until smooth. To serve, arrange 2 pear halves in each dessert dish on a scoop of ice cream. Top with chocolate-Cognac sauce. *Makes 6 servings.*

## ALSATIAN PUDDING

**½ cup soft butter or margarine**
**1¼ cups confectioners' sugar**
**4 egg yolks**
**¼ cup cold strong coffee OR ½ teaspoon instant coffee dissolved in ¼ cup water**
**12 ladyfingers**
**Rum or sherry**
**½ cup whipping cream, whipped**
**Toasted slivered almonds**

Put first 4 ingredients in blender container; cover and run on speed 6 (or high) until smooth. Arrange 3 ladyfingers in each of 4 dessert dishes or sherbet glasses. Sprinkle with rum or sherry. Spoon coffee mixture into dishes. Chill several hours. Serve topped with whipped cream and toasted almonds. *Makes 4 servings.*

## CHOCOLATE REFRIGERATOR DESSERT

**½ cup hot milk**
**2 cups miniature marshmallows**
**4 1-ounce chocolate almond candy bars**
**22 graham crackers**
**2 tablespoons confectioners' sugar**
**6 tablespoons butter or margarine, melted**
**1 cup whipping cream, Blender whipped (page 139)**

Put milk, marshmallows and candy bars (each bar broken into 4 pieces) in blender container; cover and run on speed 6 (or high) until smooth. Pour into a bowl and refrigerate while preparing crust and whipped cream.

Break 4 graham crackers into clean, dry blender container; cover and run on speed 4 (or low) until finely crumbed. Empty crumbs into a bowl. Repeat process with remaining crackers. Mix confectioners' sugar with crumbs; then stir in melted butter. Pat ⅔ of crumb mixture into an 8x8x2-inch pan. Fold whipped cream into chilled chocolate mixture; pour into crumb-lined pan. Sprinkle remaining crumbs over top. Chill 4 hours. *Makes 8 servings.*

## CHOCOLATE DAZZLER

**1 7¼-ounce package vanilla wafers**
**¼ cup butter or margarine, melted**
**3 eggs**
**3 squares (3 ounces) unsweetened chocolate, cut up**
**½ cup soft butter or margarine**
**1½ cups confectioners' sugar**
**2 cups miniature marshmallows**
**1 cup whipping cream, Blender whipped (page 139)**

Break 5 vanilla wafers into blender container; cover and run on speed 4 (or high) until finely crumbed. Empty into 8x8x2-inch pan. Repeat process with remaining wafers. Combine crumbs with melted butter; press firmly into bottom of pan.

Put eggs and chocolate in blender container; cover and run on speed 7 (or high) until very smooth. Add ½ cup butter and confectioners' sugar; cover and run on speed 7 (or high) until smooth. Spoon over crumb crust. Fold marshmallows into whipped cream; spread over chocolate layer. Chill. *Makes 12 servings.*

## QUICKIE CHOCOLATE BAVARIAN

**1½ envelopes (1½ tablespoons) unflavored gelatin**
**1 tablespoon sugar**
**2 teaspoons instant coffee**
**Dash salt**
**½ cup boiling water**
**1 6-ounce package (1 cup) semisweet chocolate pieces**
**2 egg yolks**
**1½ cups crushed ice**
**1 cup whipping cream, Blender whipped (page 139)**
**½ teaspoon vanilla**

Put first 4 ingredients in blender container; cover and run on speed 2 (or low) until well mixed. Add boiling water; cover and run on speed 5 (or high) about 40 seconds or until gelatin is dissolved. Add chocolate pieces; cover and run on speed 5 (or high) until chocolate is liquefied. Add egg yolks; cover and run on speed 5 (or high). With blender running on speed 5 (or high), slowly add crushed ice and cream; cover and run about 20 seconds or until mixture begins to thicken. Quickly pour into sherbet glasses and chill about 10 minutes. *Makes 6 servings.*

## ORANGE VELVET

½ cup sugar
2 envelopes (2 tablespoons) unflavored gelatin
⅔ cup boiling water
1 6-ounce can frozen orange juice concentrate
2¼ cups finely crushed ice
Sliced strawberries

Put sugar and gelatin in blender container; cover and run on speed 1 (or low) until well mixed. Add boiling water; cover and run on speed 1 (or low) for 1 minute or until gelatin is dissolved. Add frozen orange juice concentrate; cover and run on speed 2 (or low) until well mixed. Add crushed ice; cover and run on speed 6 (or high) about 1 minute or until mixture begins to thicken. Quickly pour into 6 individual molds or a 1-quart mold. Chill. Unmold and serve with strawberries. *Makes 6 servings.*

## RASPBERRY BAVARIAN

1 cup boiling water
1 3-ounce package raspberry-flavored gelatin
1 envelope (1 tablespoon) unflavored gelatin
1 6-ounce can frozen orange juice concentrate, thawed
½ cup cold water
1 pint vanilla ice cream, cut into chunks

Put boiling water and gelatins in blender container; cover and run on speed 1 (or low) about 1½ minutes to dissolve gelatins. Add orange juice concentrate and cold water; cover and run on speed 5 (or high) until smooth. Stop blender and add ice cream; cover and run on speed 6 (or high) until just combined. Pour immediately into a 1½-quart mold. Refrigerate until very firm. Unmold to serve. *Makes 6 servings.*

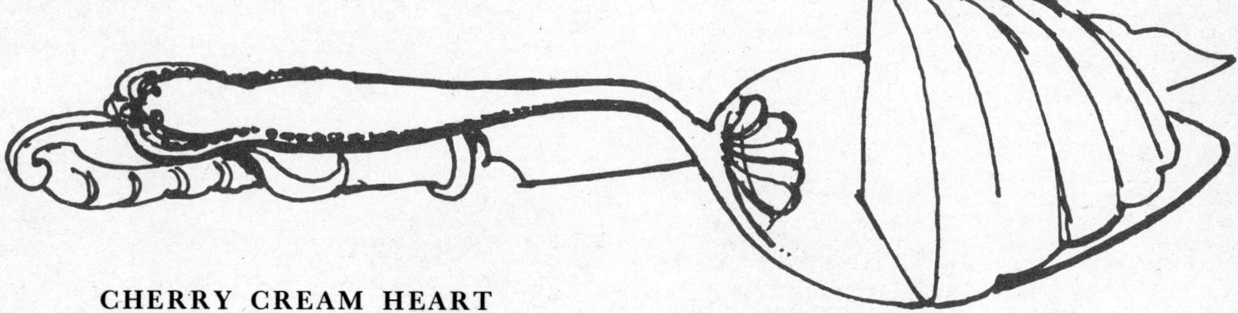

## CHERRY CREAM HEART

¼ cup cold orange juice
1 envelope (1 tablespoon) unflavored gelatin
¼ cup hot orange juice
Dash salt
½ cup dairy sour cream
2 8-ounce packages cream cheese, cubed
¾ cup sugar
1 tablespoon cornstarch
1 1-pound can pitted sour red cherries, with juice
2 tablespoons frozen orange juice concentrate

Put cold orange juice and gelatin in blender container until gelatin is moistened; add hot orange juice. Cover and run on speed 1 (or low) about 1 minute or until gelatin is dissolved. Add salt, sour cream and cream cheese; cover and run on speed 5 (or start on low, then move to high) for 2 minutes or until smooth. If necessary, stop blender during processing and push ingredients toward blades with rubber spatula. Pour into an oiled 1-quart heart-shaped mold or other 1-quart mold. Chill until firm or for several hours.

Combine sugar and cornstarch in a saucepan; add cherries and orange juice concentrate. Cook, stirring constantly, until mixture boils and thickens. Chill. When ready to serve, unmold cheese mixture and top with the cherry sauce. *Makes 8 servings.*

## APRICOT REFRIGERATOR DESSERT

30 vanilla wafers
1 egg
1 cup confectioners' sugar
½ cup soft butter or margarine
1 1-pound can apricot halves, drained
1 cup whipping cream, Blender whipped (page 139)

Break 6 vanilla wafers into blender container; cover and run on speed 4 (or low) until finely crumbed. Empty into large measuring cup and repeat process until all cookies are crumbed. Spread 1 cup of crumbs in bottom of an 8x8x2-inch pan.

Put egg, sugar and butter in blender container; cover and run on speed 5 (or start on low, then move to high) about 2 minutes or until smooth. If necessary, stop blender during processing and push ingredients toward blades with rubber spatula. Spread over the crumbs in pan.

Put apricots in blender container; cover and run on speed 4 (or high) until smooth. Spread over butter mixture in pan. Cover apricot purée with whipped cream and sprinkle with remaining crumbs. Chill at least 2 hours. Cut into squares or spoon into dessert dishes. *Makes 6–9 servings.*

*rry Cream Heart*
*nge Velvet*

### PREPARE INSTANT PUDDINGS

Put liquid and pudding mix in blender container; cover and run on speed 6 (or high) until smooth. Pour into a bowl and allow to thicken.

## CHOCOLATE POTS DE CRÈME

**1 6-ounce package (1 cup) semisweet chocolate pieces**
**1¼ cups light cream, heated to boiling**
**1 egg**
**Dash salt**
**1 teaspoon vanilla**

Put chocolate pieces in blender container. Pour hot cream over chocolate; cover and run on speed 7 (or high) about 30 seconds or until chocolate is liquefied. Add egg, salt and vanilla; cover and run on speed 6 (or high) until smooth. Pour into 6 traditional cups, demitasse cups, sherbet glasses or custard cups. Chill at least 3 hours or until mixture is like pudding. *Makes 6 servings.*

## FLUFFY CHOCOLATE BLANC MANGE

**2 cups milk**
**2 squares (2 ounces) unsweetened chocolate, cut up**
**⅓ cup sugar**
**3 tablespoons cornstarch**
**2 eggs, separated**
**¼ teaspoon salt**
**1½ teaspoons vanilla**
**2 tablespoons sugar**

Put milk, chocolate, ⅓ cup sugar, cornstarch, egg yolks and salt in blender container; cover and start on speed 1 (or low), then run on speed 6 (or high) until smooth. Empty into a saucepan and cook over low heat, stirring constantly, until thick. Remove from heat; add vanilla. Cool slightly.

Beat egg whites with electric mixer until stiff but not dry. Gradually beat in 2 tablespoons sugar; beat until egg whites stand in soft peaks. Fold egg whites into chocolate mixture. Pour into a 1-quart mold. Chill until firm. *Makes 6 servings.*

*Chocolate Pots de Crème*

## BANANA-APRICOT ICE CREAM

**1½ cups canned apricot nectar**
**½ cup sugar**
**1 tablespoon lemon juice**
**1 cup light cream**
**1 banana, peeled and quartered**

Put all ingredients in blender container; cover and start on speed 1 (or low), then run on speed 7 (or high) until smooth. Pour into a refrigerator tray; place in freezing compartment with control set at lowest temperature. Freeze until hard around outside edges and bottom, but still soft in center. Break up with a fork and put in blender container; cover and run on speed 7 (or high) until smooth and fluffy. Return to refrigerator tray; store in freezing compartment with temperature control set at normal. *Makes 1½ pints.*

## BANANA FROST

**¼ cup lemon juice**
**1 cup orange juice**
**3 ripe bananas, peeled and cut into 1-inch pieces**
**1 cup milk**
**Yellow food coloring**
**1½ cups whipping cream, Blender whipped (page 139)**
**Mandarin orange sections**

Put fruit juices and bananas in blender container; cover and run on speed 6 (or high) until bananas are completely puréed. Add milk and a few drops of yellow food coloring; cover and run on speed 6 (or high) until smooth. Fold banana mixture into whipped cream. Pour into 2 refrigerator trays; cover with waxed paper and freeze until firm. Serve garnished with Mandarin orange sections. *Makes 6 servings.*

## SHERRIED STRAWBERRY CREAM

**4 cups fresh strawberries, hulled**
**¼ cup cream sherry**
**⅓ cup confectioners' sugar**
**1 cup whipping cream, Blender whipped (page 139)**

Reserve 1 cup whole strawberries; put remaining strawberries, sherry and confectioners' sugar in blender container; cover and run on speed 6 (or high) until mixture is smooth. Pour into a bowl; chill 3–4 hours.

Fold whipped cream into strawberry mixture. Fold in whole strawberries. Pour into refrigerator tray. Freeze until mushy but not solid. *Makes 4 servings.*

*Banana Frost*

## APRICOT BANANA MOUSSE

2 tablespoons lemon juice
1 quart sweetened cooked fresh apricots, pitted, OR 2 large cans (1 lb. 13 ounces each) apricot halves, drained
2 large bananas, peeled and quartered
1 cup sugar
1 cup water
1 cup walnuts
2 cups whipping cream
2 tablespoons confectioners' sugar

Put lemon juice and apricots in blender container; cover and run on speed 6 (or high) until very smooth. Add bananas; cover and run on speed 6 (or high) until smooth. Chill. Combine sugar and water in a saucepan; boil until a thick syrup is formed. Stir sugar syrup into fruit mixture while hot. Chill thoroughly. When banana-apricot mixture is cold, whip whipping cream and confectioners' sugar together with an electric mixer until cream is stiff.

Put nuts in clean, dry blender container; cover and run on speed 4 (or low) until chopped. Stir into whipped cream. Fold 1¾ cups of the apricot mixture into whipped cream.

Pour remaining apricot mixture into a 2½-quart mold; spoon apricot-whipped cream mixture evenly over the top. Cover with foil; freeze until firm, about 4 hours. To unmold, dip mold quickly in warm water and invert on a platter. *Makes 8 servings.*

## BANANA CHOCOLATE CHIP ICE CREAM

¼ cup semisweet chocolate pieces
½ cup sugar
½ envelope (1½ teaspoons) unflavored gelatin
¼ teaspoon salt
¾ cup light cream, heated
3 medium bananas, peeled and quartered
2 eggs, separated
2 teaspoons lemon juice
1 teaspoon vanilla
2 cups whipping cream, Blender whipped (page 139)
¼ cup sugar

Put chocolate pieces in blender container; cover and run on speed 4 (or high) until coarsely chopped. Empty into a small bowl; set aside. Put ½ cup sugar, gelatin and salt in blender container; cover and run on speed 1 (or low) until well mixed. Add hot cream; cover and run on speed 2 (or low) until gelatin is dissolved and mixture is smooth. Add bananas; cover and run on speed 2 (or low) until smooth. Add egg yolks, lemon juice and vanilla; cover and run on speed 6 (or high) until smooth. Turn into a mixing bowl and chill until slightly thickened. Fold whipped cream into banana mixture. Beat egg whites in a small bowl with an electric mixer until soft peaks form; gradually add ¼ cup sugar and beat until stiff peaks form. Fold into banana mixture. Fold in chopped chocolate and turn into two refrigerator trays. Freeze until firm. *Makes about 2 quarts.*

*Raspberry Ice Cream*

*Peaches 'N' Cream*

## RASPBERRY MOUSSE

**2 10-ounce packages frozen raspberries, partially thawed**
**⅔ cup confectioners' sugar**
**⅛ teaspoon salt**
**1 cup whipping cream, Blender whipped (page 139)**

Put raspberries in blender container; cover and run on speed 6 (or high) until smooth. Add sugar and salt to whipped cream; fold in raspberries. Spoon into a refrigerator tray and freeze until ice forms around the edge. Turn into a mixing bowl and stir until smooth. Return to refrigerator tray or a 1-quart mold and freeze until firm. Unmold to serve. *Makes 6–8 servings.*

## PEACHES 'N' CREAM

**1 Cooky Crust mixture (page 177)**
**1 1-pound can peach slices**
**1 teaspoon lemon juice**
**4 cups miniature marshmallows**
**1 cup whipping cream, Blender whipped (page 139)**

Pat Cooky Crust mixture into bottom of a refrigerator tray or an 8-inch round cake pan; set aside.

Drain peaches, reserving ¼ cup syrup; heat fruit and syrup. Put in blender container; cover and run on speed 2 (or low) until puréed. Add lemon juice and marshmallows; cover and run on speed 7 (or high) until smooth. Pour into a bowl; fold in whipped cream. Pour into pan. Freeze 3–4 hours. *Makes 6 servings.*

## RASPBERRY ICE CREAM

**1 cup whipping cream, Blender whipped (page 139)**
**⅔ cup sweetened condensed milk**
**1 tablespoon lemon juice**
**1 10-ounce package frozen raspberries, thawed**

Empty whipped cream into a bowl; then put remaining ingredients in blender container in order listed; cover and run on speed 7 (or high) until smooth. Fold raspberry mixture into whipped cream. Pour into a refrigerator tray. Freeze 2–3 hours. *Makes 1 quart.*

## FRESH MINT FREEZE

**1 cup sugar**
**1 cup water**
**1 cup fresh mint leaves**
**½ cup lemon juice**
**Green food coloring**
**1 cup whipping cream, Blender whipped (page 139)**

Combine sugar and water in a saucepan; boil until sugar dissolves. Cool slightly. Put this syrup and mint in blender container; cover and run on speed 4 (or low) until mint is very fine. Cover and allow to stand until cool. Stir in lemon juice and food coloring.

Strain mixture into a refrigerator tray, discarding mint, and freeze until mushy. Turn mint ice into a chilled bowl; beat with an electric mixer until smooth. Fold in whipped cream. Return to refrigerator tray; freeze until firm. *Makes 8 servings.*

*Apricot Banana Mousse*

*Fresh Mint Freeze*

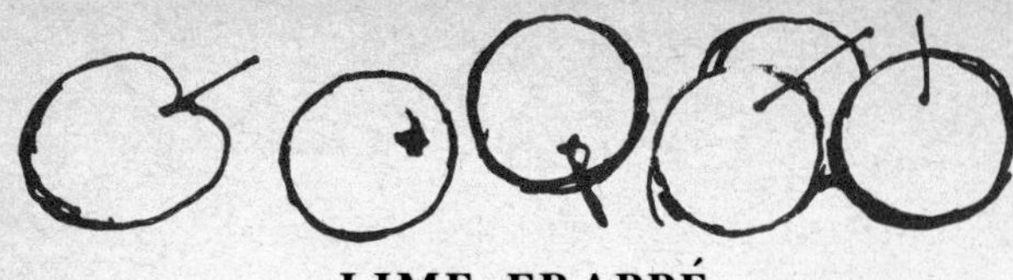

## LIME FRAPPÉ

**1 6-ounce can frozen limeade concentrate, thawed**
**¼ cup sugar**
**1 drop green food coloring**
**4 cups crushed ice**

Put all ingredients in blender container in order listed; cover and run on speed 7 (or high) until of a smooth sherbet consistency. If necessary, stop blender during processing and push ingredients toward blades with rubber spatula. Serve at once or store in refrigerator tray in freezing compartment of refrigerator. *Makes 3–4 servings.*

### LEMON FRAPPÉ

Substitute one 6-ounce can lemonade concentrate, thawed, for limeade concentrate and 1 drop of yellow food coloring for green.

### FRESH ORANGE FRAPPÉ

Put ¼ cup water and 1 large orange, peeled, quartered and seeded (in place of limeade concentrate) in blender container; cover and run on speed 3 (or low) until puréed. Add sugar and ice and run as above. Omit food coloring.

## FROZEN CHOCOLATE FRANGO

**18 graham crackers**
**4 eggs (room temperature)**
**1 cup very soft butter or margarine**
**4 squares (4 ounces) unsweetened chocolate, cut up**
**2 cups confectioners' sugar**
**2 teaspoons vanilla**
**1 cup whipping cream, Blender whipped (page 139)**
**Maraschino cherries**

Break about 4 graham crackers into blender container; cover and run on speed 4 (or low) until finely crumbed. Empty into a bowl. Repeat process until you have 1 cup crumbs. Put 18 fluted paper baking cups in muffin tins. Sprinkle half the crumbs over bottoms of the liners.

Put eggs, butter, chocolate, confectioners' sugar and vanilla in blender container; cover and run on speed 7 (or high) until perfectly smooth. If necessary, stop blender during processing and push ingredients toward blades with rubber spatula. Spoon chocolate mixture over crumbs in cupcake liners; top with remaining crumbs. Freeze until firm. When ready to serve, top each serving with whipped cream and a maraschino cherry. *Makes 18 small servings.*

## CHOCOLATE ICE CREAM

**1½ cups miniature marshmallows**
**½ cup semisweet chocolate pieces**
**1½ cups hot milk**
**2 cups whipping cream, Blender whipped (page 139)**

Put marshmallows, chocolate pieces and hot milk in blender container; cover and run on speed 2 (or low) until smooth. Pour into a bowl and cool. Fold whipped cream into cooled chocolate mixture. Pour into 2 refrigerator trays and freeze until firm, stirring occasionally. *Makes 6–8 servings.*

## TUTTI-FRUTTI TORTONI

**2 tablespoons (about 6) maraschino cherries**
**2 tablespoons seedless raisins**
**2 tablespoons toasted almonds**
**1 egg white**
**2 tablespoons sugar**
**1 cup whipping cream, Blender whipped (page 139)**

Line 8 muffin cups or custard cups with fluted paper baking cups; set aside. Put cherries, raisins and almonds in blender container; cover and run on speed 4 (or low) until coarsely chopped. If necessary, stop blender during processing and push ingredients toward blades with rubber spatula. Empty into a bowl. Beat egg white in a quart bowl with an electric mixer until soft peaks form. Gradually add sugar and beat until stiff peaks form. Fold in whipped cream, then chopped fruit and nuts. Pour mixture into prepared paper cups; freeze for several hours or until firm. *Makes 8 servings.*

## Dessert Sauces

### HARD SAUCE

**¼ cup cream**
**½ cup soft butter or margarine**
**1 teaspoon vanilla**
**2 cups confectioners' sugar**

Have all ingredients room temperature. Put ingredients in blender container in order listed; cover and run on speed 6 (or high) until smooth. If necessary, stop blender during processing and push ingredients toward blades with rubber spatula. Pour into small bowl; chill before serving. Spoon over hot steamed puddings, dessert soufflés or fruitcakes. *Makes 1¾ cups.*

**Note:** If a thicker sauce is desired, after blending stir in by hand an additional 1½ cups sifted confectioners' sugar.

#### BRANDY HARD SAUCE

Use 2 tablespoons brandy in place of vanilla in Hard Sauce and reduce cream to 2 tablespoons.

### CARDINAL SAUCE

**1 10-ounce package frozen raspberries, thawed**
**½ cup sugar**
**1 tablespoon lemon juice**
**Kirschwasser (to taste)**
**2 pints strawberries, hulled and sliced**

Put raspberries in blender container; cover and run on speed 3 (or low) until puréed. Strain to remove seeds. Add sugar, lemon juice and Kirschwasser. Add strawberries to raspberry mixture. Chill. Serve over vanilla ice cream and peach halves. *Makes about 5 cups.*

### ORIENTAL SAUCE

**1 cup sugar**
**½ cup water**
**¼ cup ginger preserves OR 2 tablespoons candied ginger**
**1 1-inch square orange rind**
**1 1-inch square lemon rind**
**1 tablespoon orange juice**
**1½ teaspoons lemon juice**
**¼ cup blanched slivered almonds**

Cook sugar and water together for 5 minutes; cool slightly. Pour into blender container. Add ginger preserves, fruit rinds and juices; cover and run on speed 4 (or high) for 15 seconds. Cool and add almonds. Serve over vanilla ice cream. *Makes 1½ cups.*

### APRICOT-HONEY TOPPING

**½ cup dried apricots**
**½ cup water**
**¼ cup honey**
**½ cup whipping cream**

Soak apricots in water at least 1 hour (if apricots are hard, soak overnight). Put honey, apricots and water in blender container; cover and run on speed 6 (or high) until smooth. Add whipping cream; cover and run on speed 5 (or high) about 20 seconds or just until sauce is fluffy and well blended. Chill. Serve over cake slices. *Makes 1¼ cups.*

### BLUEBERRY SYRUP

**1 1-pound can (2 cups) blueberries**
**½ cup light corn syrup**
**⅛ teaspoon salt**

Put all ingredients in blender container; cover and run on speed 6 (or high) until smooth. Pour into a saucepan; bring to a boil. Boil, stirring constantly, for 5 minutes. Serve warm or chilled over waffles, pancakes, ice cream, dessert soufflés, etc. *Makes about 2 cups.*

### TOASTED ALMOND-HONEY SAUCE

**1 tablespoon butter or margarine**
**1 cup blanched almonds**
**1¼ cups honey**

Put butter in a pie pan in preheated oven (300°) until melted; spread almonds over butter and bake until nuts are lightly browned, about 15 minutes. Put toasted almonds and honey in blender container; cover and run on speed 7 (or high) until almonds are chopped. Cool. Serve over ice cream. *Makes 1¾ cups.*

## NO-COOK FUDGE SAUCE

*Excellent on ice cream, cake or brownie sundaes—or use to make delicious milk and ice cream drinks.*

**¾ cup hot milk or hot coffee**
**1 cup sugar**
**2 teaspoons vanilla**
**4 squares (4 ounces) unsweetened chocolate, cut up***

Put ingredients in blender container in order listed; cover and run on speed 7 (or high) until chocolate is liquefied. Serve immediately as hot fudge sauce or chill (sauce becomes very thick when chilled). *Makes about 1½ cups.*

**Note:** To make sauce in a pint Mason jar, put ingredients in jar in reverse of order listed above (beginning with chocolate). Screw cutting assembly onto jar and run until chocolate is liquefied. Cover and store in same jar.

*Four ounces semisweet chocolate, chocolate pieces, rum chocolate, chocolate mints or any chocolate may be substituted for unsweetened chocolate.

## UNCOOKED BUTTERSCOTCH SAUCE

**1 cup evaporated milk**
**¾ cup brown sugar**
**½ cup white sugar**
**2 tablespoons soft butter or margarine**
**1 tablespoon corn syrup**
**1 teaspoon vanilla**

Put all ingredients in blender container; cover and run on speed 6 (or high) until smooth. Serve over cake or ice cream. *Makes 1½ cups.*

## MARSHMALLOW-FUDGE SAUCE

**¾ cup light cream, heated**
**4 ounces sweet chocolate, cut up**
**4 cups miniature marshmallows**

Put all ingredients in blender container in order listed; cover and run on speed 7 (or high) until smooth. Serve cold over vanilla, chocolate or peppermint ice cream. *Makes 1½ cups.*

**Note:** Half this recipe can be made in a half pint Mason jar.

## HONEY-ORANGE SYRUP

**½ cup honey**
**3 tablespoons frozen orange juice concentrate, thawed**
**⅛ teaspoon salt**

Put all ingredients in blender container; cover and run on speed 5 (or high) until mixed. Serve over ice cream or other desserts. *Makes about ¾ cup.*

*No-Cook Fudge Sauce*

## Cakes and Tortes

*Time and effort may be saved by blending butter, sugar and eggs for batters. Whether or not liquid and flour are blender-incorporated depends on the recipe.*

Nuts and Dried Fruits

*You can blender-chop nuts and fruits by adding them whole to the liquid mixture—except for a thin-battered cake. For this type of batter it is more satisfactory to chop nuts and fruits first in a dry blender (see page 12) and then mix them with the flour. This helps prevent their sinking to the bottom. Liquid ingredients may then be blended without washing the container, and added to flour as recipe recommends.*

*Add fruits and nuts to liquids at very end of mixing period. Turn to speed 6 (or high) and quickly off. Repeat if necessary. Avoid overchopping.*

Before Starting to Make Cake

1. *Have all ingredients at room temperature.*
2. *Have pans prepared as recipe directs.*
3. *Have oven heated to required temperature.*

### TWO-EGG CAKE

**2 cups sifted cake flour**
**2½ teaspoons baking powder**
**1 teaspoon salt**
**½ cup milk**
**2 eggs**
**½ cup shortening**
**1¼ teaspoons vanilla**
**1 cup sugar**

Have all ingredients room temperature. Preheat oven to 375°. Grease and line with waxed paper two 8-inch round layer cake pans. Sift flour, baking powder and salt together into mixing bowl; set aside.

Put remaining ingredients in blender container; cover and run on speed 6 (or high) until smooth. Add dry ingredients; cover container and run on speed 6 (or high) just until mixed (no longer than 60 seconds). Pour into prepared pans; bake 25 minutes or until cake tests done. Remove from pans and cool on racks.

### PINK BEAUTY CAKE

**2¼ cups sifted cake flour**
**3 teaspoons baking powder**
**½ teaspoon salt**
**1 5-ounce bottle maraschino cherries**
**Milk**
**2 eggs**
**1 teaspoon vanilla**
**½ cup soft butter or margarine**
**¾ cup sugar**

Have ingredients room temperature. Preheat oven to 375°. Grease and lightly flour two 8-inch round layer cake pans. Sift flour, baking powder and salt together into a bowl. Drain cherries, reserving syrup. Add enough milk to syrup to make ⅔ cup. Put syrup, eggs, vanilla, butter, sugar and cherries in blender container; cover and run on speed 6 (or high) just until cherries are coarsely chopped. Add to dry ingredients; mix until smooth. Pour into prepared pans; bake 30–35 minutes or until done. Cool in pans 5 minutes. Remove from pans and cool on racks.

## EASY DATE CAKE

½ teaspoon baking soda
1 cup boiling water
1 cup pitted dates
2 eggs
½ cup soft butter or margarine
1 cup sugar
1 teaspoon vanilla
1½ cups sifted flour
1 teaspoon baking powder
¼ teaspoon salt

Preheat oven to 350°. Grease a 9x9x2-inch pan. Add baking soda to boiling water; stir to dissolve. Pour over dates; allow to cool. When dates are cool, put mixture in blender container; cover and run on speed 4 (or low) until dates are chopped. Empty into a bowl.

Put eggs, butter, sugar and vanilla in blender container; cover and run on speed 6 (or high) until smooth. Sift flour, baking powder and salt into bowl with dates; add blended egg mixture and mix well. Turn into prepared pan; bake 40 minutes or until done. Remove from pan and cool on rack.

## LADY BALTIMORE CAKE

½ cup milk
½ cup water
½ teaspoon vanilla
½ teaspoon lemon extract
¾ cup shortening
2 cups sugar
3 teaspoons baking powder
¾ teaspoon salt
3 cups sifted cake flour
6 egg whites

Have all ingredients room temperature. Preheat oven to 350°. Grease and flour two 9-inch round layer cake pans. Put the first 5 ingredients in blender container; cover and run on speed 3 (or low) until shortening is creamy. Combine sugar, baking powder and salt; add to mixture in blender container. Cover and run on speed 3 (or low) about 20 seconds or until well mixed.

Sift cake flour into a mixing bowl and add blended mixture; stir until smooth. Beat egg whites in a large bowl with an electric mixer until stiff peaks form; fold into batter. Pour into prepared pans and bake 30 minutes. Remove from pans and cool on racks. Put together with Lady Baltimore Frosting (page 169).

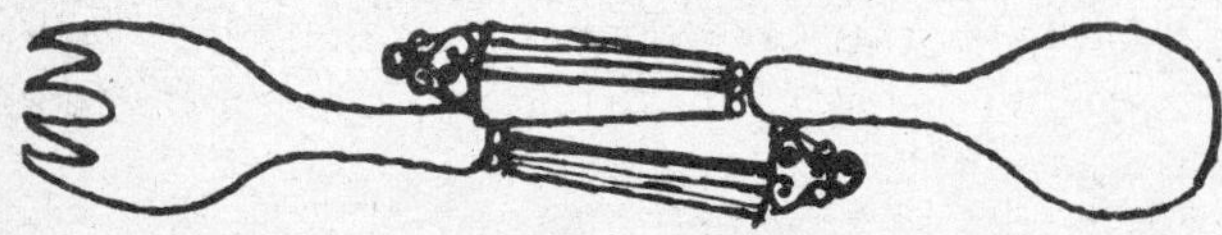

## NO-BAKE FRUITCAKE

1 pound shelled Brazil nuts OR 1 pound shelled pecans
1 1-pound box graham crackers
1 15-ounce box seedless raisins
1 cup cut-up candied mixed fruit
2 tablespoons frozen orange juice concentrate, thawed
1 envelope (1 tablespoon) unflavored gelatin
½ cup boiling water
1 8-ounce jar maraschino cherries, drained
½ cup sugar
⅔ cup molasses
¼ teaspoon cinnamon
¼ teaspoon nutmeg
¼ teaspoon cloves
⅛ teaspoon allspice
⅛ teaspoon ginger

Put ½ cup nuts in blender container; cover and run on speed 3 (or low) until ground. Empty into a large mixing bowl. Repeat process until all nuts are ground. Break 6 graham crackers into blender container; cover and run on speed 3 (or low) until finely crumbed. Empty into bowl with nuts. Repeat process until all graham crackers are crumbed. Then add the raisins and candied mixed fruit; mix until the fruit is well coated.

Put orange juice and gelatin in blender container; let stand until gelatin is moistened. Add boiling water; cover and run on speed 1 (or low) until gelatin is dissolved. Add cherries; cover and run on speed 3 (or low) until cherries are chopped. Add remaining ingredients and run on speed 6 (or high) for 1 minute. Add liquid mixture to nuts,crumbs and fruit. Mix well with spoon or hands. Press firmly into a greased or waxed paper-lined 9x5x3-inch loaf pan. Cover top of pan with waxed paper and press down firmly. Refrigerate loaf for at least 8 hours; loosen sides and remove to serving dish. Peel off waxed paper. *Makes 22-25 slices.*

### NO-BAKE FRUIT CAKE KEEPS WELL

Wrap cake after 24 hours in film or foil and store in refrigerator. Keeps well for at least 2 months. Serve two quarter-inch slices "sandwiched" with quarter-inch layer of whipped cream or dairy sour cream. Or serve half-inch slices with scoops of vanilla ice cream.

## HONEY FRUITCAKE

**¾ cup walnuts**
**1 15-ounce can sweetened condensed milk**
**¼ cup honey**
**1 tablespoon lemon juice**
**1 8-ounce package pitted dates**
**2 cups moist shredded coconut**
**½ cup cut-up candied cherries**
**½ cup cut-up candied pineapple**

Preheat oven to 325°. Line a 9x5x3-inch loaf pan with waxed paper. Put walnuts in blender container; cover and run on speed 4 (or low) until chopped. Empty into a large bowl. Put condensed milk, honey, lemon juice, dates and coconut in blender container; cover and run on speed 7 (or high) until dates are chopped. If necessary, stop blender during processing and push ingredients toward blades with rubber spatula. Add contents of blender container, cherries and pineapple to nuts. Mix thoroughly; pack into prepared pan. Bake 1 hour and 15 minutes or until a toothpick inserted in the center comes out clean. Cool in pan 5 minutes. Remove from pan; take off paper. Cool on rack.

## NUT LOAF CAKE

**2 cups pecans**
**3 eggs, separated**
**1 cup sugar**
**1 teaspoon orange extract**
**1 cup soft butter or margarine**
**1½ cups raisins**
**2 cups sifted flour**
**½ teaspoon baking powder**

Preheat oven to 325°. Grease and line with waxed paper the bottom of a 9x5x3-inch loaf pan. Put 1 cup pecans in blender container; cover and run on speed 4 (or low) until chopped. Empty into a bowl. Repeat process with remaining nuts.

Put egg yolks, ¾ cup sugar, orange extract and butter in blender container; cover and run on speed 6 (or high) until very smooth. Add raisins; cover and run on speed 4 (or low) until raisins are chopped. Sift flour and baking powder together into bowl with nuts. Add blended mixture and beat with an electric mixer just until well mixed.

Beat egg whites with an electric mixer until frothy; gradually add the remaining ¼ cup sugar while continuing to beat until egg whites will hold soft peaks. Spread beaten egg whites over batter; fold together gently. Turn into prepared pan. Bake 1 hour and 15 minutes or until done. Cool 10 minutes in pan; remove from pan and cool on rack.

## PECAN CRUNCH CAKE

**¾ cup pecans**
**1–1½ slices very dry bread**
**1¾ cups sugar**
**⅓ cup butter or margarine, melted**
**½ cup milk**
**2 eggs**
**1 teaspoon vanilla**
**⅔ cup soft butter or margarine**
**2 cups sifted cake flour**
**2 teaspoons baking powder**
**¾ teaspoon salt**

Preheat oven to 350°. Thoroughly butter the bottom and sides of a 1-quart fluted tube pan or an 8x8x2-inch pan. Put pecans in blender container; cover and run on speed 4 (or low) until very finely chopped; empty into small bowl. Break 1 slice bread into 6 pieces and drop into blender container; cover and run on speed 4 (or low) until very finely crumbed. Empty into a measuring cup. If necessary, repeat process with remaining ½ slice bread to obtain ⅓ cup crumbs.

Combine pecans, crumbs, ½ cup sugar and the melted butter. Press onto bottom and one inch up the sides of pan; set aside. Put milk, eggs, vanilla, soft butter and 1¼ cups sugar in blender container; cover and run on speed 6 (or high) until smooth. Sift flour, baking powder and salt together into a mixing bowl; add blended mixture and beat with an electric mixer until very smooth. Pour into prepared pan. Bake 60-65 minutes or until done. Cool 10 minutes in pan; remove from pan and cool on rack.

*Fresh Orange Cake (p. 15*

## CHEESECAKE

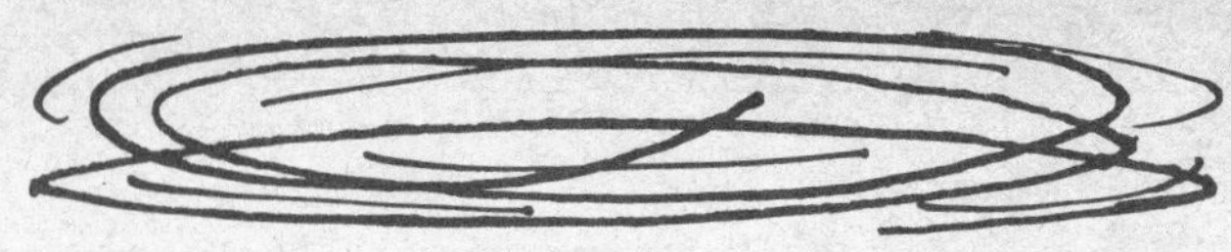

**18 zwieback**
**2 tablespoons sugar**
**⅓ cup butter, melted**
**1 cup milk**
**1 tablespoon fresh or canned lemon juice**
**4 eggs**
**½ cup sugar**
**2 tablespoons flour**
**¼ teaspoon salt**
**Small piece lemon rind***
**1 16-ounce carton creamed cottage cheese**

Have ingredients room temperature. Preheat oven to 325°. Break 4 zwieback into blender container, breaking each piece in thirds. Cover and run on speed 4 (or low) until crumbed. If necessary, turn the blender on and off several times until crumbs are fine. Empty crumbs into a 2-cup measure or small bowl. Repeat process until you have 1½ cups crumbs. Empty crumbs into a mixing bowl and stir in 2 tablespoons sugar; add melted butter and mix well. Measure ¾ cup of the crumb mixture and set aside to be used for topping. Press remaining crumb mixture into the bottom of a 9x9x2-inch cake pan or an 8-inch round pan; chill while making filling.

Put all remaining ingredients in blender container in order listed. Cover and run on speed 6 (or high) until smooth. Pour carefully over chilled crumbs. Bake - hour or until center is firm. Sprinkle the reserved ¾ cup crumb mixture evenly over the top. Cool before serving.

*Use vegetable peeler to cut a thin piece of the colored portion of the rind about the size of a 50¢ piece.

**Variation:** If a fluffy-type cheesecake is desired, separate eggs and add yolks to blender mixture. Whip egg whites with electric mixer until stiff. Fold in blender contents.

## FRESH ORANGE CAKE

**1 medium orange, cut into chunks (unpeeled)**
**1 cup plus 2 tablespoons water**
**2 eggs**
**1 package yellow cake mix**
**1½ cups sugar**
**3 tablespoons cornstarch**
**¼ teaspoon salt**
**¼ cup butter or margarine**
**1 3½-ounce can flaked coconut**
**1 package fluffy white frosting mix**

Preheat oven to 350°. Grease and flour two 8-inch round layer cake pans. Put orange chunks in blender container; cover and run on speed 3 (or low) until finely chopped. Measure ⅔ cup chopped orange and set aside. Add liquid and eggs called for on cake mix package to remaining orange in blender container. Add half the cake mix and run on speed 6 (or high) for about 20 seconds. If necessary, stop blender during processing and push ingredients toward blades with rubber spatula. Add remaining cake mix; cover and run on speed 6 (or high) for another 30 seconds. Pour batter into prepared pans. Bake as directed on package. Cool.

Combine the ⅔ cup chopped orange, sugar, cornstarch, salt and butter in a saucepan. Cook, stirring constantly, until mixture boils and thickens; cook 2 minutes. Cool and stir in coconut. Split each cake layer in half crosswise, making 4 layers. Spread each layer and top of cake with orange filling. Prepare fluffy white frosting as directed on package; spread on sides of cake. Trim with fresh orange sections, if desired.

## ORANGE-DATE LOAF CAKE

**1 cup dairy sour cream**
**2 eggs**
**½ cup soft butter or margarine**
**2 cups sugar**
**Rind of 1 orange (colored portion only)**
**1 cup walnuts**
**½ cup pitted dates**
**2 cups sifted flour**
**1 teaspoon soda**
**½ teaspoon baking powder**
**½ teaspoon salt**
**Juice of 1 orange**

Preheat oven to 350°. Grease and lightly flour a 9x5x3-inch loaf pan. Put sour cream, eggs, butter and 1½ cups sugar in blender container in order listed; cover and run on speed 6 (or high) until smooth. Add orange rind, nuts and dates; cover and run on speed 6 (or high) until all are chopped.

Sift flour, soda, baking powder and salt together into a mixing bowl; add blended mixture and mix well. Turn batter into prepared pan; bake 1 hour and 15 minutes or until cake tests done. Remove from oven and cool in pan on rack for 5 minutes. Mix orange juice and ½ cup sugar; pour over hot cake while still in pan. When cake is cool, turn out onto serving plate.

## APPLE SURPRISE CAKE

**18 graham crackers**
**2 tablespoons butter or margarine, melted**
**½ teaspoon cinnamon**
**3 eggs, separated**
**1 15-ounce can sweetened condensed milk**
**2 teaspoons lemon juice**
**4 large cooking apples, pared, cored and cubed**

Have all ingredients room temperature. Preheat oven to 350°. Break about 6 graham crackers into blender container; cover and run on speed 4 (or low) until finely crumbed. Empty into a bowl. Repeat process until all crackers are crumbed. (You should have 1 cup crumbs.) Mix melted butter and cinnamon with the crumbs. Press half this mixture evenly on the bottom of a 9-inch spring-form pan. Reserve remaining crumb mixture for later use.

Put egg yolks, condensed milk and lemon juice in blender container; cover and run on speed 6 (or high) for 2 minutes. While blender is running, add apple cubes, one at a time. Continue process until all apples are puréed; empty into a bowl.

Beat egg whites with an electric mixer until stiff but not dry; fold into egg yolk–apple mixture. Spread over crumb crust in pan. Sprinkle remaining crumb mixture evenly over top. Bake 45 minutes or until center of cake is set. Chill before serving.

## FRESH APPLESAUCE CAKE

**2 cups sifted cake flour**
**2 tablespoons cocoa**
**1½ teaspoons baking powder**
**1 teaspoon salt**
**½ teaspoon soda**
**1 teaspoon cinnamon**
**½ teaspoon cloves**
**½ teaspoon nutmeg**
**½ teaspoon allspice**
**2 eggs**
**½ cup soft shortening**
**1¾ cups sugar**
**¾ cup raisins**
**3 medium apples, pared, cored and cubed**

Preheat oven to 350°. Grease and line with waxed paper a 13x9½x2-inch pan. Sift flour, cocoa, baking powder, salt, soda and spices into medium mixing bowl. Put eggs, shortening, sugar and raisins in blender container; cover and run on speed 6 (or high) until smooth. While blender is running, add the apple cubes and run until smooth. Pour mixture over dry ingredients; mix well. Pour batter into prepared pan; bake 45 minutes. Cool in pan.

## APRICOT PINEAPPLE UPSIDE-DOWN CAKE

**2 tablespoons butter or margarine**
**½ cup firmly packed brown sugar**
**9 maraschino cherry halves**
**9 apricot halves, well drained**
**⅓ cup crushed pineapple, well drained**
**⅓ cup shortening**
**¼ cup apricot syrup**
**¼ cup maraschino cherry juice**
**1 egg**
**1¼ cups sifted flour**
**½ cup sugar**
**2 teaspoons baking powder**
**½ teaspoon salt**

Preheat oven to 350°. Melt butter in an 8x8x2-inch pan. Stir in brown sugar. Place a cherry half in each apricot half and arrange, cut side down, on top of the brown sugar mixture. Spoon crushed pineapple over all.

Put all remaining ingredients in blender container; cover and run on speed 5 (or high) about 10 seconds. If necessary, stop blender during processing and push ingredients toward blades with rubber spatula. Continue blending for 20 seconds more. Pour over apricots and pineapple. Bake 30–35 minutes or until done. Let stand 10 minutes; invert pan on plate. Serve warm with Blender Whipped Cream (page 139), if desired.

## CAKE MIXES

Use any packaged cake mix except sponge or angel cake. Preheat oven and prepare pans as directed on package. Put the liquid and any other ingredients called for on package in the blender container; add half the cake mix. Cover container and run on speed 6 (or high) for about 20 seconds. If necessary, stop blender during processing and push ingredients toward blades with rubber spatula. Add remaining cake mix; cover container and run on speed 6 (or high) about 30 seconds. Be careful not to overblend. Bake as directed on package.

## ALMOND APPLESAUCE CUPCAKES

**¾ cup unblanched almonds**
**2 eggs**
**½ cup shortening**
**1 cup firmly packed brown sugar**
**2 large cooking apples, pared, cored and cubed**
**1 cup raisins**
**1¾ cups sifted flour**
**2 teaspoons baking powder**
**½ teaspoon salt**
**¼ teaspoon soda**
**1 teaspoon cinnamon**
**½ teaspoon cloves**
**¼ teaspoon nutmeg**

Preheat oven to 350°. Line twenty-four 3-inch cupcake cups with paper liners. Put almonds in blender container; cover and run on speed 4 (or low) until chopped. Empty into a large bowl.

Put eggs, shortening and brown sugar in blender container; cover and run on speed 6 (or high) until smooth. While blender is running, gradually add apple cubes and blend until smooth. Add raisins; cover container and run on speed 4 (or low) just until raisins are chopped. Sift remaining ingredients together into bowl with nuts. Add blended mixture; beat with electric mixer just until ingredients are blended. Spoon into prepared cupcake cups, filling each half full. Bake 25–30 minutes or until done. Cool.

## BANANA CREAM CAKE

**1¼ cups walnuts**
**3–4 medium bananas, peeled and cut up**
**½ cup soft shortening**
**¼ cup milk**
**2 eggs**
**1 teaspoon vanilla**
**2 cups sifted cake flour**
**1¼ cups sugar**
**2 teaspoons baking powder**
**1 teaspoon salt**
**1 teaspoon soda**
**½ teaspoon nutmeg**
**1 cup dairy sour cream**
**⅓ cup firmly packed brown sugar**

Preheat oven to 350°. Grease and flour a 9x9x2-inch pan. Put half the walnuts in blender container; cover and run on speed 4 (or high) until chopped. Empty into a small bowl and repeat process; set aside. Put bananas in blender container; cover and run on speed 3 (or low) until puréed (it should measure 1 cup). Add shortening, milk, eggs and vanilla to banana in blender container. Cover and run on speed 5 (or high) about 20 seconds or until well blended.

Sift dry ingredients into a bowl; make a well in the center. Pour in banana mixture; stir until smooth. Add ½ cup chopped walnuts. Pour into prepared pan and bake 35–40 minutes or until done. Combine sour cream and brown sugar; spread over warm cake and sprinkle with remaining chopped walnuts. Bake 5 minutes longer or until topping is set.

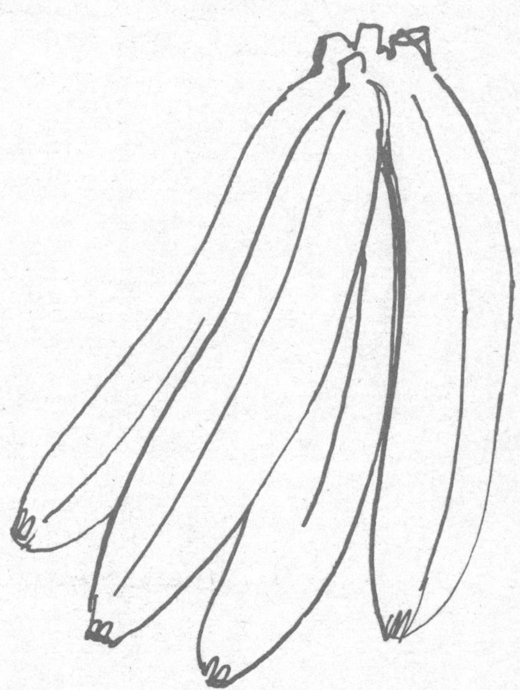

## PINEAPPLE CRUNCH CAKE

**½ cup walnuts**
**½ cup flaked coconut**
**⅓ cup firmly packed brown sugar**
**1 9-ounce can (1 cup) crushed pineapple**
**⅓ cup soft shortening**
**1 egg**
**1 teaspoon vanilla**
**½ cup sugar**
**1½ teaspoons baking powder**
**¼ teaspoon salt**
**1¼ cups sifted flour**
**3 tablespoons butter or margarine, melted**

Preheat oven to 350°. Grease and flour an 8x8x2-inch pan. Put nuts in blender container and run on speed 4 (or low) until coarsely chopped. Empty into bowl and combine with coconut and brown sugar; set aside. Drain pineapple, reserving ½ cup of the syrup. Put syrup, shortening, egg and vanilla in blender container; cover and run on speed 5 (or high) for 20 seconds or until well blended. Add sugar, baking powder and salt; cover and run on speed 5 (or high) for 10 seconds.

Sift flour into a mixing bowl. Add mixture from blender container; stir to mix. Pour half the batter into prepared pan; spoon drained pineapple over batter. Pour the remaining batter over the pineapple. Top with coconut mixture and drizzle with melted butter. Bake 35 minutes or until done. Serve with Blender Whipped Cream (page 139), if desired.

## STRAWBERRY-BANANA TORTE

**1 small angel food tube cake**
**¼ cup boiling water**
**2 envelopes (2 tablespoons) unflavored gelatin**
**½ cup creamed cottage cheese**
**¼ cup sugar**
**1 cup frozen or sweetened fresh strawberries**
**1 medium banana, peeled and quartered**
**1 cup whipping cream, Blender whipped (page 139)**
**Whole fresh strawberries**
**Banana slices**
**Lemon juice**

Slice cake crosswise into 5 equal layers. Put boiling water and gelatin in blender container; cover and run on speed 1 (or low) until gelatin is dissolved. Add cottage cheese, sugar, 1 cup strawberries and quartered banana; cover and run on speed 7 (or high) until smooth. Fold into whipped cream; chill 30 minutes or until mixture starts to thicken. Spread about ½ cup fruit mixture on each layer, including top of cake; stack layers. Chill. To serve, garnish top of torte and plate edge with whole strawberries and banana slices that have been dipped in lemon juice.

## GRAHAM NUT TORTE

**18 graham crackers**
**1 cup sifted cake flour**
**2 teaspoons baking powder**
**¾ teaspoon salt**
**1 cup milk**
**2 eggs**
**¾ cup sugar**
**1 teaspoon vanilla**
**½ cup shortening**
**1 cup pecans**

Have all ingredients room temperature. Preheat oven to 350°. Grease a 9x9x2-inch pan. Break 6 graham crackers into blender container; cover and run on speed 4 (or high) until finely crumbed. Empty into a medium bowl. Repeat process with remaining crackers. (You should have 1 cup crumbs.) Sift flour, baking powder and salt together into bowl with crumbs; mix.

Put milk, eggs, sugar, vanilla and shortening in blender container; cover and run on speed 6 (or high) until smooth. Stop blender and add pecans; cover and run on speed 6 (or high) until pecans are chopped. Pour over dry ingredients and mix lightly. Pour batter into prepared pan and bake 30 minutes or until cake tests done. Serve warm with Hard Sauce (page 153) or Blender Whipped Cream (page 139).

*Strawberry Banana To*

## CHOCOLATE CONFETTI CAKE

**2 cups sifted cake flour**
**3 teaspoons baking powder**
**¼ teaspoon salt**
**1 cup milk**
**1 teaspoon vanilla**
**1 cup sugar**
**½ cup soft butter or margarine**
**3 squares ( 3 ounces) unsweetened chocolate, cut up**
**2 egg whites**

Have ingredients room temperature. Preheat oven to 350°. Grease and lightly flour two 9-inch round layer cake pans. Sift flour, baking powder and salt into a large bowl; set aside. Put milk, vanilla, ½ cup sugar, butter and chocolate in blender container; cover and run on speed 6 (or high) until mixture is well blended and chocolate is chopped. Add to sifted dry ingredients; mix thoroughly.

Beat egg whites with an electric mixer until foamy; gradually add remaining ½ cup sugar, continuing to beat until stiff. Fold into batter. Turn into prepared pans; bake 20–25 minutes or until done. Cool 10 minutes in pans; remove from pans and cool on racks.

## CHOCOLATE ALMOND TORTE

**1⅓ cups semisweet chocolate pieces**
**½ cup sugar**
**½ cup boiling water**
**2 cups whipping cream, Blender whipped (page 139)**
**2 sticks pie crust mix, cut up**
**2 teaspoons vanilla**
**½ cup toasted slivered almonds**

Preheat oven to 425°. Put chocolate pieces, sugar and boiling water in blender container; cover and run on speed 7 (or high) until smooth. Pour off ⅓ cup of this mixture. Fold into whipped cream and chill. Add pie crust mix and vanilla to remaining chocolate mixture; cover and run on speed 6 (or high) until well blended. If necessary, stop blender during processing and push ingredients toward blades with rubber spatula.

Empty mixture onto waxed paper. Divide into 6 equal parts. Spread 1 part on the bottom of an inverted 8-inch round layer cake pan, leaving ½ inch of pan showing around edge. Bake for 5 minutes. Trim edges; cool and lift off with a spatula. Repeat until 6 layers are baked and cooled. Spread chocolate cream on layers and stack one on top of the other, ending with a cream-topped layer. Sprinkle with almonds. *Makes 9–12 servings.*

## CHOCOLATE MOLASSES CUPCAKES

**2 eggs**
**½ cup molasses**
**2 squares (2 ounces) unsweetened chocolate, cut up**
**½ cup milk**
**1½ teaspoons vanilla**
**½ cup soft shortening**
**½ cup sugar**
**2 cups sifted cake flour**
**1½ teaspoons baking powder**
**¼ teaspoon soda**
**¾ teaspoon salt**

Preheat oven to 350°. Line 24 cupcake cups with paper liners. Put first 7 ingredients in blender container in order listed; cover and run on speed 7 (or high) until chocolate is completely liquefied.

Sift remaining ingredients together into a bowl. Add blended mixture; mix until smooth. Fill cupcake cups half full. Bake 15–20 minutes or until done. Cool. *Makes 24 cupcakes.*

## SPICY MOCHA CAKE

**2 cups strong hot coffee**
**2 cups sugar**
**2 tablespoons cocoa**
**1 cup seedless raisins**
**2 eggs**
**½ cup shortening**
**½ teaspoon vanilla**
**2 cups sifted flour**
**2 teaspoons baking powder**
**½ teaspoon soda**
**½ teaspoon salt**
**1 teaspoon cinnamon**
**1 teaspoon nutmeg**
**½ teaspoon cloves**

Have all ingredients except coffee room temperature. Preheat oven to 350°. Grease and line with waxed paper a 13x9½x2-inch pan; set aside. Put coffee, 1 cup sugar, cocoa and raisins in blender container; cover and run on speed 4 (or low) until raisins are chopped. Empty into a saucepan and simmer 10 minutes; cool.

Put eggs, shortening, 1 cup sugar and vanilla in blender container; cover and run on speed 5 (or high) until smooth. Sift flour, baking powder, soda, salt and spices together into a medium mixing bowl; add blended sugar-egg mixture and coffee-raisin mixture. Stir well. Pour into prepared pan; bake about 1 hour or until cake tests done. Cool in pan.

## MARASCHINO CHOCOLATE CAKE

**1¾ cups sifted cake flour**
**1 teaspoon soda**
**¼ teaspoon salt**
**1 cup buttermilk**
**1 square (1 ounce) unsweetened chocolate, cut up**
**1 egg**
**½ cup soft butter or margarine**
**½ cup sugar**
**½ cup walnuts**
**1 5-ounce bottle maraschino cherries, with syrup**

Have ingredients room temperature. Preheat oven to 350°. Grease and lightly flour a 9x9x2-inch pan. Sift flour, soda and salt together into a bowl; set aside. Put buttermilk, chocolate, egg, butter and sugar in blender container; cover and run on speed 7 (or high) until chocolate is completely liquefied. Add walnuts and maraschino cherries; cover and run on speed 4 (or low) just until cherries and nuts are chopped. Add to flour mixture; mix well. Turn into prepared pan; bake 45 minutes or until done. Cool 10 minutes in pan; remove from pan and cool on rack.

## MOCHA ALMOND REFRIGERATOR TORTE

**1 small angel food tube cake**
**½ cup strong hot coffee**
**2 envelopes (2 tablespoons) unflavored gelatin**
**⅓ cup sugar**
**1 6-ounce package (1 cup) semisweet chocolate pieces**
**¼ cup heavy cream**
**1 teaspoon vanilla OR ½ teaspoon rum flavoring**
**2 cups crushed ice**
**¾ cup slivered almonds**

Cut cake crosswise into 5 equal layers; set aside. Put hot coffee and gelatin in blender container; cover and run on speed 1 (or low) until gelatin is dissolved. Add sugar, chocolate pieces, cream and flavoring; cover container and run on speed 7 (or high) until chocolate is liquefied. Add ice; cover container and run on speed 7 (or high) until all ice is liquefied. Let set 1 minute or until mixture begins to thicken. Quickly spread about ¾ cup filling on bottom slice of cake; sprinkle with about 2 tablespoons almonds and cover with next cake slice. Follow this procedure with remaining layers, including top of cake. Chill until serving time.

**Note:** If desired, use all filling between layers and none on top of cake. Frost top and sides with Cocoa Whipped Cream (page 139); garnish with almonds.

## CHOCOLATE LOAF CAKE

**1¾ cups sifted cake flour**
**1 teaspoon salt**
**1 teaspoon soda**
**1 cup milk**
**2 eggs**
**3 squares (3 ounces) unsweetened chocolate, cut up**
**½ cup shortening**
**1 teaspoon vanilla**
**1¼ cups sugar**

Have all ingredients room temperature. Preheat oven to 350°. Grease a 9x9x2-inch pan. Sift flour, salt and soda together into medium bowl; set aside.

Put remaining ingredients in blender container in order listed; cover and run on speed 7 (or high) until chocolate is liquefied. Pour chocolate mixture over dry ingredients and mix well. Pour into prepared pan and bake 55 minutes or until done. Cool 10 minutes in pan; remove from pan and cool on rack. Frost with Chocolate Powdered Sugar Frosting (page 168).

## ALMOND CHOCOLATE CAKE

**1 cup blanched almonds**
**½ cup milk**
**4 ounces sweet chocolate, cut up**
**4 eggs, separated**
**2 cups sugar**
**1 cup soft shortening**
**¾ cup mashed potatoes**
**2 cups sifted flour**
**½ teaspoon salt**
**½ teaspoon baking powder**
**1 teaspoon cinnamon**
**1 teaspoon cloves**

Have all ingredients room temperature. Preheat oven to 325°. Lightly grease a 10-inch tube pan. Put almonds in blender container; cover and run on speed 4 (or low) until very finely chopped. Empty into a large bowl. Put milk and chocolate in blender container; cover and run on speed 3 (or low) until chocolate is very finely grated but not liquefied. Empty into a small bowl; set aside.

Put egg yolks, sugar and shortening in blender container; cover and run on speed 6 (or high) until smooth. Add potatoes; cover and run on speed 7 (or high) until smooth. Sift flour, salt, baking powder, cinnamon and cloves together into bowl with almonds. Add chocolate mixture and egg yolk mixture; mix well. Beat egg whites with an electric mixer until stiff but not dry; fold into batter. Turn into prepared pan. Bake 1 hour and 10 minutes. Cool thoroughly in pan on a cooling rack.

## OLD-FASHIONED RED DEVIL'S FOOD CAKE

½ cup salad oil
2 eggs
1 cup milk
1 teaspoon vanilla
1¾ cups sifted cake flour
1½ cups sugar
⅓ cup cocoa
1¼ teaspoons soda
1 teaspoon salt
½ teaspoon baking powder

Preheat oven to 350°. Grease and flour two 9-inch layer cake pans. Put the first 4 ingredients in blender container; cover and run on speed 5 (or high) for 20 seconds. Sift remaining ingredients into a mixing bowl. Pour liquid mixture into dry ingredients and stir until smooth. Pour into prepared pans and bake 30–35 minutes or until done. Cool on racks.

## COCONUT CAKE

1¼ cups scalded milk
1 cup moist shredded coconut
3 cups sifted flour
1 teaspoon salt
3 teaspoons baking powder
3 eggs (room temperature)
½ cup soft shortening
1½ cups sugar
½ teaspoon vanilla
¼ teaspoon soda
¼ cup hot water

The night before the cake is to be baked, put milk and coconut in blender container; cover and run on speed 4 (or low) until coconut is chopped. Pour into a bowl; cover and refrigerate overnight. When ready to bake cake, preheat oven to 375°. Grease and line with waxed paper three 9-inch round layer cake pans. Sift flour, baking powder and salt together into a large bowl; set aside.

Put eggs, shortening, sugar and vanilla in blender container; cover and run on speed 6 (or high) until smooth. Add coconut-milk mixture; cover and run on speed 6 (or high) for 10 seconds. Dissolve baking soda in hot water. Add coconut mixture and the soda and water to sifted dry ingredients; mix until smooth with a spoon or electric mixer. Pour into prepared pans. Bake 35–40 minutes or until done. Cool 10 minutes in pans; remove from pans and cool on racks.

*Old-fashioned Red Devil's Food Cake*

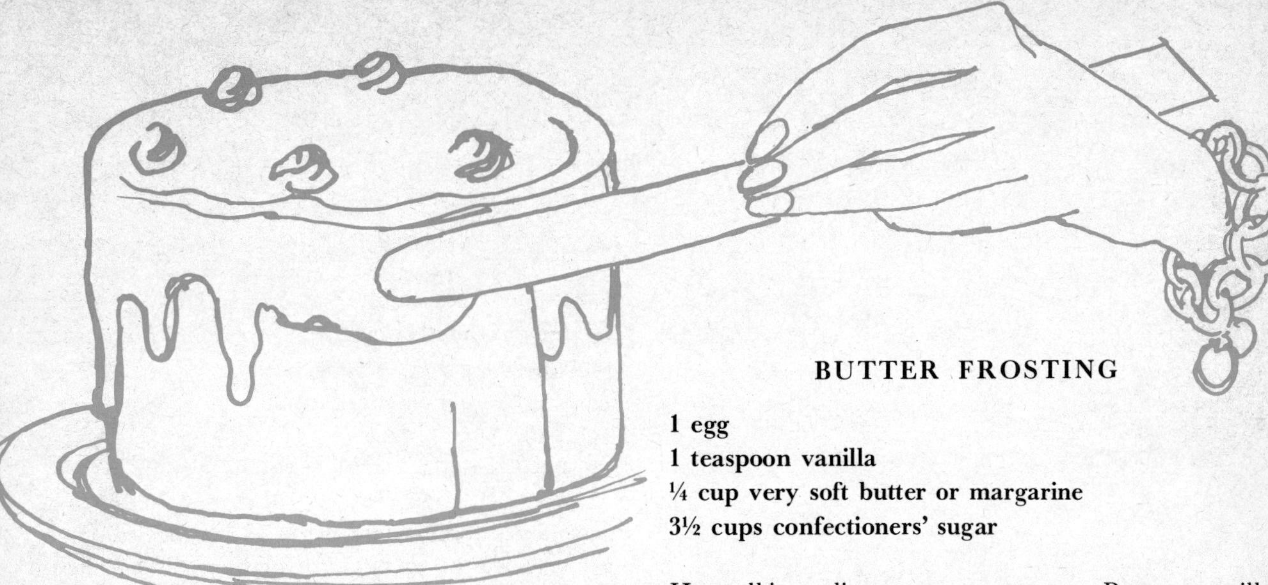

## Frostings

### CREAMY WHITE ICING

**3 tablespoons light cream**
**1 teaspoon vanilla**
**4 ounces cream cheese, cubed**
**2 tablespoons butter or margarine**
**½ teaspoon salt**
**3 cups confectioners' sugar**

Have all ingredients room temperature. Put all ingredients except confectioners' sugar in blender container; cover and run on speed 3 (or low) until smooth. Add 1 cup confectioners' sugar; cover and run on speed 7 (or high) until smooth. Gradually add remaining confectioners' sugar. If necessary, stop blender occasionally during processing and push mixture toward blades with rubber spatula. Blend until smooth. *Frosts one 8-inch layer cake.*

### SNOW WHITE FILLING

**2 tablespoons light cream**
**3–4 drops almond extract**
**1 teaspoon light corn syrup**
**Dash salt**
**1½ cups confectioners' sugar**

Put all ingredients in blender container in order listed. Cover and run on speed 5 (or high) until smooth. If necessary, stop blender during processing and push ingredients toward blades with rubber spatula. Add additional cream if necessary. *Frosts one 13x9½-inch pan of bar cookies or fills one 8- or 9-inch 3-layer cake.*

### BUTTER FROSTING

**1 egg**
**1 teaspoon vanilla**
**¼ cup very soft butter or margarine**
**3½ cups confectioners' sugar**

Have all ingredients room temperature. Put egg, vanilla and butter in blender container; cover and run on speed 2 (or low) until smooth. Add 2½ cups confectioners' sugar; cover and run on speed 6 (or high) until smooth. Add remaining confectioners' sugar and run on speed 6 (or high) until smooth. *Fills and frosts one 8- or 9-inch layer cake.*

### BUTTERSCOTCH FROSTING

**1 6-ounce package butterscotch pieces**
**2 tablespoons butter or margarine**
**3 tablespoons water**
**24 marshmallows**
**1½–2 cups confectioners' sugar**

Melt butterscotch pieces and butter with water over low heat. Put in blender container with marshmallows; cover and run on speed 6 (or high) until smooth. Pour into a bowl; stir in enough confectioners' sugar to make spreading consistency. *Fills and frosts one 8-inch layer cake or frosts one 13x9½-inch cake.*

### BUTTERSCOTCH ICING

**2 tablespoons hot milk**
**¼ cup soft butter or margarine**
**1 tablespoon light corn syrup**
**1 teaspoon vanilla**
**1 cup firmly packed brown sugar**
**1 cup confectioners' sugar**

Put milk, butter, corn syrup, vanilla and brown sugar in blender container in order listed; cover and run on speed 5 (or high) until smooth. Add confectioners' sugar; cover and run on speed 7 (or high) until smooth. *Fills and frosts one 8- or 9-inch layer cake.*

## FUDGE VELVET FROSTING

**3 tablespoons hot water**
**2 tablespoons butter or margarine, melted**
**3 squares (3 ounces) unsweetened chocolate, cut up**
**1 egg**
**1 teaspoon vanilla**
**1¾ cups confectioners' sugar**

Put hot water, melted butter and chocolate in blender container; cover and run on speed 7 (or high) until chocolate is liquefied. Add egg, vanilla and confectioners' sugar; cover and run on speed 7 (or high) until smooth. If necessary, stop blender during processing and push ingredients toward blades with rubber spatula. Cool to spreading consistency. *Fills and frosts one 8- or 9-inch layer cake.*

## ORANGE-CHOCOLATE MARSHMALLOW FROSTING

**2 tablespoons hot water**
**2 tablespoons butter or margarine, melted**
**3 squares (3 ounces) semisweet chocolate, cut up**
**Rind of ½ medium orange, cut up**
**1 tablespoon orange juice**
**2 cups miniature marshmallows**
**1½ cups confectioners' sugar**

Put hot water, melted butter and chocolate in blender container; cover and run on speed 7 (or high) until chocolate is liquefied. Add orange rind, orange juice and marshmallows; cover and run on speed 7 (or high) until marshmallows are dissolved. Add confectioners' sugar; cover and run on speed 5 (or high) until smooth. If necessary, stop blender during processing and push ingredients toward blades with rubber spatula. Cool until of spreading consistency. *Fills and frosts one 8- or 9-inch layer cake.*

## FRENCH MOCHA-CREAM FROSTING

**6 tablespoons hot coffee**
**1 6-ounce package (1 cup) semisweet chocolate pieces**
**2 tablespoons confectioners' sugar**
**½ cup soft butter or margarine**
**4 egg yolks**
**½ teaspoon vanilla**

Put coffee and chocolate pieces in blender container; cover and run on speed 7 (or high) until chocolate is liquefied. Stop blender and scrape chocolate down from sides of container with rubber spatula. Add remaining ingredients; cover and run on speed 6 (or high) until smooth. Let stand 5 minutes to thicken slightly; spread on cake. *Fills and frosts one 8- or 9-inch layer cake.*

## CHOCOLATE POWDERED SUGAR FROSTING

**¼ cup hot milk**
**6 ounces (1 cup) semisweet chocolate pieces**
**⅛ teaspoon salt**
**¼ teaspoon vanilla**
**1½–2 cups confectioners' sugar**

Put all ingredients except confectioners' sugar in blender container; cover and run on speed 7 (or high) until smooth. While blender is running, gradually add confectioners' sugar until frosting is thick enough to spread. If necessary, stop blender during processing and push ingredients toward blades with rubber spatula. *Frosts top and sides of one 9-inch square cake.*

## ORANGE FROSTING

**1 1½-inch square orange rind, cut up**
**¼ cup orange juice**
**½ teaspoon lemon juice**
**1 egg yolk**
**1¾ cups confectioners' sugar**

Put first 4 ingredients in blender container; cover and run on speed 4 (or low) until orange rind is finely chopped. Add confectioners' sugar; cover and run on speed 5 (or high) until spreading consistency. If necessary, stop blender during processing and push ingredients toward blades with rubber spatula. *Frosts one 8- or 9-inch square cake.*

## LADY BALTIMORE FROSTING

**⅓ cup seedless raisins**
**⅓ cup candied cherries**
**⅓ cup pecans**
**4 dried figs, cut up**
**2 egg whites**
**1½ cups sugar**
**¼ teaspoon cream of tartar**
**⅓ cup cold water**
**Dash salt**
**1 teaspoon vanilla**

Put first 4 ingredients in blender container; cover and run on speed 4 (or low) until chopped. If necessary, turn blender on and off several times. When chopped, empty into a mixing bowl and set aside. Put unbeaten egg whites, sugar, cream of tartar, water and salt in top of double boiler. Beat with an electric mixer to blend. Place over boiling water and cook, beating constantly, until frosting forms stiff peaks, about 7 minutes. Remove from heat; add vanilla and beat to blend. Combine ½ cup of the frosting with the chopped fruits and nuts; spread between layers of Lady Baltimore Cake (page 156). Frost top and sides with remaining frosting. *Fills and frosts one 8- or 9-inch layer cake.*

## CHOCOLATE-MINT FROSTING

**3 ⅞-ounce milk chocolate bars OR one 2½-ounce milk chocolate bar, chilled**
**½ cup pecans**
**1 package fluffy white frosting mix**
**¼ teaspoon peppermint extract**
**¼ teaspoon green food coloring**

Break chocolate bars into blender container; cover and run on speed 4 (or high) until chopped. Empty into a bowl. Put pecans in blender container; cover and run on speed 4 (or high) until finely chopped. Empty into bowl with chocolate; mix. Prepare frosting mix as directed on package; add peppermint extract and food coloring. Quickly stir in chocolate and nuts. *Fills and frosts one 8- or 9-inch layer cake.*

## CHOCOLATE-COCONUT TOPPING

**½ cup semisweet chocolate pieces**
**6 tablespoons boiling water**
**2 cups shredded coconut**

Put chocolate pieces and boiling water in blender container; cover and run on speed 6 (or high) until mixture is smooth. Add coconut; cover and run on speed 4 (or high) until coconut is chopped. If necessary, stop blender during processing and push ingredients toward blades with rubber spatula. Sprinkle over white or yellow cake while still warm. *Tops one 13x9½-inch cake.*

## STRAWBERRY FLUFF

**1 10-ounce package frozen strawberries, thawed and drained**
**1 cup whipping cream, Blender whipped (page 139)**
**⅓ cup sugar**
**½ teaspoon vanilla**
**1 egg white**

Put strawberries in blender container; cover and run on speed 2 (or low) about 20 seconds or until puréed. Empty into mixing bowl with whipped cream. Add sugar and vanilla; fold together. Beat egg white in a small bowl with an electric mixer; fold beaten egg white into whipped cream-strawberries mixture. Serve immediately. *Frosts one 10-inch tube cake.*

## SYRACUSE TOPPING

**4–6 vanilla wafers**
**9 candied cherries**
**6 marshmallows**
**¼ cup sugar**
**½ teaspoon vanilla**
**1 cup whipping cream, Blender whipped (page 139)**

Put cookies in blender container; cover and run on speed 3 (or low) until crumbed. Measure ⅓ cup; empty into bowl and set aside. Put cherries and marshmallows in blender container; cover and run on speed 5 (or high) until cut into small pieces. Empty into bowl with crumbs. Blend sugar and vanilla into whipped cream; then fold in cooky crumbs, marshmallows and cherries. *Frosts one 8- or 9-inch square cake.*

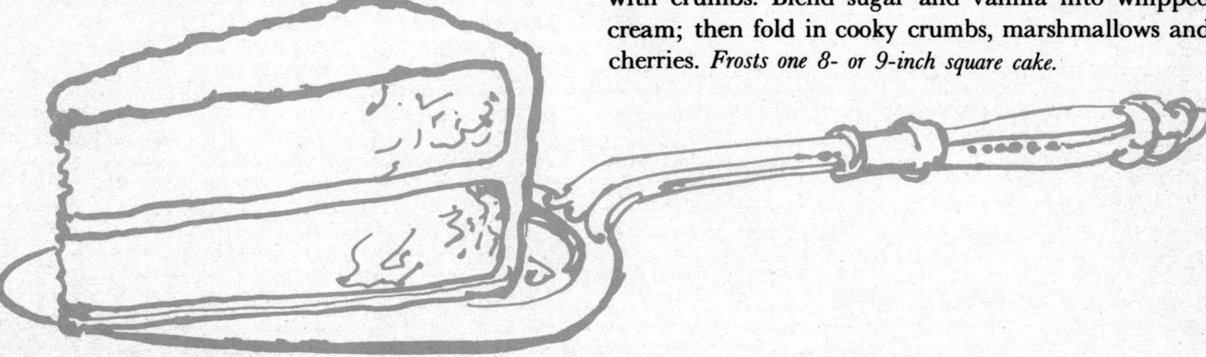

## Cookies

*You will make cookies more often and in greater variety when your blender is on the counter top day in and day out, ready for action. The blender can simplify all aspects of cooky-making, but is especially helpful when nuts or fruits are to be chopped or puréed for toppings and fillings. Follow recipes carefully for order of adding ingredients and timing.*

*To adapt your own favorite cooky recipes to blender-cooking, find one here that is similar and use that method as a guide.*

*Molasses Balls (p. 171)*

*No-Bake Date Cook (p. 171)*

*Sour Cream Cashew Drops (p. 171)*

*Cream Cheese Crisps (p. 171)*

## CREAM CHEESE CRISPS

**1½ cups corn flakes**
**1 cup sifted flour**
**2 teaspoons baking powder**
**½ teaspoon salt**
**⅓ cup soft butter or margarine**
**1 3-ounce package cream cheese, cubed**
**½ cup sugar**
**1 teaspoon lemon juice**

Have all ingredients room temperature. Preheat oven to 375°. Put half the corn flakes in blender container; cover and run on speed 4 (or low) until finely crumbed. Empty into a shallow bowl. Repeat process with remaining corn flakes. Sift flour, baking powder and salt together into a mixing bowl.

Put remaining ingredients in blender container; cover and run on speed 5 (or high) until smooth. Add to sifted dry ingredients; mix well. Shape dough into small balls; roll in crumbs. Place on ungreased cooky sheets; flatten with a fork. Bake 15 minutes or until brown. *Makes 3 dozen cookies.*

## NO-BAKE DATE COOKIES

**2 cups moist shredded coconut**
**¾ cup walnuts**
**2 eggs**
**1 cup sugar**
**¼ teaspoon salt**
**1 8-ounce package pitted dates**
**2½ cups toasted rice cereal**
**1 teaspoon vanilla**

Put 1 cup coconut in blender container; cover and run on speed 4 (or low) until chopped. Empty onto a sheet of waxed paper. Repeat process with remaining coconut; set aside. Put walnuts in blender container; cover and run on speed 4 (or low) until chopped. Empty into a bowl.

Put eggs, sugar and salt in blender container; cover and run on speed 6 (or high) for 2 minutes. Add dates; cover and run on speed 4 (or high) until dates are chopped. Pour into a large heavy frypan; cook, stirring constantly, over low heat for 10 minutes. Remove from heat; add cereal, chopped walnuts and vanilla. When cool enough to handle, pinch off portions and, with dampened hands, form into 1-inch balls. Roll in chopped coconut. *Makes about 4 dozen cookies.*

## MOLASSES BALLS

**½ teaspoon vanilla**
**¼ cup molasses**
**1 cup very soft butter or margarine**
**2 cups pecans**
**2 cups sifted flour**
**½ teaspoon salt**
**Sifted confectioners' sugar**

Preheat oven to 350°. Lightly grease cooky sheets. Put vanilla, molasses and butter in blender container; cover and run on speed 6 (or high) until very smooth. Add pecans; cover and run on speed 4 (or low) until nuts are finely chopped. If necessary, stop blender during processing and push ingredients toward blades with rubber spatula.

Sift the flour and salt together into a bowl. Add molasses mixture; mix well. Shape into 1-inch balls. Place 2 inches apart on cooky sheets. Bake 12–15 minutes. Remove to cooling racks; cool slightly, then roll in confectioners' sugar. *Makes 5 dozen cookies.*

## SOUR CREAM CASHEW DROPS

**2 cups sifted flour**
**1 teaspoon baking powder**
**¾ teaspoon soda**
**¼ teaspoon salt**
**1 egg**
**½ cup soft butter**
**1 cup firmly packed brown sugar**
**1 teaspoon vanilla**
**½ cup dairy sour cream**
**1½ cups salted cashew nuts (6¾-ounce can)**

Preheat oven to 375°. Grease cooky sheets. Sift flour, baking powder, soda and salt together into mixing bowl. Put egg, butter, brown sugar, vanilla and sour cream in blender container; cover and run on speed 3 (or low) until smooth. Stop blender and add nuts. Cover and run on speed 4 (or low) until nuts are coarsely chopped. (Watch carefully so nuts do not become finely chopped; turn on and off quickly several times.) Pour into flour mixture and stir to mix. Drop by teaspoonfuls onto cooky sheets. Bake about 10 minutes. Cool and frost with Creamy White Icing (page 167). *Makes 7 dozen cookies.*

## BANANA DROP COOKIES

**2½ cups sifted flour**
**2 teaspoons baking powder**
**½ teaspoon salt**
**¼ teaspoon soda**
**2 eggs**
**⅔ cup soft shortening**
**1 cup sugar**
**2 medium bananas, peeled and cut into 2-inch pieces**
**¾ teaspoon vanilla**

Have all ingredients room temperature. Preheat oven to 400°. Grease cooky sheets. Sift flour, baking powder, salt and soda together into a mixing bowl; set aside. Put remaining ingredients in blender container in order listed; cover and run on speed 6 (or high) until smooth. Add blended mixture to flour and mix well. Drop by teaspoonfuls onto cooky sheets. Bake 10–12 minutes or until done. *Makes 5 dozen cookies.*

## SOUR CREAM ORANGE DROPS

**1 egg**
**¼ cup orange juice**
**½ cup dairy sour cream**
**½ cup soft butter or margarine**
**¾ cup sugar**
**1 cup raisins**
**¼ cup pecans**
**2 cups sifted flour**
**1 teaspoon salt**
**½ teaspoon soda**

Have ingredients room temperature. Preheat oven to 375°. Grease cooky sheets. Put first 5 ingredients in blender container; cover and run on speed 6 (or high) until smooth. Add raisins and pecans; cover and run on speed 4 (or high) just until chopped. Sift flour, salt and soda together into a bowl; add blended mixture. Mix well. Drop by teaspoonfuls onto prepared cooky sheets. Bake 10 minutes or until done. *Makes 4 dozen cookies.*

## OATMEAL SURPRISE COOKIES

**4 cups corn flakes**
**2 cups quick-cooking rolled oats**
**2 cups sifted flour**
**1 teaspoon soda**
**¼ teaspoon salt**
**¼ teaspoon nutmeg**
**1 cup butter or margarine, melted**
**2 cups firmly packed brown sugar**
**2 eggs**

Preheat oven to 350°. Grease cooky sheets. Put 2 cups corn flakes in blender container; cover and run on speed 4 (or low) until finely crumbed. Empty into a bowl. Repeat process with remaining corn flakes. Add rolled oats to crumbs. Sift flour, soda, salt and nutmeg together into bowl with cereals; mix. Put butter, brown sugar and eggs in blender container; cover and run on speed 6 (or high) for 30 seconds. Add to flour mixture; mix thoroughly. Drop dough by teaspoonfuls onto cooky sheets; flatten with a fork. Bake 10–12 minutes. *Makes 6 dozen cookies.*

## OATMEAL BANANA COOKIES

**1½ cups sifted flour**
**1 cup sugar**
**1 teaspoon salt**
**½ teaspoon soda**
**¼ teaspoon nutmeg**
**¾ teaspoon cinnamon**
**1¼ cups soft butter or margarine**
**1 egg**
**3 bananas, peeled and quartered**
**½ cup walnuts**
**1¾ cups quick-cooking rolled oats**

Preheat oven to 400°. Sift flour, sugar, salt, soda, nutmeg and cinnamon together into a large bowl. With pastry blender or two knives cut in ¾ cup butter until mixture is the texture of coarse meal. Put egg, bananas and remaining butter in blender container; cover and run on speed 6 (or high) until smooth. Add nuts; cover and run on speed 4 (or low) until nuts are coarsely chopped. Add banana mixture and rolled oats to sifted flour mixture; mix thoroughly. Drop by teaspoonfuls 1½ inches apart onto ungreased cooky sheets. Bake 15 minutes or until done. *Makes 5 dozen cookies.*

## APPLE COOKIES

**1½ cups sifted flour**
**1 teaspoon baking powder**
**½ teaspoon soda**
**1½ cups rolled oats**
**¼ cup milk**
**2 medium apples, pared, cored and cubed**
**¾ cup raisins**
**1 egg**
**1 cup sugar**
**½ cup shortening**
**1 teaspoon salt**
**1 teaspoon cinnamon**
**½ teaspoon nutmeg**
**¼ teaspoon cloves**
**1 cup pecans**

Have all ingredients room temperature. Sift flour, baking powder and soda together into large mixing bowl. Add rolled oats; mix. Set aside.

Put milk in blender container; cover and run on speed 4 (or high); gradually add apple cubes and raisins; run until finely chopped. Stop blender and add egg, sugar, shortening, salt and spices; cover and run on speed 6 (or high) until well mixed. Add pecans and run on speed 6 (or high) until nuts are coarsely chopped. Pour over dry ingredients and mix well; chill. Preheat oven to 375°. Grease cooky sheets; drop dough by teaspoonfuls onto cooky sheets. Bake 15 minutes or until done. *Makes 5 dozen cookies.*

## CHOCOLATE BUTTERSCOTCH COOKIES

**¾ cup pecans**
**½ cup semisweet chocolate pieces**
**½ cup butterscotch pieces**
**½ cup soft butter or margarine**
**½ cup sugar**
**¼ cup firmly packed brown sugar**
**1 egg**
**1 teaspoon vanilla**
**1 cup sifted flour**
**½ teaspoon soda**
**½ teaspoon salt**

Preheat oven to 375°. Grease cooky sheets. Put pecans in blender container; cover and run on speed 4 (or low) until chopped. Empty into mixing bowl; add chocolate and butterscotch pieces to nuts. Put all remaining ingredients in blender container; cover and run on speed 5 (or high) until smooth. If necessary, stop blender during processing and push ingredients toward blades with rubber spatula. Empty into bowl with nuts and chocolate and butterscotch pieces. Mix well. Drop from a teaspoon, 2 inches apart, onto cooky sheets and bake 10–12 minutes or until lightly browned. *Makes 3½ dozen cookies.*

## CHOCOLATE DELIGHTS

**9–10 soda crackers**
**¾ cup walnuts**
**1 cup (6 ounces) semisweet chocolate pieces**
**3 egg whites**
**1 cup confectioners' sugar**
**1 teaspoon vanilla**

Preheat oven to 325°. Grease cooky sheets. Break 5 soda crackers into blender container; cover and run on speed 4 (or low) until finely crumbed. Empty into a bowl. Repeat process with remaining crackers. (You should have ½ cup crumbs.) Put nuts in blender container; cover and run on speed 4 (or low) until chopped. Add to cracker crumbs.

Put chocolate pieces in blender container; cover and run on speed 4 (or low) until chocolate is fine. Add to crumbs and nuts. Beat egg whites with an electric mixer until they form soft peaks; add sugar, 2 tablespoons at a time, continuing to beat until stiff but not dry. Fold in crumb mixture and vanilla. Drop by teaspoonfuls onto cooky sheets. Bake 12 minutes. *Makes 3 dozen cookies.*

## COCONUT-CHERRY CHEWS

**2 cups moist shredded coconut**
**½ cup sweetened condensed milk**
**10 candied cherries**
**1 teaspoon almond extract**

Preheat oven to 325°. Grease cooky sheets. Put 1 cup coconut in blender container; cover and run on speed 4 (or low) until chopped. Empty into a bowl. Put milk, remaining 1 cup coconut, cherries and almond extract in container; cover and run on speed 6 (or high) until blended and cherries are chopped. Add to chopped coconut; mix well. Drop by teaspoonfuls onto cooky sheets; bake 10 minutes. Cool; remove to cooling racks. *Makes 3 dozen cookies.*

## PEANUT DROP COOKIES

**1 egg**
**½ cup sugar**
**¼ teaspoon vanilla**
**2 teaspoons flour**
**1½ cups salted peanuts**

Preheat oven to 350°. Grease cooky sheets. Put all ingredients except peanuts in blender container; cover and run on speed 6 (or high) for 2 minutes. Add peanuts; cover and run on speed 4 (or low) until nuts are coarsely chopped. Drop by teaspoonfuls, 2 inches apart, onto cooky sheets. Bake 10–12 minutes. Let cool 1 minute before removing to cooling racks. *Makes 3 dozen cookies.*

*Raisin Bars*

## SUGAR COOKIES

**5 cups sifted flour**
**5 teaspoons baking powder**
**½ teaspoon salt**
**½ cup milk**
**3 tablespoons lemon juice**
**Rind of 1 lemon (colored portion only)**
**1½ cups sugar**
**1 pound soft butter or margarine**

Have all ingredients room temperature. Sift flour, baking powder and salt together into a large mixing bowl; set aside. Put remaining ingredients in blender container; cover and run on speed 6 (or high) until smooth. Add blended mixture to dry ingredients; stir until well mixed. Chill.

Preheat oven to 400°. Roll small portions of chilled dough very thin, using as little flour as possible on pastry cloth and rolling pin. Cut with small cooky cutters. Place 2 inches apart on ungreased cooky sheets. Bake about 8 minutes or until lightly browned. *Makes 9 dozen cookies.*

## CHEWY BUTTERSCOTCH SQUARES

**½ cup walnuts**
**¼ cup butter or margarine, melted**
**1 6-ounce package (1 cup) butterscotch pieces**
**2 eggs**
**½ teaspoon vanilla**
**1 cup firmly packed brown sugar**
**1 cup sifted flour**
**1 teaspoon baking powder**
**½ teaspoon salt**

Preheat oven to 350°. Grease a 13x9½x2-inch pan. Put nuts in blender container; cover and run on speed 4 (or low) until chopped. Empty into a large bowl. Put melted butter, butterscotch pieces, eggs, vanilla and brown sugar in blender container in order listed; cover and run on speed 7 (or high) until smooth.

Sift flour, baking powder and salt together into bowl with nuts. Add blended butterscotch mixture; mix well. Spread in prepared pan. Bake 25 minutes or until done. *Makes about 2 dozen squares.*

## RAISIN BARS

**2 tablespoons milk**
**1 teaspoon vanilla**
**1 egg**
**1 cup sugar**
**½ cup soft butter or margarine**
**2 cups sifted flour**
**1 teaspoon baking powder**
**1 teaspoon salt**
**½ cup water**
**1 tablespoon lemon juice**
**1½ cups raisins**
**¼ cup firmly packed brown sugar**
**1 teaspoon cornstarch**
**½ teaspoon ginger**
**¼ teaspoon salt**

Put first 5 ingredients in blender container; cover and run on speed 6 (or high) until smooth. Sift flour, baking powder and salt into a bowl; add blended mixture and mix well. Chill.

Meanwhile, put all remaining ingredients in blender container in order listed; cover and run on speed 4 (or low) until raisins are chopped. Pour into a saucepan; simmer about 10 minutes or until thickened, stirring frequently. Cool.

Preheat oven to 375°. Grease a 9x9x2-inch pan. Spread about ⅔ of chilled dough in the bottom of prepared pan with spatula or back of spoon. Cover with raisin filling. Roll remaining dough ⅛-inch thick; cut into ½-inch wide strips. Arrange crisscross fashion over filling. Bake 30 minutes or until browned. Cool in pan. *Makes 36 bars.*

*wy Butterscotch Squares (p. 175)*
*onut-Cherry Chews (p. 174)*

## DATE-HONEY BARS

**2 tablespoons honey**
**1 egg, separated**
**¼ cup soft butter or margarine**
**1 cup confectioners' sugar**
**¾ cup pitted dates**
**1½ cups sifted flour**
**½ cup sugar**
**1 teaspoon baking powder**
**½ teaspoon salt**
**½ cup quick-cooking rolled oats**
**½ cup shortening**
**¼ cup milk**
**1 teaspoon vanilla**

Preheat oven to 400°. Grease and line with waxed paper a 9x9x2-inch pan. Put honey, egg white and butter in blender container; cover and run on speed 6 (or high) until smooth. Add confectioners' sugar and dates; cover and run on speed 6 (or high) until dates are finely chopped and mixture is well blended. If necessary, stop blender during processing and push ingredients toward blades with rubber spatula. Empty into a bowl; set aside.

Sift together flour, sugar, baking powder and salt. Add rolled oats. Cut in shortening until mixture is crumbly. Put milk, vanilla and egg yolk in blender container; cover and run on speed 5 (or high) until smooth. Add to flour mixture and stir until flour is well moistened. Spread half the dough on bottom of prepared pan. Spread honey-date filling over dough. Pat remaining dough over filling. Bake 25–30 minutes. *Makes 18 bars.*

## CHOCOLATE BROWNIES

**2 eggs**
**2 squares (2 ounces) unsweetened chocolate, cut up**
**¼ cup soft shortening**
**1 cup sugar**
**½ cup sifted flour**
**¼ teaspoon salt**
**½ cup walnuts**

Have all ingredients room temperature. Preheat oven to 350°. Grease an 8x8x2-inch pan; set aside. Put eggs, chocolate, shortening and sugar in blender container; cover and run on speed 7 (or high) until chocolate is liquefied. Add flour and salt; cover and run on speed 7 (or high) just until mixed. If necessary, stop blender during processing and push ingredients toward blades with rubber spatula. Add walnuts; cover container and run on speed 7 (or high) just until all nuts are chopped. Spread batter in prepared pan. Bake 35 minutes or until done. *Makes 16 squares.*

## CRUMB BROWNIES

**36 graham crackers**
**1 15-ounce can sweetened condensed milk**
**1 4-ounce can moist shredded coconut**
**⅓ cup walnuts**
**1 teaspoon vanilla**
**1 12-ounce package (2 cups) semisweet chocolate pieces**

Preheat oven to 350°. Grease and lightly flour an 8x8x2-inch pan. Break about 5 graham crackers into blender container; cover and run on speed 4 (or low) until finely crumbed. Empty into a bowl. Repeat process until all crackers are crumbed. (You should have 2 cups crumbs.)

Put all remaining ingredients in blender container in order listed; cover and run on speed 7 (or high) until chocolate and nuts are finely chopped. If necessary, stop blender during processing and push ingredients toward blades with rubber spatula. Add to crumbs; mix well. Spread evenly in prepared pan. Bake 40 minutes or until done. Cut into squares while still warm. Sprinkle with confectioners' sugar, if desired. *Makes 16 squares.*

## BROWNIE DREAMS

**½ cup nuts**
**½ cup moist shredded coconut**
**1½ cups sifted flour**
**½ teaspoon soda**
**½ teaspoon salt**
**½ cup soft shortening**
**2 squares (2 ounces) unsweetened chocolate, cut up**
**2 eggs**
**½ cup milk**
**1 cup firmly packed brown sugar**
**1 teaspoon vanilla**

Have all ingredients room temperature. Preheat oven to 350°. Grease a 13x9½x2-inch pan. Put nuts in blender container; cover and run on speed 4 (or low) until coarsely chopped; empty into small bowl. Put coconut in blender container; cover and run on speed 4 (or low) until finely chopped; add to nuts. Set aside.

Sift flour, soda and salt into medium bowl. Put remaining ingredients in blender container; cover and run on speed 7 (or high) until smooth. Pour over flour mixture and mix thoroughly. Spread batter evenly in prepared pan. Sprinkle nut-coconut mixture over top. Bake 15–18 minutes or until done. Cut into squares while warm. *Makes 40 bars.*

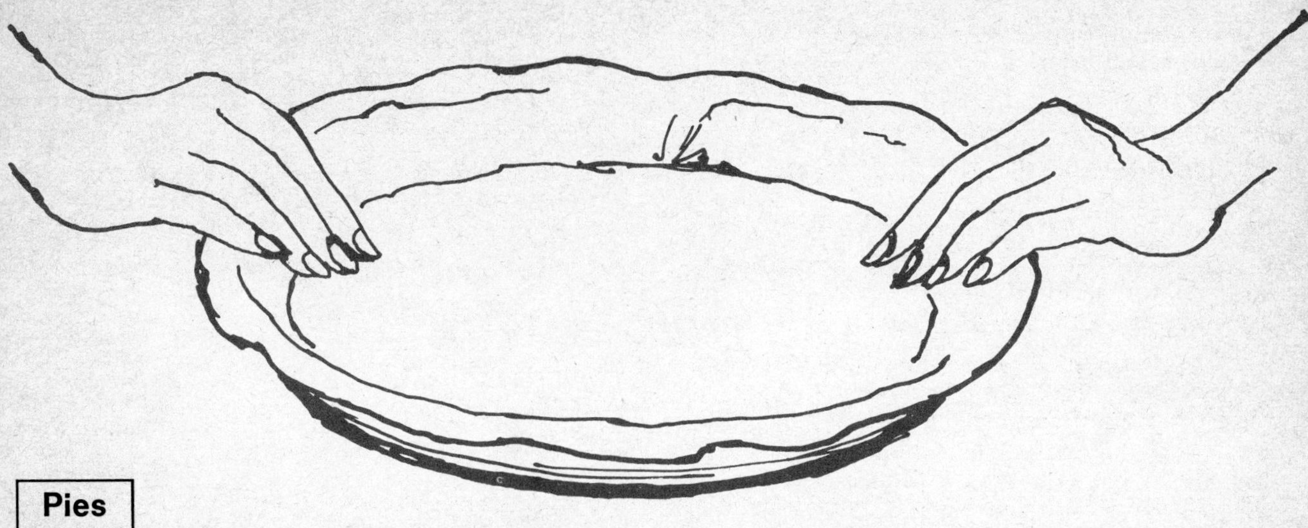

# Pies

*There is only one risk when the blender begins working for you as a pie-maker. The process becomes such fun you never want to stop. And since some of the most luscious pies are made with crumb crusts and creamy fillings, the finished products are devilishly tempting. Choose a fruit chiffon pie when you want something especially good but not too high in calories. Choose any of those in this section to create a sensation.*

## GRAHAM CRACKER CRUMB CRUST

**16-18 graham crackers**
**3 tablespoons sugar**
**½ teaspoon cinnamon**
**½ cup butter or margarine, melted**

Break 4 graham crackers into blender container; cover and run on speed 4 (or low) until crackers are finely crumbed. Empty into a bowl. Repeat process until all crackers are crumbed. (You should have 1 cup crumbs.) Add sugar and cinnamon to cracker crumbs; mix. Add melted butter and mix well. Press firmly onto bottom and sides of 9-inch pie pan. Chill until firm. *Makes one 9-inch pie shell.*

### CHOCOLATE-GRAHAM CRUST

After crumbing crackers, put 1 cut-up square (1 ounce) unsweetened chocolate in blender container; cover and run on speed 3 (or low) until chocolate is finely grated. Stir into cracker crumbs. Complete crust as directed.

### FILBERT CRUST

Use 11 graham crackers instead of 16 in Graham Cracker Crumb Crust recipe. After crumbing crackers, put 1 cup filberts in blender container; cover and run on speed 4 (or high) until nuts are chopped very fine. Add to cracker crumbs. Complete crust as directed.

## COOKY CRUST

**20-25 cookies (vanilla or chocolate wafers or gingersnaps)**
**⅓ cup butter or margarine, melted**

Break 5 cookies into blender container; cover and run on speed 4 (or high) until finely crumbed. Empty into a measuring cup. Repeat process until you have 1¼ cups cooky crumbs. Empty cooky crumbs into a bowl; add melted butter and mix well. Press onto sides and bottom of a 9-inch pie pan. Chill. *Makes one 9-inch pie shell.*

## NUT CRUST

**1½ cups walnuts or pecans**
**3 tablespoons sugar**
**⅓ cup butter or margarine, melted**

Put half the nuts in blender container; cover and run on speed 4 (or low) until nuts are finely ground. Empty into a bowl. Repeat process with remaining nuts. Stir in sugar; add melted butter and mix well. Press firmly onto sides and bottom of 9-inch pie pan. Chill. *Makes one 9-inch pie shell.*

## FRESH COCONUT PIE SHELL

**⅓ cup cubed fresh coconut (½-inch cubes)**
**1½ cups sifted flour**
**½ teaspoon salt**
**½ cup shortening (not butter or margarine)**
**3 tablespoons cold water**

Preheat oven to 450°. Put coconut in blender container; cover and run on speed 4 (or low) until coconut is finely grated. Set aside. Mix flour and salt in a medium bowl; cut in shortening with a pastry blender or two knives until the size of peas. Mix grated coconut with flour mixture. Sprinkle water over all; mix with a fork until dough holds together. Shape into a ball. Roll out and fit into a 10-inch pie pan; crimp edges. Prick bottom of shell with sharp-tined fork. Bake 12-15 minutes or until browned. Cool. *Makes one 10-inch pie shell.*

## CHOCOLATE COCONUT PIE SHELL

**1½ cups shredded coconut**
**2 squares (2 ounces) unsweetened chocolate**
**2 tablespoons butter or margarine**
**2 tablespoons water**
**⅔ cup confectioners' sugar**

Put ½ cup coconut in blender container; cover and run on speed 3 (or low) until coconut is finely chopped. Empty into a bowl. Repeat process until all coconut is chopped. Melt chocolate and butter in water. Put in blender container with half the coconut and all the sugar; cover and run on speed 1 (or low) until well mixed. If necessary, stop blender during processing and push ingredients toward blades with rubber spatula. Pour into a bowl. Add the remaining coconut and mix well. Spread onto the bottom and sides of a well-buttered 9-inch pie pan. Chill until firm. *Makes one 9-inch pie shell.*

### GRATE FRESH COCONUT

Put about ½ cup cubed coconut meat in blender container; cover and run on speed 3 (or low) until grated. If necessary, stop and start blender to toss coconut toward blades. Empty into a bowl and repeat until you have the amount you need.

## BAKED PECAN PIE SHELL

**⅓ cup pecans**
**7 tablespoons butter or shortening**
**3–3½ tablespoons hot milk**
**1¼ cups sifted flour**
**½ teaspoon salt**

Preheat oven to 425°. Put pecans in blender container; cover and run on speed 4 (or high) until nuts are finely chopped. Empty onto waxed paper or into a bowl; set aside. Put butter in blender container; add 3 tablespoons hot milk. Cover and run on speed 2 (or low) until mixture is smooth. Sift together flour and salt into a bowl. Add butter mixture and quickly stir into a smooth dough, adding additional milk if needed. Shape into a flat round and place between 2 pieces of waxed paper. Roll to ⅛-inch thickness, peel off top piece of paper and sprinkle with half the chopped pecans. Replace the waxed paper and gently roll nuts into the dough. Turn pastry over and repeat process. Remove top paper and fit pastry into a 9-inch pie pan. Remove other piece of paper; trim and flute edge. Prick shell with a fork. Bake 8–10 minutes or until pastry is lightly browned. Cool. *Makes one 9-inch pie shell.*

*Chilled Cherry Cheese Pie (p. 184) in Graham Cracker Crust (p. 177)*

*Coffee Chiffon Pie (p. 181)*
*in Chocolate Cooky Crust (p. 177)*

*Fresh Coconut Chiffon Pie (p. 182)*
*in Fresh Coconut Pie Shell (p. 178)*

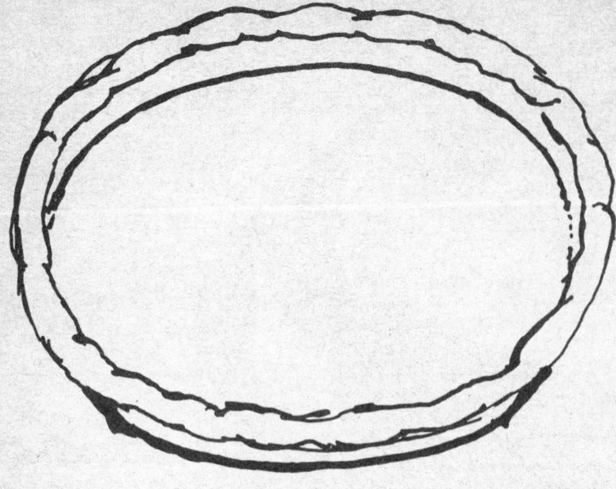

## PECAN PIE

**3 eggs**
**½ cup heavy cream**
**½ cup dark corn syrup**
**¼ teaspoon salt**
**¼ teaspoon cinnamon**
**1 cup sugar**
**½ teaspoon vanilla**
**2 tablespoons soft butter or margarine**
**1½ cups pecans**
**1 unbaked 9-inch pie shell**

Preheat oven to 400°. Put all ingredients except pie shell in blender container in order listed; cover and run on speed 3 (or low) until nuts are coarsely chopped, about 3 seconds. Pour into unbaked pie shell; bake about 35 minutes or until crust is browned and filling is puffed. Cool. *Makes one 9-inch pie.*

## WALNUT PIE

**4 eggs**
**½ cup soft butter or margarine**
**¾ cup sugar**
**¼ teaspoon salt**
**¼ cup light corn syrup**
**½ cup whipping cream**
**1 teaspoon vanilla**
**2 cups walnuts**
**1 unbaked 9-inch pie shell**
**1½ cups whipping cream, Blender whipped (page 139)**

Preheat oven to 375°. Put first 7 ingredients in blender container; cover and run on speed 7 (or high) for 2 minutes. Add walnuts; cover and run on speed 4 (or low) just until walnuts are coarsely chopped. Pour into unbaked pie shell. Bake 40 minutes. Cool. Top with whipped cream. *Makes one 9-inch pie.*

## HEAVENLY CHOCOLATE NUT PIE

**¾ cup walnuts**
**1½ squares (1½ ounces) unsweetened chocolate, cut up**
**½ cup boiling water**
**⅔ cup sugar**
**1½ teaspoons vanilla**
**¼ cup butter or margarine**
**1 cup sifted flour**
**¾ cup sugar**
**1 teaspoon baking powder**
**½ teaspoon salt**
**¼ cup soft butter or margarine**
**½ cup milk**
**1 egg**
**1 unbaked 9-inch pie shell**

Preheat oven to 350°. Put nuts in blender container; cover and run on speed 4 (or low) until nuts are finely chopped. Empty into a bowl; set aside. Put chocolate and boiling water in blender container; cover and run on speed 7 (or high) until chocolate is liquefied. Add ⅔ cup sugar, vanilla and ¼ cup butter; cover container and run on speed 6 (or high) until smooth. Pour mixture into a cup; set aside. Sift flour, ¾ cup sugar, baking powder and salt together into another bowl. Put ¼ cup soft butter, milk and egg in blender container; cover and run on speed 5 (or high) until smooth. Add to sifted dry ingredients and stir just until smooth; pour into unbaked pie shell. Pour chocolate mixture carefully over this batter and sprinkle chopped nuts over all. Bake 50-60 minutes or until the center springs back when touched lightly. If desired, serve with whipped cream. *Makes one 9-inch pie.*

## GINGER PECAN CREAM PIE

**8-10 gingersnaps**
**½ cup pecans**
**½ cup moist shredded coconut**
**1 quart vanilla ice cream**
**1 Gingersnap Cooky Crust (page 177)**

Break 4-5 gingersnaps into blender container; cover and run on speed 4 (or low) until finely crumbed. Empty into a measuring cup. Repeat process until you have ½ cup crumbs. Put pecans and coconut in blender container; cover and run on speed 4 (or low) until nuts are chopped. Mix with gingersnap crumbs. Soften ice cream slightly; spread half in Cooky Crust and sprinkle with half of crumb mixture. Repeat with remaining ice cream and crumbs. Freeze. *Makes one 9-inch pie.*

## CHOCOLATE-RUM MARBLE PIE

**¾ cup hot milk**
**1 envelope (1 tablespoon) unflavored gelatin**
**¼ cup cold milk**
**1 cup sugar**
**⅛ teaspoon salt**
**¼ cup rum**
**2 eggs, separated**
**2 cups (12 ounces) semisweet chocolate pieces**
**1 cup whipping cream**
**1 teaspoon vanilla**
**1 10-inch baked pie shell**

Put hot milk and gelatin in blender container; cover and run on speed 1 (or low) for 1 minute or until gelatin is dissolved. Add cold milk, ¼ cup sugar, salt, rum, egg yolks and chocolate pieces; cover and run on speed 7 (or high) until chocolate is liquefied. Beat egg whites in a small bowl with an electric mixer until foamy; gradually add ½ cup sugar and beat until stiff peaks form. Fold egg whites into chocolate mixture. Wash and dry blender container; blender whip cream (see page 139) with remaining ¼ cup sugar and vanilla. Spoon the chocolate mixture and whipped cream alternately into baked pie shell. Swirl with a spoon. Chill until firm. *Makes one 10-inch pie.*

## FRENCH VELVET CHOCOLATE PIE

**2 eggs**
**¾ cup sugar**
**½ cup soft butter or margarine**
**2 squares (2 ounces) unsweetened chocolate, melted**
**½ teaspoon vanilla**
**1 9-inch crumb crust or baked pie shell**
**1 pint vanilla ice cream, softened**

Put eggs, sugar, butter, chocolate and vanilla in blender container. Cover and run on speed 6 (or high) until completely smooth, with no sugar granules. Pour into pie shell. Refrigerate for at least 2 hours. Spread softened ice cream on top; serve at once. *Makes one 9-inch pie.*

## CHOCOLATE CHIFFON PIE

**¼ cup cold water**
**1 envelope (1 tablespoon) unflavored gelatin**
**½ cup hot milk**
**2 squares (2 ounces) unsweetened chocolate, cut up**
**1 cup sugar**
**1 teaspoon vanilla**
**¼ teaspoon salt**
**4 eggs, separated**
**1 9-inch Graham Cracker Crumb Crust (page 177), chilled**

Put cold water and gelatin in blender container and let stand until gelatin is moistened; add hot milk and run on speed 1 (or low) until gelatin is dissolved, about 1 minute. Add chocolate; cover and run on speed 7 (or high) until chocolate is liquefied. Add ½ cup sugar, vanilla, salt and egg yolks; cover and run on speed 7 (or high) 2 minutes longer. Chill until mixture is thick but not firmly set.

Beat egg whites in a medium bowl with an electric mixer until soft peaks form; gradually add ½ cup sugar and beat until stiff peaks form. Fold chilled chocolate mixture carefully but thoroughly into egg whites. Pour into prepared pie shell; chill until firm. Serve topped with whipped cream, if desired. *Makes one 9-inch pie.*

## COFFEE CHIFFON PIE

**1 envelope (1 tablespoon) unflavored gelatin**
**¼ cup sugar**
**1½ teaspoons instant coffee**
**⅛ teaspoon salt**
**1 cup boiling water**
**4 eggs, separated**
**1 teaspoon vanilla**
**¼ cup sugar**
**1 9-inch Chocolate Coconut Pie Shell (page 178)**

Put first 4 ingredients in blender container; cover and run on speed 1 (or low) until well mixed. Add boiling water; cover and run on speed 1 (or low) for 1 minute or until gelatin is dissolved. Add egg yolks and vanilla. Cover and run on speed 5 (or high) for 1 minute. Empty into a bowl and chill, stirring occasionally, until mixture mounds when dropped from a spoon. Beat egg whites in a small bowl with an electric mixer until soft peaks form; gradually add ¼ cup sugar and beat until stiff peaks form. Fold into gelatin mixture. Turn into pie shell and chill for several hours or until firm. Garnish with whipped cream, if desired. *Makes one 9-inch pie.*

## FRESH COCONUT CHIFFON PIE

**¼ cup cold water**
**1½ envelopes (1½ tablespoons) unflavored gelatin**
**3 tablespoons boiling water**
**4 eggs, separated**
**1 teaspoon vanilla**
**¼ teaspoon salt**
**¾ cup sugar**
**1 cup cubed fresh coconut**
**1 10-inch baked Fresh Coconut Pie Shell (page 178), chilled**

Soften gelatin in cold water and let stand in blender container until gelatin is moistened; add boiling water, cover and run on speed 1 (or low) until gelatin is dissolved. While continuing to run, add egg yolks, one at a time. Stop blender; add vanilla, salt and ½ cup sugar; cover and run on speed 5 (or high) until smooth. Add coconut; cover and run on speed 3 (or low) until coconut is finely grated. Chill in refrigerator until mixture begins to thicken.

Beat egg whites in a medium bowl with an electric mixer until soft peaks form; gradually add remaining ¼ cup sugar and beat until stiff peaks form. Fold chilled gelatin mixture into beaten egg whites. Pour into pie shell. Chill until firm. Top with sweetened whipped cream and mandarin orange sections. *Makes one 10-inch pie.*

## CREAMY COCONUT PIE

**2 tablespoons soft butter or margarine**
**2½ cups moist shredded coconut**
**3 eggs**
**1 tablespoon lemon juice**
**¾ cup sugar**
**12 ounces cream cheese, cubed**

Have all ingredients room temperature. Preheat oven to 350°. Spread soft butter evenly over bottom and sides of a 9-inch pie pan. Sprinkle 1½ cups coconut over pan and pat firmly into butter. Chill while making filling.

Put eggs, lemon juice, sugar and cream cheese into blender container; cover and run on speed 6 (or high) until smooth. Add 1 cup coconut; cover and run on speed 3 (or low) until coconut is very finely grated. Pour mixture into prepared pie shell and bake 25 minutes or until set. Cool. Serve topped with whipped cream. *Makes one 9-inch pie.*

**Note:** This filling is also good in Vanilla Cooky Crumb Crust (page 177).

## PEPPERMINT PIE

**1 cup peppermint candy pieces**
**¼ cup cold water**
**1 envelope (1 tablespoon) unflavored gelatin**
**2 egg yolks, beaten**
**1¼ cups milk**
**½ cup whipping cream, whipped**
**Red food coloring**
**2 egg whites**
**⅛ teaspoon salt**
**¼ cup sugar**
**1 9-inch baked pie shell**
**6 tablespoons butter or margarine**
**6 tablespoons confectioners' sugar**
**1½ squares (1½ ounces) chocolate, melted**
**1 egg yolk**

Put half the candy in blender container; cover and run on speed 4 (or high) until finely crushed. Empty into a measuring cup. Repeat process with remaining candy until you have ½ cup; set aside. Put cold water and gelatin in blender container and let stand until gelatin is moistened. Cook beaten egg yolks and milk over low heat, stirring constantly, until mixture thickens slightly and coats a metal spoon. Pour over gelatin in blender container; cover and run on speed 1 (or low) about 1 minute or until gelatin is dissolved. Add crushed candy and run on speed 5 (or high) about 1 minute or until candy is dissolved. Empty into a bowl and chill until slightly thickened, then fold in whipped cream. Add a few drops of red food coloring. Beat egg whites in a small bowl with an electric mixer until soft peaks form; gradually add sugar and beat until stiff peaks form. Fold into gelatin mixture. Spoon into baked pie shell and chill several hours or until firm.

When ready to serve, put butter, confectioners' sugar and chocolate in blender container. Cover and run on speed 2 (or low) until smooth. Add egg yolk and run on speed 2 (or low) until blended. Spread over chilled pie. *Makes one 9-inch pie.*

*Peppermint Pie (p. 182)* *Angel Pie (p. 183)*

## PEANUT BUTTER CHIFFON PIE

**½ cup sugar**
**1 envelope (1 tablespoon) unflavored gelatin**
**⅔ cup boiling water**
**2 eggs, separated**
**⅔ cup peanut butter**
**1 cup whipping cream, whipped**
**OR 1 cup dairy sour cream**
**1 9-inch baked pie shell**

Put sugar and gelatin in blender container; cover and run on speed 1 (or low) until well mixed. Add boiling water; cover and run on speed 1 (or low) until gelatin is dissolved. Add egg yolks and run on speed 5 (or high) until smooth. Add peanut butter; cover and run on speed 1 (or low) a few seconds or until smooth. Pour into a bowl. Chill until slightly thickened. Beat egg whites in a small bowl with an electric mixer until stiff peaks form. Gently fold egg whites and whipped cream or sour cream into gelatin mixture. Pour into pie shell and chill until firm. *Makes one 9-inch pie.*

## ANGEL PIE

**30 crisp round crackers**
**2 cups pecans**
**3 egg whites**
**1 cup sugar**
**1 teaspoon vanilla**
**2 tablespoons sugar**
**1 teaspoon vanilla**
**¼ teaspoon almond extract**
**1 cup whipping cream, whipped**

Preheat oven to 350°. Break 5–6 crackers in blender container; cover and run on speed 4 (or high) until finely crumbed. Empty into a measuring cup. Repeat process until you have 1 cup crumbs. Put ½ cup pecans in blender container; cover and run on speed 4 (or high) until finely chopped. Empty into a bowl. Repeat process until all pecans are chopped. Beat egg whites in a small bowl with an electric mixer until soft peaks form; gradually add 1 cup sugar and beat until stiff peaks form. Add 1 teaspoon vanilla. Fold in cracker crumbs and 1 cup chopped pecans gradually. Spoon mixture into an 8-inch pie pan, pushing it up the sides to form a shell. Bake 30 minutes. Cool thoroughly. Fold 2 tablespoons sugar and flavorings into whipped cream. Spoon into cooled meringue shell; sprinkle with remaining chopped pecans. Chill several hours. *Makes one 8-inch pie.*

**Note:** If desired, fresh raspberries or sliced strawberries, nectarines or peaches may be arranged in shell before cream is spooned in.

## LEMON FLUFF PIE

**1 envelope (1 tablespoon) unflavored gelatin**
**1 6-ounce can frozen lemonade concentrate, thawed**
**1 cup sugar**
**4 eggs, separated**
**1 9-inch Graham Cracker Crumb Crust or Cooky Crust (page 177)**

Soften gelatin in 4 tablespoons thawed lemonade concentrate; set over hot water until dissolved. Put gelatin mixture and remaining lemonade concentrate in blender container; cover and run on speed 1 (or low) about 1 minute. Add ½ cup sugar and egg yolks; cover and run on speed 5 (or high) for 2 minutes. Chill until thick but not firmly set.

Beat egg whites in a medium bowl with an electric mixer until soft peaks form; gradually add ½ cup sugar and beat until stiff peaks form. Fold chilled lemon mixture gently but thoroughly into egg whites. Pour into prepared pie shell. Chill until firm. Garnish with whipped cream and fresh strawberries, if desired. *Makes one 9-inch pie.*

## CHILLED CHERRY CHEESE PIE

**1 8-ounce package cream cheese, cubed**
**1 15-ounce can sweetened condensed milk**
**⅔ cup lemon juice**
**1 teaspoon vanilla**
**1 9-inch Graham Cracker Crumb Crust (page 177), chilled**
**1 1-pound 6-ounce can cherry pie filling**

Put cheese, milk, lemon juice and vanilla in blender container; cover and run on speed 5 (or high) about 2 minutes or until smooth. Pour into the crumb crust and chill 2–3 hours. Spread with cherry pie filling and serve. *Makes one 9-inch pie.*

## BANANA FLUFF PIE

**2 egg whites**
**2 large bananas, peeled and cut into 1-inch pieces**
**1 cup sugar**
**⅛ teaspoon salt**
**1 tablespoon lemon juice**
**20 drops yellow food coloring**
**1 9-inch baked pie shell**
**1 cup whipping cream, Blender whipped (page 139)**
**Shaved semisweet chocolate**

Preheat oven to 375°. Put egg whites, bananas, sugar, salt, lemon juice and food coloring in blender container; cover and run on speed 6 (or high) until thick and creamy, about 3 minutes. Turn into pie shell; bake 25-30 minutes. Cool. Spread whipped cream on pie. Sprinkle shaved chocolate on top. *Makes one 9-inch pie.*

## SOUR CREAM RAISIN PIE

**1 cup dairy sour cream**
**2 eggs**
**1 cup seedless raisins**
**2 thin slices lemon with rind**
**¼ teaspoon salt**
**½ teaspoon nutmeg**
**1 teaspoon cinnamon**
**1 teaspoon cornstarch**
**¾ cup sugar**
**1 9-inch unbaked pie shell**

Preheat oven to 450°. Put all ingredients except pie shell in blender container; cover and run on speed 6 (or high) until raisins and lemon are chopped. Pour into pie shell. Bake at 450° for 10 minutes; reduce heat to 350° and bake 25 minutes longer or until set. Cool. If desired, serve topped with whipped cream. *Makes one 9-inch pie.*

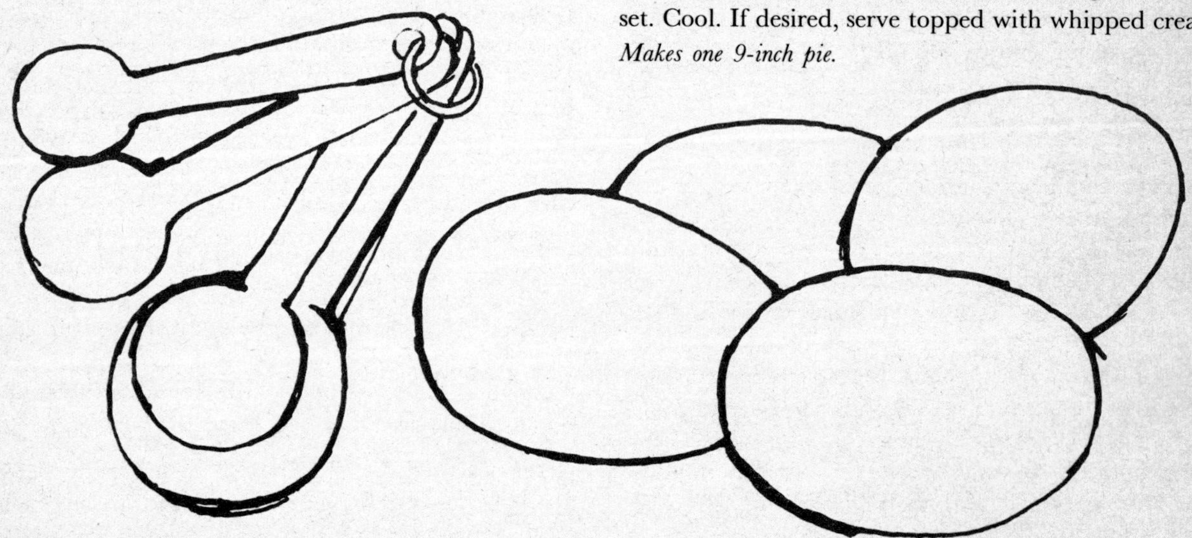

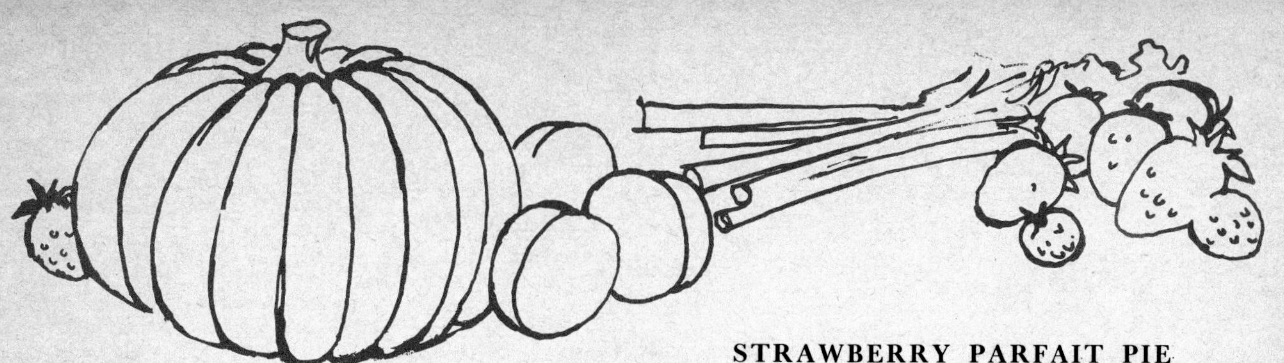

## APRICOT CHIFFON PIE

**¼ cup water**
**1 envelope (1 tablespoon) unflavored gelatin**
**1 1-pound can apricot halves**
**¼ cup orange juice**
**1 tablespoon lemon juice**
**½ cup sugar**
**⅛ teaspoon salt**
**½ cup whipping cream, whipped**
**1 9-inch Baked Pecan Pie Shell (page 178)**

Put water and gelatin in blender container and let stand until gelatin is moistened. Drain apricots, reserving syrup. Add water to syrup to make 1¼ cups; heat. Add hot apricot syrup to softened gelatin; cover and run on speed 1 (or low) about 1 minute or until gelatin is dissolved. Add orange juice, lemon juice, sugar, salt and apricot halves. Cover and run on speed 6 (or high) about 1 minute or until smooth. Pour into a bowl and chill until syrupy; fold in whipped cream. Pour mixture into pie shell and chill for several hours or until firm. Top with additional whipped cream, if desired. *Makes one 9-inch pie.*

## PUMPKIN PIE

**1 cup light cream**
**2 eggs**
**1 1-pound can pumpkin OR 2 cups cooked pumpkin**
**⅔ cup firmly packed brown sugar**
**1 teaspoon cinnamon**
**½ teaspoon ginger**
**¾ teaspoon nutmeg**
**⅛ teaspoon cloves**
**¾ teaspoon salt**
**1 9-inch unbaked pie shell**

Preheat oven to 350°. Put all ingredients except pie shell in blender container in order listed; cover and run on speed 5 (or high) until well mixed. Pour into unbaked pie shell; bake 50-60 minutes or until a silver knife inserted in center comes out clean. Cool. *Makes one 9-inch pie.*

## STRAWBERRY PARFAIT PIE

**1 3-ounce package strawberry-flavored gelatin**
**¾ cup boiling water**
**¾ cup crushed ice**
**1 pint vanilla ice cream, cut into chunks**
**1 cup sliced fresh strawberries**
**1 9-inch baked pie shell, cooled**
**Blender Whipped Cream (page 139)**
**Whole strawberries**

Put boiling water and strawberry gelatin in blender container; cover and run on speed 3 (or low) until dissolved, about 30 seconds. While blender is running, add crushed ice and ice cream chunks, a few at a time; continue to run on speed 3 (or low) until all ice cream is dissolved. Pour mixture into a bowl and chill until it mounds slightly when spooned, about 15–20 minutes. Fold in sliced berries. Pour into cooled pie shell. Chill 20-25 minutes, or until firm. Garnish with whipped cream and whole berries. *Makes one 9-inch pie.*

## RHUBARB CUSTARD PIE

**2 eggs**
**1¼ cups sugar**
**10 pieces zwieback, quartered**
**3 cups fresh rhubarb, cut into ¾-inch pieces**
**1 9-inch unbaked pie shell**
**2 tablespoons butter or margarine**
**Nutmeg**

Preheat oven to 400°. Put eggs in blender container; cover and run on speed 2 (or low). While blender is running, add sugar. Run on speed 6 (or high) and add broken zwieback, a few pieces at a time, while blender is running. Run until well blended, switching blender on and off several times if necessary to crumb all zwieback.

Put rhubarb in mixing bowl; add egg mixture and stir well. Let stand 10 minutes. Pour rhubarb mixture into pie shell; dot with butter and sprinkle with nutmeg. Bake 15 minutes, then reduce heat to 375° and bake 35 minutes longer, or until a silver knife inserted in center comes out clean. Serve slightly warm or cool. *Makes one 9-inch pie.*

# Pretty and Special Preserves and Relishes

*In this age, when the supermarket has replaced the family food cellar, few women bother to do any large-scale pickling or preserving. Many, however, still get pleasure from making superlative relishes and jams in small quantities, either for their own tables or to be presented as gifts. The recipes that follow have been carefully selected to justify that "little extra" effort involved. All the hard work is done by the blender, and the results are sure to bring both satisfaction and compliments to the cook.*

## GARLIC MUSTARD

**1 6-ounce jar dark prepared mustard**
**1 clove garlic**
**1 teaspoon seasoned salt**

Put all ingredients in blender container; cover and run on speed 2 (or low) until garlic is completely blended with mustard. Serve with hot meat or cold cuts. *Makes ¾ cup.*

## GARDEN RELISH

**½ medium head cabbage, coarsely cut**
**2 carrots, cut into 1-inch pieces**
**1 green pepper, seeded and cut up**
**1 medium onion, quartered**
**¾ cup vinegar**
**¾ cup sugar**
**2 teaspoons salt**
**½ teaspoon mustard seed**
**½ teaspoon celery seed**

Fill blender container to top cup marking with cut cabbage, carrots, green pepper and onion; add cold water just to cover vegetables. Cover container and turn to speed 7 (or high) just until all vegetables go through blades once (do not overblend or vegetables will be liquefied). Pour into a colander or sieve to drain; turn drained vegetables into a bowl. Repeat this process until all vegetables are chopped. Put remaining ingredients in blender container; cover and run on speed 1 (or low) about 10 seconds. Pour over chopped vegetables; mix well. Refrigerate at least 2 hours before serving. *Makes about 5 cups.*

## QUICKY CORN RELISH

**2 cups vinegar**
**1 tablespoon dry mustard**
**1 tablespoon celery seed**
**1 tablespoon salt**
**1¼ cups firmly packed light brown sugar**
**¼ sweet red pepper, seeded and cut into 1-inch pieces**
**1 small green pepper, seeded and cut into 1-inch pieces**
**1 large onion, cut into 1-inch pieces**
**4 cups cooked or canned sweet corn, drained**

Put all ingredients except corn in blender container; cover and run on speed 4 (or high) until vegetables are chopped. Pour into a 3-quart saucepan; add corn. Cook slowly for 20 minutes. Pour into sterilized hot jars and seal at once. *Makes 4 pints.*

## HORSERADISH-BEET RELISH

**1 tablespoon vinegar**
**1 tablespoon sugar**
**2 cups canned diced beets, drained**
**⅛ teaspoon pepper**
**1 teaspoon salt**
**¼ cup prepared horseradish**

Put all ingredients in blender container in order listed; cover and run on speed 6 (or high) until beets are finely chopped. If necessary, stop blender during processing and push ingredients toward blades with rubber spatula. Refrigerate 2-3 days. Serve with roast beef, pork, lamb, tongue or corned beef. *Makes 1½ cups.*

*From left to right: Quicky Corn Relish (p. 187), Garden Relish (p. 187), Pineapple-Cherry Marmalade (p. 189), Fresh Cranberry-Orange Relish (p. 188), Apricot Jam (p. 189)*

## GREEN PEPPER RELISH

**8 green peppers, seeded and cut up**
**3 medium onions, cut up**
**½ cup sugar**
**1 teaspoon salt**
**1½ cups white vinegar**
**½ teaspoon celery salt**

Fill blender container to top cup marking with cut vegetables; fill with enough cold water to cover vegetables. Cover container and run on speed 7 (or high) just until vegetables are coarsely chopped. Drain in a colander or sieve and turn into a large saucepan. Repeat process with remaining vegetables until all are chopped. Cover vegetables with boiling water and let stand 15 minutes; drain. Cover with fresh boiling water and let stand 15 minutes longer; drain. Add remaining ingredients; mix. Bring to a boil; simmer uncovered 30 minutes. Pack into jars while hot and seal immediately. *Makes 3 pints.*

## FRESH CRANBERRY-ORANGE RELISH

**1 orange**
**¾ cup sugar**
**2 cups raw cranberries**

Quarter orange and remove seeds; remove and discard rind from three sections. Put orange sections and sugar in blender container; cover and run on speed 2 (or low) until puréed. Add 1 cup cranberries. Cover and run on speed 4 (or high) until cranberries are chopped; empty into a bowl. Put remaining cranberries in container; cover and run on speed 4 (or high) until chopped. Add to mixture in bowl. Chill. *Makes about 1½ cups.*

## ZIPPY RELISH FOR MEATS

**2 medium turnips, pared and cut up**
**½ medium onion, cut up**
**¼ cup vinegar**
**1½ tablespoons sugar**
**1 tablespoon prepared horseradish**
**½ teaspoon salt**

Put all ingredients in blender container; cover and run on speed 4 (or high) until vegetables are chopped. If necessary, stop blender and push ingredients toward blades with rubber spatula. Store in refrigerator. Delicious with roast beef, corned beef or ham. *Makes 1½ cups.*

## RAW APPLE CHUTNEY

**2 apples, cored and quartered**
**1 green pepper, seeded and cut up**
**½ clove garlic**
**1 tablespoon sugar**
**1 tablespoon vinegar**
**1 tablespoon lemon juice**
**¼ teaspoon salt**
**¼ teaspoon ginger**
**⅛ teaspoon white pepper**
**¾ teaspoon paprika**
**½ cup raisins**

Put apples, green pepper and garlic in blender container; fill with water to cover. Cover container and run on speed 7 (or high) just until apples and pepper are coarsely chopped. Be careful not to overblend or they will be liquefied. Drain in a colander or sieve; turn into a bowl. Add remaining ingredients; mix well and chill. *Makes 2½ cups.*

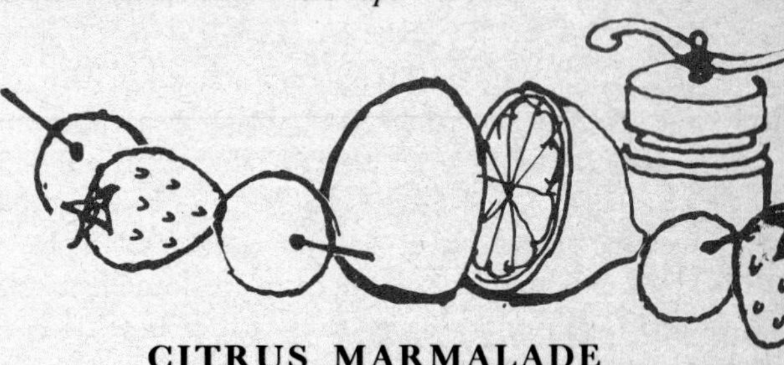

## CITRUS MARMALADE

**4 large oranges**
**2 lemons**
**1½ cups water**
**⅛ teaspoon baking soda**
**5 cups sugar**
**1 1¾-ounce package powdered pectin**

Remove colored outer portion of orange and lemon rinds with a vegetable peeler. Put ½ cup water and ⅓ of the rind in blender container; cover and run on speed 3 (or low) until rind is coarsely cut. Empty into a large saucepan. Repeat process two more times with remaining water and rind. Add soda; bring to boil and simmer 20 minutes. Meanwhile, remove and discard white portion of rind from oranges and lemons. Cut each piece of fruit into 8 pieces and remove seeds. Put half the fruit in blender container; cover and run on speed 5 (or high) until puréed. Add to cooked rind mixture. Repeat process with remaining fruit. Simmer 10 minutes longer. Add sugar and pectin. Bring to a full rolling boil, then boil 1 minute (accurate timing is important). Remove from heat and cool 10 minutes. Ladle into hot sterilized glasses and cover with hot paraffin. *Makes six or seven 6-ounce glasses.*

## APPLE BUTTER

**½ cup water**
**1 teaspoon vinegar**
**¾ teaspoon cinnamon**
**Dash salt**
**⅛ teaspoon cloves**
**Small piece lemon rind (colored portion only)**
**½ cup firmly packed brown sugar**
**3 large tart apples, pared, cored and cut into 1-inch pieces**

Put all ingredients except apples in blender container; add half the apples. Cover container and run on speed 6 (or high) until smooth. Add remaining apples; cover and run on speed 6 (or high) until smooth. Pour into a saucepan and cook until thick, 30-40 minutes. Seal in sterilized jars. *Makes 1 pint.*

## APPLE-PINEAPPLE CONSERVE

**1 large orange**
**3 medium apples, cored and quartered**
**1 small pineapple, pared and cut up**
**1 cup water**
**3 cups sugar**
**¾ cup shredded coconut**

Remove colored outer portion of rind from half the orange with vegetable peeler; reserve. Remove and discard rest of rind. Cut orange into 8 pieces. Fill blender container to 3-cup mark with cut fruit; add water. Cover and run on speed 4 (or high) a few seconds or until fruit is coarsely chopped. Drain in a colander or sieve, reserving liquid. Repeat process with remaining fruit, using reserved liquid instead of water. Put fruit and liquid in a 3-quart saucepan; stir in sugar and cook until thickened, about 30-40 minutes. As mixture thickens, stir frequently to prevent sticking. Stir in coconut; return to boil. Pour, boiling hot, into hot sterilized jars and seal immediately. *Makes four ½-pint jars (1 quart).*

## APRICOT JAM

**3 1-pound cans apricot halves**
**2 tablespoons lemon juice**
**2 cups sugar**

Drain apricots, reserving 1 cup syrup. Put reserved apricot syrup, lemon juice and drained apricots in blender container; cover and run on speed 7 (or high) until smooth. Pour into a saucepan and add sugar. Bring to a boil, then cook over low heat until thick. Pour into sterilized jars; seal. *Makes about 1½ pints.*

## PINEAPPLE-CHERRY MARMALADE

**1 No. 2½ can (3¾ cups) crushed pineapple, with juice**
**Juice of 2 lemons**
**1 8-ounce jar maraschino cherries**
**7½ cups sugar**
**1 6-ounce bottle liquid pectin**

Put pineapple and lemon juice in blender container. Drain cherries, reserving juice; add enough water to juice to make ¾ cup. Add this liquid and cherries to blender container; cover and run on speed 6 (or high) just until cherries are chopped. Pour into a large saucepan; add sugar. Bring to boiling, stirring constantly; boil 2 minutes. Remove from heat and stir in pectin. Fill hot sterilized jars and seal at once. Or put in a large container, cool, then refrigerate. *Makes 4½ pints.*

## SUNSET JAM

**2 pounds firm ripe pears, pared, cored and cut up**
**1 8-ounce can crushed pineapple, with syrup**
**3 tablespoons lemon juice**
**¾ cup maraschino cherries, drained**
**7½ cups sugar**
**1 6-ounce bottle liquid pectin**

Put pears, pineapple and lemon juice in blender container; cover and run on speed 7 (or high) until smooth. Add maraschino cherries; cover and run on speed 7 (or high) just until cherries are chopped. Pour into saucepan; stir in sugar. Bring to a boil, stirring constantly; boil hard for 1 minute. Remove from heat and stir in pectin. Stir and skim for 5 minutes. Ladle into hot jars; seal. *Makes 3½ pints.*

# *Baby Pleasers*

*When you blender-prepare baby foods, you can cut the cost in half—and, perhaps even more important in a crowded kitchen, you can clear the shelves of many of those little jars and cans.*

*You can easily adjust your baby's diet to his changing needs. When the doctor recommends new foods, small amounts may be blended into the combinations that your child already likes. Then the new food may be increased gradually until the recommended amount is accepted. When the time comes for junior foods, you can again make the transition by easy stages. The final change from baby foods to the full spread of the family table can be achieved the same easy way—by a gradual process of adding ingredients and coarsening textures.*

*Follow your doctor's orders for foods to be blended. Formulas given here indicate relative quantities for good consistencies. Cereal, of course, may be included in any fruit, vegetable or meat purée.*

*When possible, do your blending in small Mason jars for convenience and economy. Put solids in first, then liquids. You can feed the baby right from the jar and refrigerate any leftovers in the same jar.*

## CHICKEN SOUP

**½ cup milk**
**2 tablespoons chicken broth**
**2 tablespoons cubed cooked chicken**
**2 tablespoons cubed cooked carrot**
**1 teaspoon butter or margarine**
**1 teaspoon uncooked quick-cooking wheat cereal**

Put all ingredients in blender container; cover and run on speed 4 (or low) until chicken and carrot are finely chopped. Pour into a saucepan; cook 5 minutes, stirring constantly. *Makes 2 servings.*

## TODDLER'S SANDWICH

**2 peach halves, cooked or canned**
**¼ cup cottage cheese**
**2 tablespoons peanut butter**

Put all ingredients in blender container. Cover and run on speed 6 (or high) until smooth. Chill. Spread on bread. *Makes about ⅔ cup.*

## MEATS FOR BABY

**½ cup cubed cooked meat**
**Dash salt**
**2 tablespoons milk, formula or liquid from boiled meat**

Put all ingredients in blender container. (Or put all ingredients into a small standard Mason jar and screw on cutting assembly.) Cover container and run on speed 2 (or low) until perfectly smooth. *Makes 1 serving.*

**Note:** To test for smoothness, take a small amount of purée between your fingers; rub fingers together. If any large particles can be felt, process again.

## BABY BACON

**½ cup milk**
**½ cup diced cooked sweet potato**
**¼ teaspoon salt**
**2 slices bacon, fried crisp**

Put all ingredients in blender container in order listed; cover and run on speed 2 (or low) until smooth. Pour into a small saucepan; cook over low heat until warmed. *Makes 1 serving.*

## CHICKEN TREAT

**¼ cup chicken broth**
**1 egg**
**¼ teaspoon salt**
**½ cup cubed cooked potatoes**
**½ cup cubed cooked chicken**

Preheat oven to 350°. Butter 2 custard cups. Put all ingredients in blender container in order listed; cover and run on speed 2 (or low) until smooth. Pour into prepared custard cups; set cups in pan containing 1½ inches hot water. Bake 25 minutes or until knife inserted in center comes out clean. *Makes 2 servings.*

## "MEAL-IN-ONE"

**½ cup milk**
**½ cup cubed cooked beef or veal**
**2 tablespoons cooked carrots or peas**
**4 tablespoons cooked rice**

Put all ingredients in blender container in order listed; cover and run on speed 2 (or low) until very smooth. If necessary, stop blender during processing and push ingredients toward blades with rubber spatula. Heat before serving. *Makes 2-3 servings.*

## VEGETABLES FOR BABY

**½ cup freshly cooked vegetables**
**2 tablespoons milk, formula or cooking liquid**
**Dash salt**

Put all ingredients in blender container. (Or put all ingredients into a small standard Mason jar and screw on cutting assembly.) Cover container and run on speed 2 (or low) until perfectly smooth. *Makes 1 serving.*

**Note:** To test for smoothness, take a small amount of purée between your fingers; rub fingers together. If any large particles can be felt, process again.

Junior or toddler foods should contain some larger particles, so they require less blending.

## FRESH BANANA APPLESAUCE

**1 tablespoon lemon juice**
**1 tablespoon sugar**
**1 small banana, peeled and quartered**
**1 small apple, peeled, cored and cubed**

Put all ingredients in blender container in order listed; cover and run on speed 2 (or low) until smooth. If necessary, stop blender during processing and push ingredients toward blades with rubber spatula. *Makes 2 servings.*

## BANANA-LIME MOLD

**1 cup boiling water**
**1 3-ounce package lime-flavored gelatin**
**1 banana, peeled and quartered**
**1 cup crushed ice**

Put boiling water and gelatin in blender container; cover and run on speed 1 (or low) until gelatin is dissolved. Add banana and crushed ice; cover and run on speed 7 (or high) until perfectly smooth. Pour into a small mold or bowl; chill until firm. *Makes 6 servings.*

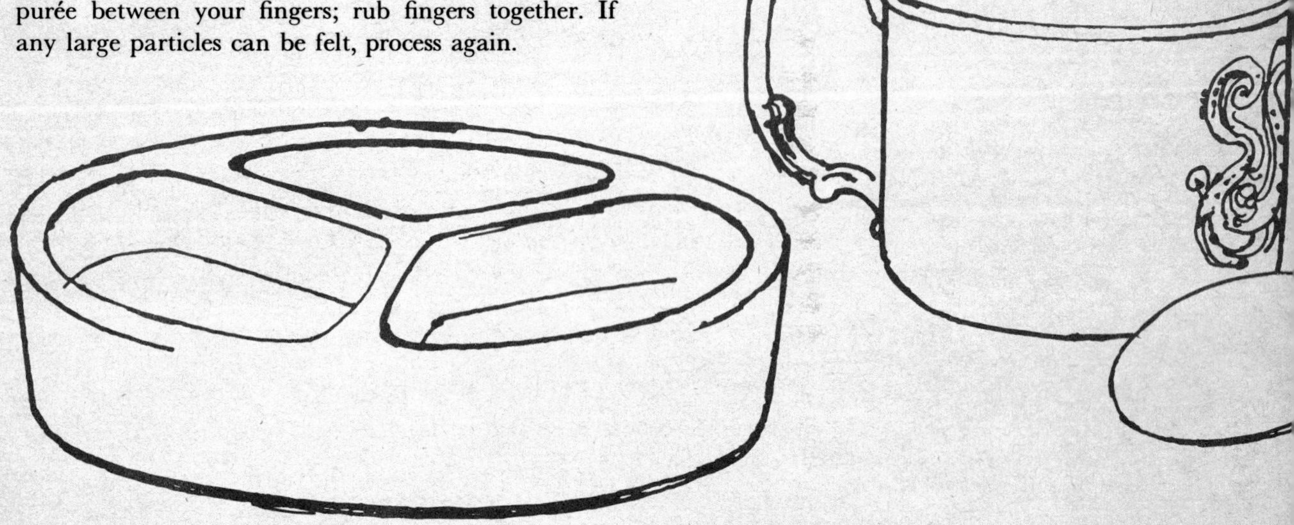

## APRICOT PUDDING

**½ cup dried apricots**
**1½ cups milk**
**¼ cup sugar**
**2 tablespoons cornstarch**

Soak apricots in milk overnight in refrigerator. When ready to prepare pudding, put apricots with milk and remaining ingredients in blender container; cover and run on speed 7 (or high) until smooth. Pour into a saucepan; bring to a boil, stirring constantly. Cool to lukewarm before serving. *Makes 4 servings.*

## PEACH PUDDING

**1 cup milk**
**1 cup peach syrup**
**3 peach halves, cooked or canned**
**¼ cup sugar**
**3½ tablespoons cornstarch**

Put all ingredients in blender container in order listed; cover and run on speed 6 (or high) until smooth. Pour into the top of a double boiler; cook over hot water until thickened. Pour into a bowl; cool. *Makes 3 cups.*

**Note:** This pudding may be frozen for later use. To save space, use an ice cube tray.

## COTTAGE CHEESE CUSTARD

**¾ cup hot milk**
**½ cup creamed cottage cheese**
**2 tablespoons light corn syrup**
**1 egg**
**Nutmeg (optional)**

Preheat oven to 325°. Butter 3 custard cups. Put all ingredients except nutmeg in blender container; cover and run on speed 6 (or high) for 1 minute. Pour into prepared custard cups and sprinkle with nutmeg, if desired; set cups in pan containing 1½ inches hot water. Bake 40 minutes or until knife inserted in center comes out clean. Cool to lukewarm before serving. *Makes 3 servings.*

## FRUITS FOR BABY

**¾ cup freshly cooked fruit***
**½ teaspoon sugar**
**2 teaspoons liquid from fruit**

Put all ingredients in blender container. (Or put all ingredients into a small standard Mason jar and screw on cutting assembly.) Cover container and run on speed 2 (or low) until perfectly smooth. *Makes 1 serving.*

* Fresh uncooked fruits prescribed by your pediatrician may also be processed by this method.

**Note:** To test for smoothness, take a small amount of purée between your fingers; rub fingers together. If any large particles can be felt, process again.

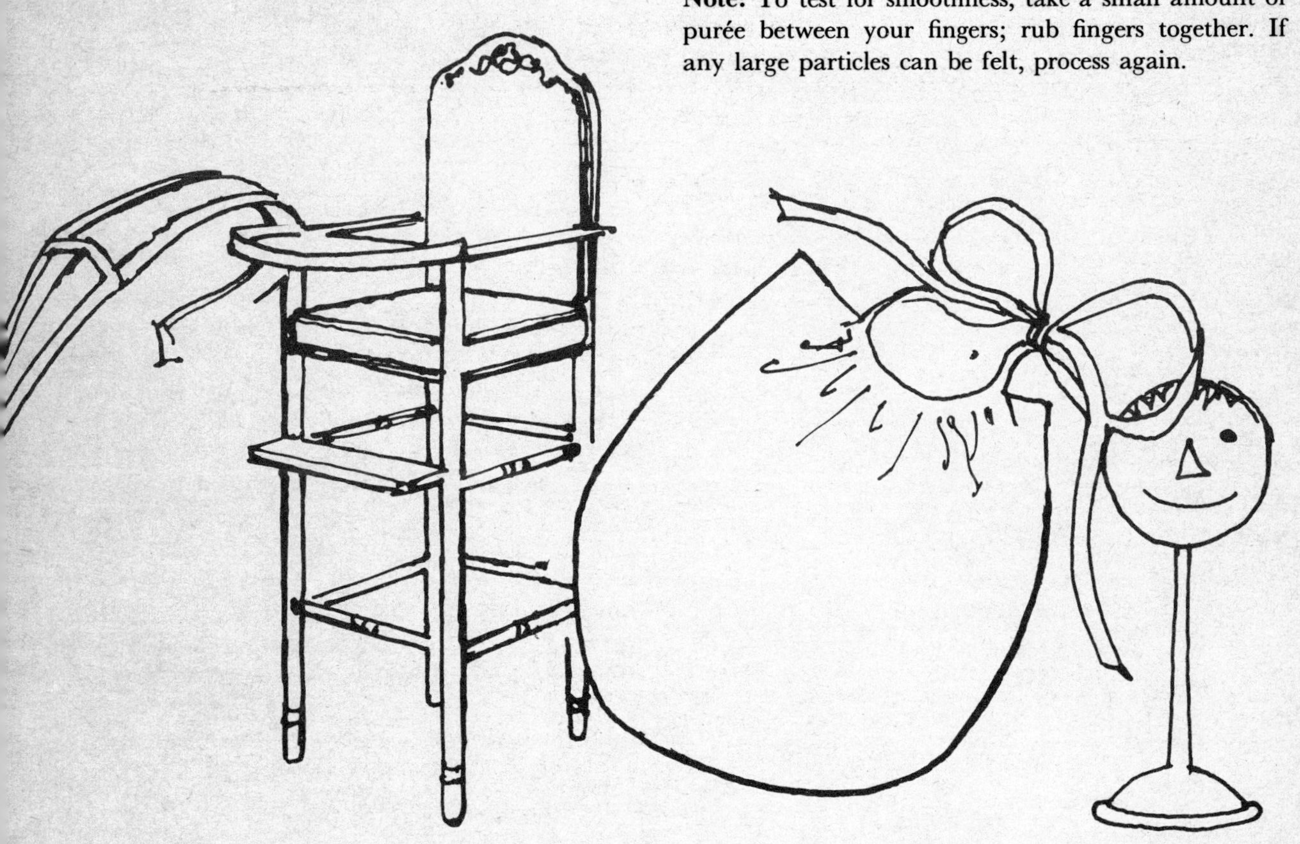

# Calculations for the Calorie Counter

*The wise calorie counter will reduce the quantities of all foods eaten and will avoid excess amounts of fat, sugar and starch. Even if you are dieting, it is important to maintain the proper balance of daily requirements from the "Basic Four" food groups.*

*The low-calorie diet, like any other diet with a restricted choice of foods, tends to become monotonous. But the blender, by changing textures and facilitating new combinations, can make even the most limited range of foods attractive. The recipes that follow have been specially developed to give maximum satisfaction with a minimum number of calories, and they will suggest other combinations that can be created from the foods that make up the low-calorie list. Happily, these recipes produce dishes that will be welcomed by the whole family.*

## NIPPY DIP

*(about 12 calories per tablespoon)*

**2 cups creamed cottage cheese**
**2 teaspoons garlic salad dressing mix**
**4 sprigs parsley**
**¼ green pepper, seeded**
**1 tablespoon lemon juice**
**2 teaspoons Worcestershire**
**Few drops Tabasco**

Put all ingredients in blender container in order listed; cover and run on speed 2 (or low) until well mixed. If necessary, stop blender during processing and push ingredients toward blades with rubber spatula. Empty into serving dish; cover and chill at least 1 hour. Serve with crisp raw vegetables or melba toast. *Makes 2 cups.*

## SEAFOOD COCKTAIL SAUCE

*(about 14 calories per tablespoon)*

**½ cup catsup**
**1 tablespoon prepared horseradish**
**1 tablespoon lemon juice**
**1 thin slice onion**
**1½ teaspoons brown sugar**
**½ teaspoon Worcestershire**
**¼ teaspoon salt**
**Dash monosodium glutamate**
**3 drops Tabasco**

Put all ingredients in blender container; cover and run on speed 7 (or high) until onion is liquefied. *Makes ¾ cup.*

## CUCUMBER SOUP OR COCKTAIL

*(about 50 calories per cup)*

**2 cups buttermilk**
**1 cucumber, pared and cut into chunks**
**¼ green pepper, seeded**
**¼ medium onion**
**3 sprigs parsley**
**¾ teaspoon salt**
**½ teaspoon celery seed**
**¼ teaspoon pepper**
**¼ teaspoon dill weed**

Put first 5 ingredients in blender container; cover and run on speed 3 (or low) until vegetables are finely chopped. Add remaining ingredients; cover and run on speed 4 (or high) for 30 seconds or until blended. Chill. *Makes 4 cups.*

## JELLIED CONSOMMÉ

*(about 50 calories per serving)*

**1½ cups hot water**
**2 chicken bouillon cubes**
**2 envelopes (2 tablespoons) unflavored gelatin**
**3 cups tomato juice**
**2 teaspoons lemon juice**
**1 teaspoon sugar**
**1 green pepper, seeded and cut up**
**2 teaspoons aromatic bitters**

Put hot water, bouillon cubes and gelatin in blender container; cover and run on speed 1 (or low) until bouillon cubes and gelatin are dissolved. Empty into a saucepan.

Put remaining ingredients except bitters in blender container; cover and run on speed 4 (or low) until green pepper is chopped. Add to mixture in saucepan; cover and simmer 6-8 minutes or until pepper is tender. Strain. Stir in bitters. Cool. Chill until set. Before serving, beat lightly with a fork; garnish with lemon slices. *Makes 5 servings.*

## BOSTON CLAM CHOWDER

*(about 61 calories per serving)*

**2 7½-ounce cans minced clams**
**½ cup water**
**1 medium onion, cubed**
**1 carrot, cut into 1-inch pieces**
**¼ teaspoon salt**
**¼ teaspoon white pepper**
**½ teaspoon thyme**
**2 cups skim milk**

Drain clams, reserving ½ cup liquid. Put reserved clam liquid and remaining ingredients except clams and milk into blender container; cover and run on speed 4 (or low) until vegetables are chopped. Pour into a saucepan; cook, covered, over low heat about 20 minutes or until vegetables are tender. Add clams. Gradually add milk, stirring constantly. Simmer 5 minutes. *Makes 6 servings.*

## CRUNCHY TOMATO SALAD

*(about 28 calories per serving)*

**1 3/5-ounce package strawberry-flavored dietary gelatin**
**1 1-pound can (2 cups) tomatoes, heated**
**¼ small onion, cut up**
**1 teaspoon prepared horseradish**
**2 medium sweet pickles**
**¼ small head cabbage, cut up**
**1 canned pimiento**
**½ teaspoon salt**
**Dash cayenne**
**½ teaspoon celery seed**

Put gelatin in blender container. Add hot tomatoes; cover and run on speed 4 (or high) until gelatin is dissolved and tomatoes are puréed. Add remaining ingredients; cover and run on speed 4 (or high) until vegetables are chopped. Cool until mixture begins to thicken. Pour into 6 individual molds. Chill until firm. *Makes 6 servings.*

## PERFECTION SALAD

*(about 12 calories per serving)*

**½ cup very hot water**
**1 envelope (1 tablespoon) unflavored gelatin**
**1 cup cold water**
**3 tablespoons cider vinegar**
**1 tablespoon lemon juice**
**¾ teaspoon liquid non-caloric sweetener OR 6 non-caloric sweetening tablets**
**3 stalks celery, cut into 1-inch pieces**
**¼ small head cabbage, coarsely sliced**
**½ canned pimiento**

Put hot water and gelatin in blender container; cover and run on speed 1 (or low) until gelatin is dissolved, about 1 minute. Add all remaining ingredients; cover and run on speed 4 (or high) just until the vegetables are coarsely chopped. Pour into an oiled 1-quart mold. Chill until firm. To serve, unmold on a chilled plate. *Makes 8 servings.*

## MOLDED BEET SALAD

*(about 20 calories per serving)*

**1 1-pound can sliced beets**
**1 envelope (1 tablespoon) unflavored gelatin**
**3 beef bouillon cubes**
**1 cup boiling water**
**3 tablespoons lemon juice**
**½ teaspoon dill weed**

Drain beets, reserving liquid. Soften gelatin in ½ cup beet juice in blender container. Add bouillon cubes and boiling water; cover and run on speed 4 (or high) until gelatin and bouillon cubes are dissolved. Add beets and remaining beet juice, lemon juice and dill weed; cover and run on speed 4 (or high) until beets are finely chopped. Cool until mixture begins to thicken. Pour into a 4-cup mold or 6 individual molds. Chill until firm. *Makes 6 servings.*

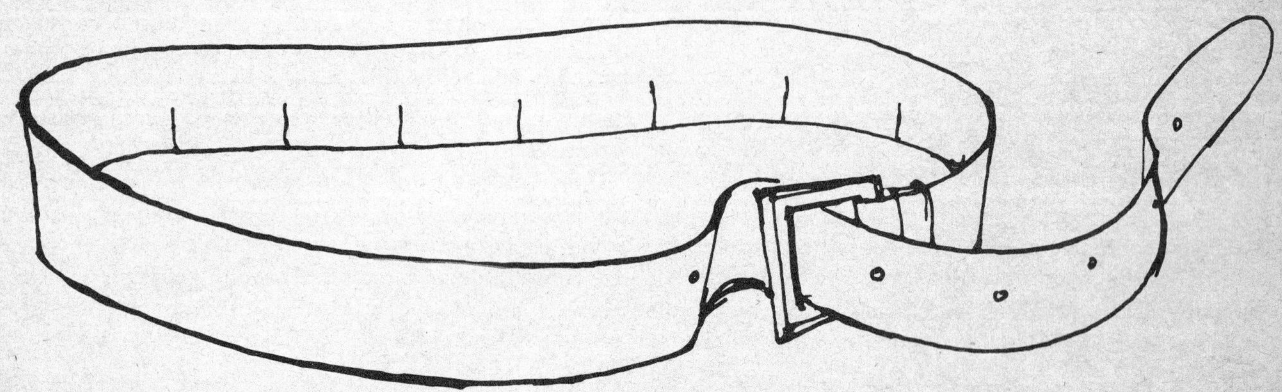

*Perfection Salad (p. 196)*

## CREAMY DIET DRESSING

*(about 8 calories per tablespoon)*

**1 cup creamed cottage cheese**
**½ small onion, cut up**
**2 canned pimientos**
**8 sprigs parsley**
**1 teaspoon salt**
**⅔ cup sauerkraut juice**

Put all ingredients in blender container in order listed; cover and run on speed 2 (or low) until smooth. *Makes 2 cups.*

## DIET THOUSAND ISLAND DRESSING

*(about 6 calories per tablespoon)*

**1 10½-ounce can condensed tomato soup, undiluted**
**½ cup tarragon vinegar**
**1 medium dill pickle**
**1 celery stalk, cut up**
**6 sprigs parsley**
**1 clove garlic**
**1 tablespoon Worcestershire**
**1 teaspoon paprika**
**1 teaspoon prepared mustard**
**Dash cayenne**

Put all ingredients in blender container in order listed; cover and run on speed 4 (or high) until vegetables are chopped. *Makes about 2½ cups.*

## GERMAN MEATBALLS

*(about 150 calories per serving)*

**2 medium potatoes, cut into pieces**
**½ medium onion, cut up**
**1 1-inch square lemon peel**
**4 sprigs parsley**
**1 egg**
**1 pound lean ground beef**
**½ teaspoon salt**
**¼ teaspoon pepper**
**½ teaspoon caraway seed**
**2 tablespoons flour**
**2 tablespoons butter or margarine**
**2 beef bouillon cubes**
**2 cups hot water**

Put a few pieces of potato in blender container; cover and run on speed 3 (or low) until chopped. Empty into measuring cup. Repeat process until you have 1 cup. Put onion, lemon peel, parsley and egg in blender container; cover and run on speed 4 (or high) until vegetables are chopped. If necessary, stop blender during processing and push ingredients toward blades with rubber spatula. Combine with chopped potatoes, ground beef, seasonings and caraway seed. Form into sixteen ½-inch balls; dip in flour and brown in butter. Dissolve bouillon cubes in hot water and add to meatballs. Cover and simmer for 30 minutes. *Makes 8 servings.*

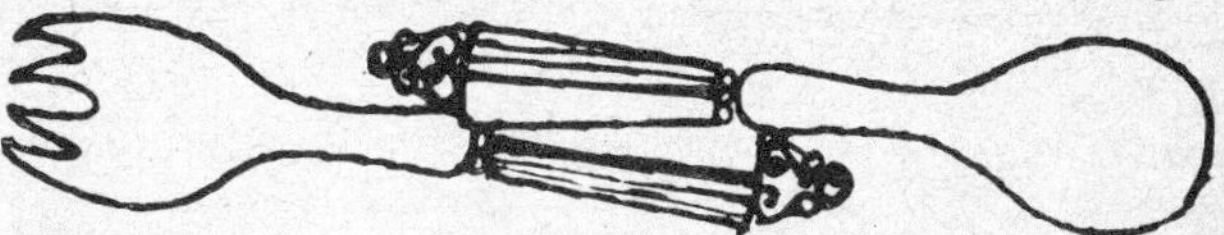

## DEVILED VEAL CUTLET

*(about 200 calories per serving)*

**1 pound lean veal cutlets, ¼-inch thick**
**2 tablespoons flour**
**¾ teaspoon salt**
**¼ teaspoon pepper**
**2 tablespoons butter or margarine**
**1 carrot, cut up**
**1 stalk celery, cut up**
**1 medium onion, cut up**
**1½ cups water**
**2 teaspoons prepared horseradish**
**1 teaspoon prepared mustard**
**½ cup yogurt**

Pound cutlets very thin. Combine flour, salt and pepper; dip cutlets in mixture and brown in butter. (Reserve remaining flour.) Meanwhile, put carrot, celery, onion and water in blender container; cover and run on speed 4 (or high) until vegetables are chopped. Add to browned cutlets in frypan; cover and simmer 25 minutes. Put horseradish, mustard, yogurt and remainder of flour in blender container; cover and run on speed 4 (or high) until well mixed. Add to meat in frypan and cook, stirring constantly, until well mixed and thickened. *Makes 5 servings.*

## JELLIED CHICKEN LOAF

*(about 110 calories per serving)*

**1 envelope (1 tablespoon) unflavored gelatin**
**¼ cup cold water**
**2 chicken bouillon cubes**
**1¾ cups boiling water**
**1 cup cut-up cooked chicken**
**2 tablespoons lemon juice**
**½ green pepper, seeded and cut up**
**¼ medium onion, cut up**
**2 canned pimientos**
**3 sprigs parsley**
**2 stalks celery with leaves, cut up**
**½ teaspoon thyme**

Soften gelatin in cold water in blender container. Add bouillon cubes and boiling water; cover and run on speed 3 (or low) until gelatin and bouillon are dissolved. Add chicken; cover and run on speed 4 (or high) about 30 seconds or until chicken is chopped. Empty into a mixing bowl and chill until mixture begins to thicken.

Put remaining ingredients in blender container; cover and run on speed 4 (or high) until vegetables are chopped. If necessary, stop blender during processing and push ingredients toward blades with rubber spatula. Fold vegetables into thickened gelatin. Pour into a 9x5x3-inch loaf pan. Chill until firm. *Makes 8 servings.*

## HAM-SPINACH SOUFFLÉ

*(about 150 calories per serving)*

**½ pound spinach (4 firmly packed cups)**
**½ cup milk**
**3 eggs, separated**
**2 slices dry bread or toast**
**¼ medium onion, cut up**
**1 cup cubed ham**
**¼ teaspoon salt**
**⅛ teaspoon pepper**

Preheat oven to 350°. Put about 1 cup spinach in blender container, pushing it toward blades. Add milk and egg yolks; cover and run on speed 2 (or low) until spinach is puréed. Slowly add remaining spinach while blender is running. Break bread into container while blender is running. Add onion, ham and seasonings while blender is still running. If necessary, stop blender during processing and push ingredients toward blades with rubber spatula. Pour into large bowl. Beat egg whites in small bowl with an electric mixer until stiff peaks form; fold into spinach mixture. Pour into a 1-quart casserole and bake for 45–50 minutes or until firm. *Makes 6 servings.*

*Jellied Chicken Loaf*

## FOIL-BAKED FISH

*(about 200 calories per serving)*

**1 pound frozen fish fillets, thawed**
**½ lemon, cut up and seeded**
**3 sprigs parsley**
**1 stalk celery, cut up**
**1 clove garlic**
**2 tablespoons Worcestershire**
**1 teaspoon salt**
**1 teaspoon oregano**
**½ teaspoon basil**
**¼ teaspoon thyme**
**¼ cup soft butter or margarine**

Cut fish into serving-size portions and place each on a square of foil. Put remaining ingredients in blender container; cover and run on speed 4 (or high) until lemon and celery are chopped. Stop blender during processing and push ingredients toward blades with rubber spatula. Top each portion of fish with a heaping tablespoon of mixture. Wrap, using a double fold, and bake 30 minutes. *Makes 5 servings.*

## CRAB-STUFFED TOMATOES

*(about 150 calories per serving)*

**4 medium tomatoes**
**1 7½-ounce can crab meat, drained (bony tissue removed)**
**½ medium onion, cut up**
**½ green pepper, seeded and cut up**
**1 stalk celery, cut up**
**1 slice bread, torn into pieces**
**1 egg**
**2 tablespoons salad dressing**
**½ teaspoon salt**
**1 teaspoon Worcestershire**
**Dash Tabasco**
**Grated Parmesan cheese**

Preheat oven to 350°. Cut off stem end of tomatoes and scoop out pulp; invert on paper towel to drain. Put remaining ingredients except cheese in blender container; cover and run on speed 4 (or high) until well blended. Stop blender during processing and push ingredients toward blades with rubber spatula. Fill tomatoes with mixture; sprinkle with cheese. Bake for 45 minutes. *Makes 4 servings.*

*Hurry-up Jambalaya*

## HURRY-UP JAMBALAYA

*(about 180 calories per serving)*

**¼ medium onion, cut up**
**1 stalk celery, cut up**
**6 sprigs parsley**
**¼ green pepper, seeded**
**1 1-pound can (2 cups) tomatoes**
**1 teaspoon salt**
**1 teaspoon chili powder**
**Dash cayenne**
**½ cup packaged pre-cooked rice**
**2 cups cooked cleaned shrimp**

Put onion, celery, parsley, green pepper and 1 cup tomatoes in blender container. Add seasonings; cover and run on speed 4 (or high) until vegetables are chopped. Empty into large saucepan and cook for 5 minutes. Add remaining tomatoes and bring to a boil. Add rice and shrimp and bring to a boil. Turn off heat and let stand, covered, for 5 minutes. *Makes 4 servings.*

## MUSHROOMS IMPERIAL

*(about 110 calories per serving)*

**1 pound (about 12) large mushrooms**
**1 10½-ounce can condensed mushroom soup, undiluted**
**½ small onion, cut up**
**2 hard-cooked eggs, shelled and quartered**
**1 4½-ounce can (about 1 cup) cooked, cleaned shrimp**
**2 sprigs parsley**
**1 tablespoon lemon juice**
**½ teaspoon curry powder**
**¼ cup milk**
**2 teaspoons lemon juice**

Preheat oven to 350°. Wash mushrooms and remove stems. Put ½ cup mushroom soup, onion, eggs, shrimp, parsley, 1 tablespoon lemon juice and curry powder in blender container; cover and run on speed 3 (or low) until eggs and shrimp are finely chopped. If necessary, stop blender during processing and push ingredients toward blades with rubber spatula. Fill mushroom caps with this mixture. Place in a shallow baking pan and bake 20 minutes. Meanwhile, put milk, remaining soup and 2 teaspoons lemon juice in blender container; cover and run on speed 4 (or high) until well mixed. Empty into a saucepan and heat. To serve, spoon sauce over mushrooms. *Makes 4 servings.*

## COTTAGE CHEESE OMELET

*(about 147 calories per serving)*

**1 tablespoon butter or margarine**
**3 eggs, separated**
**3 tablespoons water**
**½ teaspoon salt**
**Dash pepper**
**½ cup creamed cottage cheese**
**½ canned pimiento**
**1 teaspoon cut chives**

Preheat oven to 350°. Melt butter in a heavy griddle or 10-inch skillet which may be put in the oven. Beat egg whites with an electric mixer until stiff but not dry; set aside. Put egg yolks, water, salt, pepper and cottage cheese in blender container; cover and run on speed 7 (or high) for 1 minute. Add pimiento and chives; cover and run on speed 4 (or low) just until pimiento is chopped. Spread egg yolk mixture over egg whites and fold in gently. Slide carefully onto heated griddle; cook 30 seconds; lower heat and cook slowly for 10 minutes or until lightly browned on bottom.

Then place in oven and bake 10 minutes, or until dry and lightly browned on top. Loosen edges with a spatula, make a quick shallow cut through center and fold one half over. Gently slip onto a warm serving platter. Serve immediately. *Makes 3 servings.*

## SPANISH GREEN BEANS

*(about 30 calories per serving)*

**1 10-ounce package frozen cut green beans**
**1 slice bacon, cut up**
**½ green pepper, seeded and cut up**
**¼ small onion**
**2 medium tomatoes, cut up, OR 1 cup canned tomatoes**
**Salt and pepper**

Cook beans according to package directions; drain. Cook bacon in small frypan until crisp. Meanwhile, put green pepper and onion in blender container; cover and run on speed 4 (or high) until chopped. Empty into frypan with bacon and sauté until tender. Put tomatoes in blender container; cover and run on speed 2 (or low) until puréed. Add to pepper and onion; simmer 5 minutes. Pour over cooked green beans and heat. *Makes 4 servings.*

## ORANGE BEETS

*(about 100 calories per serving)*

**8-10 medium beets, pared and cut up**
**2 tablespoons butter or margarine**
**¾ cup orange juice**
**½ small orange with rind**
**1 teaspoon flour**
**½ teaspoon salt**

Put a few beets in blender container; cover and run on speed 3 (or low) until finely chopped. Empty into large measuring cup. Repeat process until you have 2½ cups. Empty into frypan with butter and sauté 5 minutes. Meanwhile, put orange juice, orange, flour and salt in blender container; cover and run on speed 4 (or high) until mixed. Pour over beets and mix well. Simmer about 5 minutes or until tender. *Makes 6 servings.*

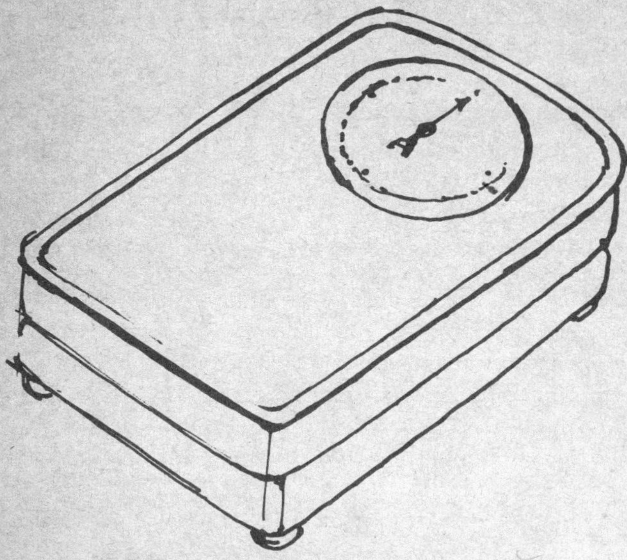

## RUBY RED APPLE DESSERT

*(about 50 calories per serving)*

**4 large cooking apples, pared and cut up (about 4 cups)**
**¼ lemon, cut up and seeded**
**2 cups water**
**1 3/5-ounce envelope cherry-flavored dietary gelatin**
**1 teaspoon liquid non-caloric sweetener**

Put about 2 cups apple pieces, half the lemon and 1 cup water in blender container; cover and run on speed 4 (or high) until apples are chopped. Empty into a saucepan and repeat process with remaining apple, lemon and water. Cook 10 minutes. Add gelatin and sweetener; cool. *Makes 6 servings.*

## SLIM JIM PARFAIT

*(about 120 calories per serving)*

**½ cup yogurt**
**1 cup creamed cottage cheese**
**½ teaspoon liquid non-caloric sweetener**
**3 small slices pineapple**
**1 pint strawberries, hulled**
**¼ teaspoon liquid non-caloric sweetener**

Put yogurt, cottage cheese and ½ teaspoon non-caloric sweetener in blender container; cover and run on speed 2 (or low) until smooth. Add pineapple; cover and run on speed 4 (or high) until chopped. Empty into a bowl and refrigerate. Put ½ cup berries in blender container and add ¼ teaspoon sweetener; cover and run on speed 2 (or low) until puréed. Empty into a bowl. Slice remaining strawberries into purée. Refrigerate. At serving time, layer cheese mixture and berries in parfait glasses. *Makes 4 servings.*

## STRAWBERRY SHERBET

*(about 45 calories per serving)*

**1 pint strawberries, hulled**
**1 3/5-ounce package strawberry-flavored dietary gelatin**
**½ cup hot water**
**2 tablespoons lemon juice**
**1½ cups buttermilk**
**⅛ teaspoon cinnamon**
**2 egg whites**

Put berries in blender container; cover and run on speed 2 (or low) until crushed. If necessary, stop blender during processing and push berries toward blades with rubber spatula. Empty into a mixing bowl. Put gelatin and hot water in blender container; cover and run on speed 1 (or low) until gelatin is dissolved. Add lemon juice, buttermilk, cinnamon and crushed berries; cover and run on speed 4 (or high) until mixed. Pour into a 9x5x3-inch pan. Freeze until firm.

Break into chunks and put ¼ at a time in blender container; cover and run on speed 7 (or high) until smooth. Empty into a mixing bowl and repeat until all is smooth. If necessary, stop blender during processing and push mixture toward blades with rubber spatula. Beat egg whites in small bowl with an electric mixer until soft peaks form; fold into strawberry mixture. Return to pan and freeze until firm. Remove from freezer to refrigerator 1 hour before serving. *Makes 1 quart; 8 servings.*

Frozen Strawberry Whip

Mocha Moüsse

Carrot Custard

## FROZEN STRAWBERRY WHIP

*(about 80 calories per serving)*

**2 tablespoons lemon juice**
**½ cup boiling water**
**1 envelope (1 tablespoon) unflavored gelatin**
**2 egg whites**
**1 10-ounce package frozen strawberries, cut into pieces**

Put lemon juice, boiling water and gelatin in blender container; cover and run on speed 1 (or low) for 1 minute or until gelatin is completely dissolved. Add egg whites and frozen fruit; cover and run on speed 7 (or high) until container feels cool to the touch. Pour into bowl or mold. Chill until firm. *Makes 4 servings.*

## MOCHA MOUSSE

*(about 91 calories per serving)*

**3 tablespoons boiling water**
**2 squares (2 ounces) unsweetened chocolate, cut up**
**1 tablespoon liquid non-caloric sweetener**
**1 tablespoon instant coffee**
**2 eggs, separated**

Put all ingredients except eggs in blender container; cover and run on speed 7 (or high) until chocolate is liquefied. Add egg yolks; cover and run on speed 7 (or high) for 1 minute. Beat egg whites with an electric mixer until stiff but not dry; fold in chocolate mixture. Chill until set. *Makes 4 servings.*

## CARROT CUSTARD

*(about 110 calories per serving)*

**8-10 medium carrots, cut up**
**¼ small onion, cut up**
**2 tablespoons butter or margarine**
**2 eggs**
**1 cup milk**
**1 teaspoon salt**
**Dash pepper**

Preheat oven to 350°. Put a few pieces of carrot in blender container; cover and run on speed 3 (or low) until finely chopped. Empty into a large measuring cup. Repeat process until you have 2½ cups. Add onion with the last of the carrots. Empty into a frypan and sauté in butter for 5 minutes. Put remaining ingredients in blender container; cover and run on speed 5 (or high) until mixed. Add carrots; cover and run on speed 5 (or high) a few seconds. Pour into a 1-quart casserole. Bake 45-50 minutes. *Makes 6 servings.*

# Index